Testimonials

"Living the Truth in Love is challenging. The demands of the Gospel are difficult enough without making it undesirable by our misery. One's first encounter with Christ is through the members of His Body, and Dr. Anne DeSantis has rightfully emphasized the importance of not distorting the image of our loving, just, and merciful God."

– Fr. Matthew Phelan, Vicar Provincial of the Mercedarian Friars, USA

Drawing upon contemporary papal writings, most especially that of Pope Francis, sacred scripture, the Church Fathers and the lives of the saints, Dr. Anne DeSantis has skillfully created a framework for Pastoral Care based on the virtue of affability. The need for healing is great, and affability is a choice we must make in our dealings with others, if we are to bring Jesus to those we meet each day. This book is a roadmap for missional mercy offered in Christ's name."

– Dr. Mary Amore, Executive Director, Mayslake Ministries

"In such a divided world, division that also affects the Church, the virtue of affability in the practice of evangelization is essential to credibility of the faithful. DeSantis shows us that now is the time to hone this virtue and gives stunning examples of the saints for us to follow."

– Carmina Chapp, Ph.D., Dean, School of Theological Studies, St. Charles Borromeo Seminary

"Anne DeSantis' *The Virtue of Affability* offers a profound exploration of how kindness and approachable demeanor can transform modern evangelization. This timely guide emphasizes affability as essential for healing divisions and fostering meaningful connections, drawing from scripture, saints' lives, and Pope Francis' teachings. DeSantis inspires readers to embody compassion, highlighting how affability bridges gaps and renews faith in today's complex world. A must-read for fostering genuine love and mercy in everyday life."

– Dr. Sebastian Mahfood, OP, co-author with Ronda Chervin of *Catholic Realism: A Framework for the Refutation of Atheism and the Evangelization of Atheists*

"Dr. Anne DeSantis, in this important work, contributes much to the theological study on the virtue of affability and provides valuable insight and practical wisdom on why it is necessary for all to Christians to practice and employ along their journey of faith."

– Bill Snyder, Founder and CEO, Patchwork Heart Ministry

The Virtue of Affability or Friendliness and its Relevance in Modern Evangelization

Anne DeSantis, Th.D.

En Route Books and Media, LLC
Saint Louis, MO

✶ENROUTE
Make the time

En Route Books and Media, LLC
5705 Rhodes Avenue
St. Louis, MO 63109

Contact us at contactus@enroutebooksandmedia.com

Cover Credit: His Holiness Pope Francis I greets prayers gathered before St Peter's Basilica in Vatican City, on April 04, 2013.

Copyright 2024 Anne DeSantis

Nihil Obstat: Rev. Eric J. Banecker, Censor Librorum
Archdiocese of Philadelphia, January 9, 2026

Imprimatur: Most Reverend Nelson J. Perez, D.D.,
Archbishop of Philadelphia, January 13, 2026

ISBN-13: 979-8-88870-283-3
Library of Congress Control Number: 2024951596

All rights reserved. No part of this book may be reproduced, stored in a retrieval system, or transmitted in any form, or by any means, electronic, mechanical, photocopying, or otherwise, without the prior written permission of the author.

This book is dedicated to my devoted and loving husband Angelo,
my beautiful children, Alaine, and her husband Zac,
my daughter Shawn

to my caring book director:
Mary Amore, D. Min.

to Mercedarian friar and dear friend for his ongoing prayers, care, and
support:
Fr. Matthew Phelan, O. de M.

and to good friends who have supported me through their prayers and
friendship:
Sarah Carney
Dr. Carmina Chapp
Derek Fiorenza
Mickey Kelly
Bill Snyder
Teresa Winslow
and others

In addition, in a particular way, I dedicate this book to:
the marginalized
the poor
the lonely
the rejected
those who lack support
those who have no friends
and
and those who lack faith

Table of Contents

Introduction 1

Chapter One: Demeanor and Sincerity of Action Affects Society When Neglected 19
   I. Positive Demeanor is Relevant and Effective in Evangelization 19
   II. The Role of Holy Scripture, the Medieval Period, the Reformation, and Modern Church History and Affability ... 29
   III. The Universal Call to Holiness and Friendliness 33
   IV. The Effects to Society When Affability is Neglected 40

Chapter Two: Church Teachings on Human Interaction, Community, and the Desire of Love 49
   I. Church Teachings on Love of God and Neighbor 49
   II. Communio Theology 55
   III. Ecclesiology and Soteriology in Relation to Communal Outreach 61
   IV. The Desire to Love is Expressed within Community 69

Chapter Three: Biblical Sources that Demonstrate Friendliness is an Integral Part of the Call to Holiness 75
   I. The Old Testament and the Virtue of Friendliness 75
   II. The New Testament and Affability 84
   III. The Church Fathers 94
   IV. The Life of Christ and Outreach to the Marginalized 104

Chapter Four: Evangelization and Friendliness through Faith 107
  I. Human Development and Affability 107
  II. Happiness Through a Living Faith 117
  III. The Teachings of St. Teresa of Calcutta 124
  IV. St. Francis Cabrini: A Life of Compassion 130

Chapter Five: Teachings on Living a Virtuous Life 133
  I. What is a Virtuous Life According to the Church? 133
  II. The Effects of Bullying and Gossip on the Human Person .. 138
  III. Illuminations from St. John Paul II and Pope Emeritus
       Benedict XVI 146
  IV. Pope Francis Teachings on Holiness of Life 154

Chapter Six: St. Thomas Aquinas on Friendliness 161
  I. The Virtue of Affability According to St. Thomas Aquinas ... 161
  II. Comparison: Aristotle and St. Thomas Aquinas 169
  III. St. Thomas Aquinas and the Virtues 177
  IV. Living Out the Virtue of Friendliness 180

Chapter Seven: Teachings of Pope Francis Related to Exercising
    Mercy and Sensitivity 189
  I. What is Love? 189
  II. *Amoris Laetitia* and Exercising Mercy 202
  III. Mercy and Sensitivity 225
  IV. The Practicality of Mercy 227

Table of Contents

Chapter Eight: On-going Conversion 233
    I. Prayer: The Key to Conversion 233
    II. Our Baptismal Call to Holiness 240
    III. Catechizing the Young and Newly Initiated Catholics on
        Conversion of Life 249
    IV. Creating a Gentler World through Mercy 257

Chapter Nine: Loving and Serving as Catholics 267
    I. Church Teachings on Loving and Serving Others 267
    II. Lessons from the Lives of the Saints 270
    III. Exercising Kindness, Goodness, and Charity 279
    IV. A Living and Breathing Faith 285

**Chapter Ten: Faith Interweaved through Daily Action and Sincere
    Charity** 293
    I. Outreach to the Marginalized 293
    II. Compassion as Primary in Making Outreach 299
    III. Friendliness and Charity: God's Call to the Faithful 306
    IV. A Message for the Academic World 309

Conclusion 315

Bibliography 337

Introduction

Human behavior, development, psychology, physiology integrate with the human spirit encompassing both body and soul acting together in being fully alive. When Father, Son, and Holy Spirit come together dwelling inside a human soul, miracles can happen in terms of animating the life of faith and in doing what is good. The Holy Trinity[1] is one God in three Divine Persons, Father, Son, and Holy Spirit, consubstantial and undivided. The Father, Son, and Holy Spirit are instrumental in every action of our lives of faith. These three persons of the Trinity are distinct from one another and are foundational as Christians live the Gospel. Sanctifying grace[2] is a habitual gift and super-natural disposition enabling us to live with God and act by his love in doing his will and is an action of the spirit within us. The relation between the Holy Trinity and sanctifying grace relates to the movement of the Lord in the lives of his followers who love and live by his commands. In meditating upon the modern world and its need for greater outreach to the marginalized, we fervently pray and call to the Lord for his guidance in living daily the Corporal and Spiritual Works of Mercy[3] toward all we encounter. Prayers to Our Father in Heaven and through the activity of sanctifying grace in our lives, we can begin the journey of true evangelization[4] to the rejected and outcast of the world. Tangible care, concern,

---

[1] Catechism of the Catholic Church. Second Edition. 266. Liberia Editrice Vaticana. 1994. *This book will refer to this source as: CCC.
[2] Ibid., 2000.
[3] CCC, 2447.
[4] Ibid., 905.

and action helps to allow the grace of God to work in our souls in doing good.

As committed Catholics, friendly demeanor combined with sincere attitude toward others is impactful to the human person and evidence can be detected of this in weighing the societal consequences when neglected. An examination on the role of how human behavior, decisions, and the treatment of others is a topic for exploration related to analyzing how the Gospel is being lived out. This book will explore the writings of Pope Francis and selected saints expressing that affability is a virtue[5] which impacts human relations for the good of the world. It explores Holy Scripture, the medieval period, the reformation, and the modern Church of the late twentieth century and the twenty-first century. Affability is the human virtue which has to do with being approachable to others in giving them the respect they deserve. Friendly interactions influence the lives of the giver and the receiver, which offers encouragement and produces joy. Evidence of this rests not only on the tenets of the Gospel and of the teachings of the Church, but also through modern studies related

---

[5] "Human virtues are firm attitudes, stable dispositions, habitual perfections of intellect and will that govern our actions, order our passions, and guide our conduct according to reason and faith." CCC, 1804. (Although "virtues" are part of man's vocation in the life of spirit as Catholics, it is possible for non-Catholics to live lives of virtue since moral virtues are "acquired through human effort" and are part of the natural law of faith. As Catholics, given the gift of the Holy Spirit, our lives of virtue are ignited more fully through the spirit living within us.)

to the neuroscience of emotion[6] and other areas related to psychology.

The question at hand: Are the virtues of affability and friendliness at their core Catholic and are they relevant to the way individuals treat one another? Affability, kindness, and the concept of treating people with sincerity are impactful to society. When these cores are neglected and when Catholics do not take the call to kindness and sacrifice toward others seriously, human society suffers and so do efforts to evangelize. Depression, anxiety, and civil unrest occurs when people are viewed as faceless and actions toward individuals no longer matters. The virtue of friendliness is key in terms of making greater outreach to the marginalized. The happiness of others is of value as we are not only body but also soul and spirit. Just as when the incarnation occurred and God became man, the human person is also incarnational. For this reason, our brothers and sisters deserve love and care at all times. Pursuing the good helps to guide in the human condition of life on earth and enables one to find true happiness. This book will combine the theology of the teachings of Pope Francis' *Amoris Laetitia* and St. Thomas Aquinas *Summa Theologica*. This study integrates additional aspects of Church teachings including Holy Scripture, specific periods of Church history and the Church Fathers.

---

[6] Diana Fosha, Daniel J. Siegel, Marion F. Solomon, *The Healing Power of Emotion. Affective Neuroscience, Development and Clinical Practice* (New York: W.W. Norton and Company, 2009).

The New Evangelization[7] is best established as an authentic experience of relational justice which engenders the manifestation of joy. Divine charity affirms that this apprehension of joy in the other, is best situated as a spontaneous grace-filled participation of the created with the uncreated. Thus, as affability was the evangelical modality demonstrated by Christ, that which was revealed in the Gospels and the teachings of the Catholic Church, it must perpetually be upheld as the foundation of the evangelization and joy to those Christ calls through his Body, the People of God.

The Argument

The argument of this book is in tracing the effects of affability as a moral virtue of justice as an effective method of modern evangelization in the 21st century and beyond through the lens of Pope Francis. An examination of affability and its role throughout the centuries will also be discussed. Affability as tethered to charity, joy, and justice will be demonstrated to overcome apologetic encounters that emphasize utility and pleasure of the self at the expense of others. Affability necessitates mutual evangelical efforts by engaging all members of the Church.

Why a book on affability in evangelization? The time is right for just such an academic endeavor. In the first fifteen years following

---

[7] "The New Evangelization calls each of us to deepen our faith, believe in the Gospel message and go forth to proclaiming the Gospel. The focus of the New Evangelization calls all Catholics to be evangelized and to go forth to evangelize." USCCB website, March 2024. https://www.usccb.org/beliefs-and-teachings/how-we-teach/new-evangelization

the Second Vatican Council[8], Catholics were seemingly affable and active in reaching out to people trying to make them feel welcomed into the Church. This effort led to a fair amount of confusion, and somewhat of a watering-down of the Catholic faith in a quest to be relevant to people during that time period. Those partaking in the evangelization, while well-meaning, were not necessarily prepared theologically. The papacy of St. John Paul II brought a call for a New Evangelization that had a strong grounding in the truths of the faith. His work to explain the faith in light of Vatican II led to a renewal in catechesis and a greater interest in the study of theology by the laity. Pope Benedict continued this trend, particularly through his interest in engaging people in the liturgical life of the Church. With Pope Francis, we see a return to a centering on affability and approachability, but now with a more focused theological foundation partially because of the work of his two predecessors. Being affable does not mean falling into emotivism[9] or relativism[10], as it did in the past. It follows the work of St. John Paul II, who grounded the Church, and Pope Benedict, who added even more knowledge and

---

[8] The Second Vatican Council is the most recent ecumenical council of the Church. The dates of the council are October 11, 1962-December 8, 1965. The founder of the council is St. John XXIII. https://www.vatican.va/archive/hist_councils/ii_vatican_council/index.htm

[9] Emotivism is a theory which regards ethical and value judgements as an expression or feeling of action as opposed to assertion. https://britannica.com/topic/emotivism.

[10] Relativism is a doctrine which states that knowledge, morality, and truth exist only as a reaction to society, historical contexts, and culture. This theory believes there are no absolutes. https://www.oxford-reference.com/display/10.1093/oi/authority.20110803100412717

theological understanding. Now Pope Francis sends members of the Church out as missionaries. It is appropriate to do a careful study of the proper role that affability has played in evangelization throughout the history of the Church, and how it is essential today. This is, in part, what this book will focus on.

The virtue of friendliness and its relevance is at the center of this book along with ways to achieve this end in the universal Church. Pope Francis' teachings on kindness, demeanor, and positive interactions is monumental to bringing healing and restoration to those who feel left out, alone, and misunderstood by others and the world. Positive emotion sparked through affability is a missing piece needed more than ever in the work of evangelization. In addition to Pope Francis, a host of others will be discussed who have had massive impact on the role of affability as a justice given.

Joy is a key element in how those who have been affected by trauma and other horrific events of life can find healing. When we, as people of faith, have the capacity to offer empathy, active listening, care, and affability to someone on the verge of despair, positive things begin to happen. The Holy Spirit works in the hearts of those who recognize this reality that being a devout Catholic or person of faith involves active love and care for the marginalized. Jesus gives many examples in the New Testament of how this concept can be lived out by us today. The way we treat one another is *relevant* and *necessary* in creating a kinder world. This is the will of God[11] to learn not just know the faith and catechesis well, but that in exercising it we may become friendlier people toward everyone. Being Catholic

---

[11] Matthew: 7:12, NOAB.

means not only living one's baptismal call to live within the realm of the sacramental life, but in being kind, loving, and affable, as well. The happiness of others and each one of us is of utmost importance in order to be healed of the sadness that sin has created. Molding into the likeness of Christ over a lifetime calls each member of the human family to live the Beatitudes[12] which in turn is a call to love, charity, and sincere kindness. The Beatitudes impels the faithful to live the lessons of love given by Jesus on the Sermon of the Mount[13].

Major Source Work

This book is both a research project and a pastorally written paper bringing together sources from a variety of subject matters. Since the book is being written on the topic of the moral virtue of affability and its relevance in modern evangelization, I have focused on areas of both academic and pastoral theologies. Church documents, Holy Scripture, and commentaries have been used to define what affability is both literally and practically, so the reader has full knowledge of the definition of the word and how it applies in real-life situations related to the evangelical works of the Church. I explore affability from its beginning; namely in Holy Scripture through the Modern Church.

---

[12] Matthew: 5:3, NOAB.
[13] Matthew Chapter 5 – 7, NOAB.

A Pastoral Approach

Although the book is a research project, the pastoral sources[14] of this presentation are imperative since the topic has to do with the field of pastoral theology and evangelization. The writings of Pope Francis have a major impact on the book since he has written extensively on making outreach to the marginalized, and he has offered practical suggestions for individuals and families in finding hope and healing when crises occur. The major source work from Pope Francis includes: *Amoris Laetitia, Evangelii Gaudium, Laudato Si,* and *Fratelli Tutti*. Additionally, I have included other minor sources from Francis as secondary sources[15] for this project. St. Pope John Paul II and Pope Emeritus Benedict XVI have also contributed to the meaning of friendship and affability, and their writings lay the groundwork for Pope Francis, as mentioned.

The reason behind my centering on the writings of Pope Francis as the title of my book suggests, is because his writings are relevant to modern evangelization in the 21st Century . With this said, "modern" refers to evangelization which is happening as this project is being written in 2024. The focal point of writing is geared for the current time and beyond as we proceed into the future. The research gathered for this book has led me to aim on what the Church can do at this time to help to make better pastoral outreach to those who have either left the Church, those who are not Catholic, and those who feel distanced from the Church. The methodology is to inform

---

[14] See the bibliography.
[15] Ibid., p. 268-273.

the academic world and those who are interested in learning more about how to bridge the gap between the Church and those who are away from the faith. I reiterate often throughout the book that the people whom we are trying to invite back are closer than we realize. They are our family members, extended family, friends, neighbors, and various others. This project is geared to help the faithful to recognize the impact of simple one-to-one contact demonstrating affability as a way to open new doors to those who have distanced themselves from the Catholic faith. The choice of tone and dialogue in this book is *purposefully* basic and understandable so that it can be read and understood by those who are not "academics" but also people of good will who wish to learn more about the moral virtue of affability and its relevance in the modern world.

The source work from Pope Emeritus Benedict XVI and St John Paul II are included since both have highly respected writings to add on the topics of friendliness and charity toward others related to family life and culture. Their writings are included as a major source for this project. St. Thomas Aquinas, the Church Fathers, Communio Theology, and additional chapters on selected saints have been included to add more depth to this book.

Additional Source Work

Since this project is research based, I have included biblical, historical, and theological sources to gain understanding on where the Church stands on this topic. The goal is to add useful information to the field of theology to help bring greater awareness to the academic world and the entire Church. My hope is to not only present the true teachings of the Church but to do so in a relatable manner. This will bring greater clarity to the reader no matter their level of education or understanding.

The decision to incorporate information on the neuroscience of emotion, from the field of psychology, was included to consider how emotions play a substantial role in helping those who have been traumatized. Having a basic grasp of the role of emotions enables one to develop more knowledge on how to approach challenging situations in which families are suffering through. Human development and psychology sources are both major and secondary in this book. These areas of study will aid in bringing greater overall understanding of the human person.

Understanding the Choice of Source Work as a Useful Guide

When reading this book, the reader should keep in mind the pastoral nature of the project in order to embrace more fully why specific sources were utilized to create the thesis. Although it has been written as a pastoral project overall, there is a strong research element creating it into an academic piece. The mix of resources ranging from encyclicals to Church documents, biblical sources, and lives of the saints offers education and a call to action for the academic world and the Church. The source work points to the teachings of the Catholic Church presented in a crystal-clear way to make a difference for the those who are marginalized and feel hopeless. Another aspect of the book is its prayerful approach in inviting the faithful to partake in the mission of mercy through the valuable moral virtue of friendliness.

Pope Francis and Renewal

As emphasized, one of the key contributors to this topic of the treatment of others as having highest importance is the Holy Father, Pope Francis. He speaks of the church as a field hospital[16]. Francis and members of the Church are workers in this hospital, and we are all spiritual health-care workers. Pope Francis recognizes that it is not an easy task to love everyone regardless of the various facets of life which separates humans, and he has made this aspect of human life the centerpiece of his pontificate. In this book, I will thoroughly explore the writings of Pope Francis and his passion for educating the world on living as people of compassion and mercy.

Francis has spoken a great deal on these issue in his writings, in his personal life, during interviews and in his homilies since he became pope. We are to be ministers of mercy in our everyday lives, as exemplified by charitable actions. These acts include how we listen, care, and love others. Being a minister of God's mercy encompasses affability to a great degree. Francis affirms in his writings that to be authentically Catholic, one can never exclude being a genuinely loving person and caring about the welfare of the marginalized.[17] He has made this the core of his ministry. Attempting to bring happiness to the poor and suffering is a life mission that every person is invited to partake. The pope's teachings point to genuine care of all aspects of the lives of the vulnerable and uncared for. Pope Francis also calls

---

[16] Pope Francis, General Audience. https://www.vatican.va. August 28, 2019.

[17] *Amoris Laetitia*, p. 27

God's people to care for all living creatures and the environment as part of living out this call, as well. Friendship with Jesus is the avenue to achieve this type of missionary discipleship. Francis writes:

> I invited all Christians everywhere at this very moment to a renewed personal encounter with Jesus Christ, or at least an openness to letting him encounter them: I ask all of you to do this unfailingly each day.[18]

Pope Francis talks about this renewal to encounter Christ daily in all situations of life, this means in every aspect of living including normal interactions humans have with one another which have immense value. Francis continues to speak about the aspects of encountering Christ throughout his pontificate as it leads to communion with others.[19] This is where people living out the Gospel make a major imprint on the world at large. Pope Francis preaches that by example, the way we treat everyone matters to God, and it should matter to us as baptized members of the Church. This teaching is having an influence on society now, and it will continue to add meaning to life experiences in the future.

Added Perspectives

In addition to the papal perspective, this book will explore other areas of study such as social psychology, and social justice since there

---

[18] *Evangelii Gaudium*, p. 1.
[19] *Amoris Laetitia*, p. 243.

is a great deal to explore on the topic of the relevance of friendly human interactions and its impact on people within societies. Papal writings and selected saints will be included to highlight these points. Research from reputable writings of theology will be presented to support the book at hand. The combination of sources and opinions of those who have knowledge of the Christian meaning of affability are included in this presentation. The writings of Pope Francis offer support on the effects of love, good relationships, and human intimacy and how they positively affect the human person. In this light, this book offers research on the writings of both Pope Francis and St. Thomas Aquinas' *Summa Theologica* regarding the virtue of friendliness and its impact on the human person. These additional facets of study and reflection will add relevant information in the presentation of this topic. The understanding brought forth will make a difference for the rejected of our world. Additionally, greater comprehension of affability's role in Church history will be solidified and fully discussed.

Evangelization and Spirituality

The full scope of this writing looks at all of these aspects not only for research but more importantly as an invitation to present to the modern world that the most effective method of evangelization is a pastoral caring about people regardless of religion, race, creed, sexuality, or anything that separates. The world is in dire need of kindness, sincerity, and genuine love. To love[20] is to *will the good of the*

---

[20] CCC, 733.

other according to the Catechism of the Catholic Church, and being affable partially fulfills this need. Views of love and friendship from biblical to modern times will be presented in this book to broaden understanding of this virtue.

Evangelization[21] occurs when the faithful fulfill their prophetic mission by participating in the evangelical work of the Church, which is the proclamation of Christ by word and testimony of life. The relationship between love and evangelization is both an individual calling from the Lord and one that is communal and universal to God's people. Evangelization is in proclaiming Christ and the Gospel to all the world which can be done through an affable spirit of joy. A pastoral method of evangelization is relevant and urgently needed right now. Tying these concepts together with the virtue of affability is a way that Catholics can live out the mission of being ministers of the Gospel message to the marginalized. This invitation is not just for Catholics[22], it is for all members of the human family. In this regard, the proclamation of the Gospel is meant for every person. The Catholic Church openly invites everyone to become professed members of the Church through these efforts of evangelization. The Catholic religion contains the deposit of faith, the truth, and the real presence of Christ in the Eucharist. With respect for those who follow other faiths and systems of belief, we present all that we believe to the world as those who love the Church and its mission. In this

---

[21] Ibid., 905.

[22] "Catholics" refers to those who are professed, baptized members of the Catholic Church who are living out the sacramental life of the Church. Throughout this book, the term "Catholics" is used to describe members of the Church.

regard, our faith is monumental, and the universal Church is a sign and sacrament for those who believe and a testimony to those who do not.

One major Catholic source referenced in the book is *Amoris Laetitia* by Pope Francis otherwise known as *The Joy of Love*. This piece by our Holy Father focuses on family, marriage, love, and overcoming challenges which encompasses the array of emotional challenges families may face through life. Francis speaks of the faithfulness of love and how accompaniment is imperative in living out a relationship with Christ. In terms of this book, *Amoris Laetiti*a integrates pastoral perspectives and offers ways the faithful can become empathetic, forgiving, and kind in all interactions since this is how the human family must be formed in order to be fruitful. Not only does this pertain to how families interact at home, but it is also related to the whole of human society and how it will thrive to create a more just world. Popes such as St. John Paul II and Pope Emeritus Benedict XVI have also written on similar topics which include the relevance of affability and openness toward others which is discussed in throughout this book.

Human feelings[23] have a profound impact on this study in combination with faith. Dysfunctional families are everywhere both

---

[23] "In the Christian life, the Holy Spirit himself accomplishes his work by mobilizing the whole being, with all its sorrows, fears, and sadness, as is visible in the Lord's agony and passion. In Christ, human feelings are able to reach their consummation in charity and divine beatitude." CCC, 1769. (In addition, the role of "human feelings" are neutral in terms of the moral goods, but their role can lead to the good when directed toward the will of God through the gifts of the Holy Spirit. This is their role in terms of human

inside the Church and outside and this creates many tensions in terms of human interactions and the fostering of healing. In dysfunctional families, shame can creep in, and there may be no safe place to discuss feelings within the unit. Families and individuals may need accompaniment to discuss feelings to find healing especially related to trauma. There are people who suffer in life because of relationship issues, depression, anxiety, and other factors. Pastoral care combined with a caring Catholic approach aids in better understand the reality of the human condition and the ways in which people suffer immensely due to an array of psychological and human factors. Prayer is needed since patience is necessary in dealing with people who have become isolated and challenged in terms of living life. Although some may find this hard to conceive, there are people that because of life's circumstances find themselves marginalized and alone through no fault of their own.

How will all these aspects tie together in reference to the scope of this project? The lens of the study is the Catholic faith, and everything within the book's analysis begs to ask the question of how it affects the living out and proclaiming the Gospel of Christ. The combination of primary and secondary sources will prove that within the scope of study, answers can be found. A nucleus of the book is on the relevance of affability and how working in the field hospital of mercy should not being ignored on how people can be helped and shown the love of God in everyday ways. A major focus of the scope of this

---

reason. The role of feelings in terms of the proclamation of the Gospel are always directed toward the good in order to follow Christ more closely and live in his spirit. Emotions are also neutral but are best directed and ordered toward the moral goods and in following God's law of love.)

project are the function of emotions and how trauma and tragedy can be worked through when human interaction is positive, empathetic, and kind. Our faith points to the recognition that friendly and kind interactions have a considerable impact on the human family person by person.

In an analysis of the questions at hand, respect for human life is primary when considering the virtue of affability. Human spirituality and psychology are interwoven and must be integrated into our human dialogue and work in society. Whether through work or in one's personal life, being a peacemaker and recognizing the suffering many people have encountered assists those following Christ to be a true peacemaker for God. Authentic evangelization takes into consideration modern science, living faith, human care, and dialogue with everyone, especially those who feel left-out, forsaken, and uncared for. The happiness of the forsaken is work for all members of the Church. It matters to God how people are treated even in the smallest interactions. The Catholic Church can provide love, which is so needed, and it is a major calling to the entire world to model after the kingdom of the Lord.

Chapter One

Demeanor and Sincerity of Action Affects Society When Neglected

I. Positive Demeanor is Relevant and Effective in Evangelization

This chapter will explore when kind demeanor[1] of action and sincerity toward neighbor in society is not present in community small or large negative consequences occur. According to the teachings of Pope Francis, every encounter we have with others in our daily journey has an impact on evangelization. In his dialogue with fellow priests, he begs the question, *"Do people leave us looking like they heard the good news?"*[2] This is a relevant question for all the faithful. This question also ties into the key focus as to why and how positive demeanor and interactions have a major impact on evangelization.

---

[1] Kind action or kindness is defined in the Catechism of the Catholic Church as one of the fruits of the Spirit. These gifts are "perfections that the Holy Spirit forms in us as the first fruits of eternal glory." CCC 1832. (In addition, kindness may be described as materializing charity toward others through tangible actions and outward signs. Kind action may also involve inward signs such as prayer or other charitable gestures toward a person or persons.)

[2] Pope Francis. *I Ask You Shepherds. Reflections on Pastoral Ministry*, p. 28.

According to Pope Francis, we are all invited to be missionary disciples[3] in our world today. Francis has written at length about the consumerism, and the complacency of the human heart that neglects concern for the poor.[4] From this attitude stems the reasons why people gradually give in to the desire to do good and the inclination to make any kind of outreach to those who are less fortunate. There is a joy that comes with evangelization which he also speaks of[5] for it brings not only joy but also great happiness in daily living which is the antidote to breaking the cycle of laziness and of sin. When the human heart is fulfilled as a missionary disciple of Christ, tendencies toward vice decrease and evangelization efforts flourish.

The reason positive demeanor or affability is relevant in the modern world is because it affects every person alive. Whether Catholic or non-Catholic, man, or woman, young or old, and whatever vocation a person is living out, friendliness is and will continue to be relevant in efforts to evangelize. A friendly smile and reaction to even a stranger is an avenue to demonstrate and model Christ in a world desperately in need of tangible actions of God's unconditional love. Its reverberations are infinitely numerous.

We are members of what Francis refers to as God's family[6]. In this family, every member is important and has immense value. He

---

[3] Pope Francis. *Evangelii Gaudium*, p. 11. A "missionary disciple" is one who takes on the challenge of being a part of making outreach to the marginalized of our world through prayerful efforts which spring into action.

[4] Ibid., p. 1.

[5] Ibid., p. 5.

[6] United Stated Conference of Catholic Bishops*. *Pope Francis and the Family*, p. 70. *This book will refer to this source as: USCCB.

Chapter One: Demeanor and Sincerity of Action

describes the Church's task as one of exhibiting and practicing mercy in everyday living. People suffer because of the effects of sin. Participating in the mission of Christ is remedy which enables everyone to take part in being a faithful member of God's holy family. In delving deeper into the relevance of the issues being discussed, families are experiencing challenges which have never been encountered until now due to the demands of a fast-paced and ever-changing society. Francis speaks of the current reality[7] of the family in *Amoris Laetitia*. He states:

> It is also evident that the principal tendencies in anthropological-cultural changes are leading individuals in personal and family life to receive less and less support from social structures than in the past.[8]

Sadly, many lives are getting caught up in materialism, and life's goals are reflected and can be centered more upon power, pleasure, and popularity as opposed to the simpler things of life which bring more joy. When this happens and when selfishness prevails, the number of marriages tends to decrease[9], and family life declines, as well.

Francis recognizes this trend as one that needs to be addressed not only in educating the faithful on the depths and beauty of the vocation of marriage but also in bringing to the forefront the current

---

[7] *Amoris Laetitia*, p. 28.
[8] Ibid., p. 28.
[9] *Amoris Laetitia*, p. 29.

realities of the family and the effects of the tensions of our modern world. Respect for one another within family life and in relationships formed around the family aides in more initiative-taking in living out a joy-filled life. Where there is more happiness and positive interaction within the family unit, all other relationships are affected in an encouraging way. Extended family, neighbors, co-workers, and friends are drawn to a God-centered and peaceful domestic church which creates a better overall society.

Effective evangelization consists in one that is focused on the teachings of the church, the Gospel, and of imitating Jesus Christ. This kind of evangelization begins with the family unit, the domestic church[10], and extends to community, and to the world. Francis speaks of Jesus as the one who restores and fulfills God's plan[11]. Even with all the modern challenges that families face, the key to this specific type of evangelization is accompaniment. Through God's grace, families and individuals can be led back to Christ and his Church when led astray. The Gospels clearly present Jesus as the means of restoring grace and leading those on a bad path to be brought back to God's original plan of holiness of life.

These teachings stem from objective truths[12] of our faith which are found in the teachings of the Catholic Church. The truths of our

---

[10] CCC, 1656.

[11] *Amoris Laetitia*, p. 53. The plan of God for humankind is in living a virtuous life which is sacrificial toward others in imitation of Christ. The eternal plan is heaven.

[12] "The disciple of Christ consents to 'live in the truth,' that is in the simplicity of a life in conformity with the Lord's example, abiding in his truth." CCC, 2470.

Chapter One: Demeanor and Sincerity of Action

faith are objective, meaning they are not affected by feelings or opinions; they are based on the teachings of Christ and his Church. There are, indeed, moral absolutes[13] of our faith in avoiding sin and in doing good to follow the will of God in all things. With this said, one of those "moral absolutes" is in adhering to one of the primary teachings of Holy Scripture found in Matthew 25[14], known as the Judgement of the Nations. This teaching refers to Jesus separating of the sheep from the goats in living a sacrificial life aimed at care for the poor, the sick, and the outcast. This decision to care for those who suffer and are in need is a *major* part of all evangelization efforts. One goal of this book is to educate others on this fundamental aspect of basic Christian morality which is justice given through affability.

Evangelization must start with the domestic church which is why the family, and all members of the family unit are of prime importance. Francis speaks of the family as the image of God[15] and a

---

[13] "Moral absolutes" are those truths which cannot be comprised within our faith. According to the Catechism of The Catholic Church, "The natural law is immutable, permanent throughout history. The rules that express it remain substantially valid. It is a necessary foundation for the erection of moral rules and civil Law." CCC, 1979.

[14] Matthew 25: 31-46, *NOAB*. (In these passages, Jesus takes his places when he returns as King with his angels as he sits upon the throne. Two groups will be divided. The sheep and the goats. The sheep will be praised and welcomed for serving and taking care of those in need. The goats will go into the fiery furnace into hell.)

[15] The human person, created by God, "is and ought to be the principle, the subject, and the object of every social organization." In addition, "The human person needs life in society in order to develop in accordance with his nature." CCC, 1892, 1891. (As God's highest form of creation, the human person finds fulfillment in God and beatitude.)

communion of persons. We have been made in his image and likeness[16]. Mother, father, children, and extended family make up societies, and as Catholics, efforts to evangelize begin here. Pope Francis speaks of the covenant of marriage:

> The sacrament of marriage is not a social convention, an empty ritual or merely the outward sign of a commitment. The sacrament is a gift given for the sanctification and salvation of spouses, since their mutual belonging is a real representation, through the sacramental sign, of the same relationship between Christ and the Church.[17]

When evangelization efforts begin within the family, it is a mutual effort of members of that family to show the love of God to a world in need of accompaniment and care. In speaking of marriage, Francis teaches that God's grace makes it possible for not only parents to partake in this special mission, but also to engage children, family, and friends to be missionaries of mercy to a hurting world.

This relationship that Francis speaks of between Christ and his Church is a real and active journey that strives to care for every member of society starting each household. This mutual belonging to one another, as couples partake in marriage, may be imitated in various ways to those in need and those who do not have the support they deserve. This sacramental sign of marriage is for all the world

---

[16] We are made in God's image and likeness, and are therefore every human life is intimately and eternally valuable to God, our Creator. Genesis 1:26-27, *NOAB*.

[17] Ibid., p. 59.

to see and to continue in the mission to serve. The world observes the beauty of marriage and family as a sign of God's love working actively through love.

In this key relationship of family life, the way husbands and wives interact with one another and with their children on a day-to-day basis is integral to evangelization efforts. Interaction includes living together, eating together, dialogue, relationships with those outside of the family, and more. When these interconnections are positive and life-giving and when the virtues of faith are exercised in vocational life, growth occurs in various aspects including evangelization efforts. There will always be frictions in family life and in life in general, which is expected, but when positive demeanor is present, God's grace is continually at work. This book will present how this call to holiness through genuine friendliness has been in existence within the Church for centuries from the beginning.

Why is positive interaction relevant in evangelization? It is true because accompaniment is an art which will continue to be effective since the poor will always be with us[18] as Jesus has taught. The poor include those who are materially poor and those who are poor in spirit. Close family members may also be poor in spirit. There are also those who do not have the support they deserve, and those for whom society has rejected. As Christians, our primary purpose is *to serve* in imitation of Christ. Pope Francis has stated that the role of Christians including clergy is for the service of the people[19]. A large

---

[18] Matthew: 26:11, NOAB.

[19] Reginald Alva, "The Church's Mission with the Marginalized: An Analysis in the Light of the Teachings of Pope Francis' Evangelii Gaudium."

part of this service is the way we interact and treat people on a basic level. Do we listen and engage? Do we smile and show that we care when we have conversations with others? These are important questions for everyone to answer. When a person is sincere and show they are genuine toward another, the Holy Spirit is at work in the hearts of those who are open to the marginalized. This is how positive interaction prevails for those who feel left out and rejected. The family of God can together work to repair the bonds which have been broken in family life through prayer and outreach.

Why is friendliness effective in evangelization? It is effective because it is integral to giving others the justice they deserve. Justice is the moral virtue which consists in the constant and firm will to give their due to God and neighbor. [20] Justice is *more* than this, as it brings harmony and promotes equality of people. In an equivalent way, affability or friendliness accomplishes the same task through honoring of another through kind-actions and in a spirit of giving. A simple smile gives justice to one another by recognizing human dignity. This is why friendliness should be a part of every evangelization effort. The truth alone[21] will only go so far in evangelization efforts as those who feel rejected and marginalized are not always open to simply

---

International Review of Mission. Vol. 109, Issue 1. International Review of Mission. May 2020, p. 2.

[20] CCC, 1807.

[21] The "truth alone" in this context refers to the idea that in addition to all of Church teachings and the doctrines of faith, those who are away from the Church need to see faith in action demonstrated by the faithful in tangible real-life ways which enable them to experience Christ in daily life. Simply presenting Catholic doctrine, Holy Scripture, and the Catechism may not be enough to reach them in evangelization efforts.

"hearing" the Gospel. A better method of outreach is most likely established through experiencing the kindness and goodness of others. Catechesis and education often takes place after friendships are established.

One may ask the question, "How are we to respond in situations where the person or persons we are attempting to evangelize are clearly in a state of sin or those who are enemies of the faith"? This may seem as a challenging question to answer, but there are proper ways to deal with these circumstances. Affability or openness displayed toward those who reject faith is not an acceptance of sinful actions. It is not a "green light" for behaviors or deeds which are contrary to the faith. There are a variety of scenarios which could happen in light of handling these circumstances, perhaps too many to list. One example is a how to interact with a person who does not uphold to pro-life values[22] and may believe that an anti-life mentality is a "kinder" choice. These are challenging conditions which require prayer, contemplation, and education in dealing with a paganistic culture. Being kind and affable toward others is not an acceptance of sin. While we must always adhere and live by Christian moral values, to reach those who reject the faith, we may consider opening

---

[22] The proper way to interact with those who do not uphold prolife values is through education, respectful dialogue, prayer, kindness, keeping the doors of communication open, and through the work of the Holy Spirit. Many modern pro-life nonprofits and organizations offer free resources, counseling, care, and education to combat a society with an "anti-life" mentality. These organizations are often Catholic, Christian, or secular and offer essential services.

dialogue in order to educate, catechize, and to shed light when someone is in darkness.

The art of accompaniment, which is the conscious decision to walk with one another, begins at home within the family unit and extends to everyone in the community. Accompaniment is a major part of efforts to evangelize the lonely and forsaken as it involves developing genuine relationships especially those who may have experienced trauma and challenging times. Focusing on one-to-one friendship fosters accompaniment in highlighting the virtue of affability. Each person has his/her own hopes, dreams, and experiences. People within communities, are not objects or mission projects;[23] they are human beings and children of God.

Centering on assets and not problems[24] are part of offering positive demeanor toward others in daily life. These concepts are extremely relevant in evangelization. Accompaniment at its core is love. When we, as Catholic Christians, focus on the virtue of affability as an act of love, it aids in bringing evangelization to *higher levels*. We can focus on the good and on positive facets of specific situations helping those who feel alone and rejected to feel better about their relationship with God and in gaining confidence to move forward in faith. Despite any circumstances which can hold someone back, seeking to find good in situations helps to create dialogue when done in a spirit of love and compassion.

---

[23] Kim Lamberty, *"The art of accompaniment."* An International Review. Sage. 2015, p. 43.

[24] Ibid., p.43.

No one has the answers to all of life's questions, especially those who have suffered greatly and may feel lost. Love *does* have the answers all people search for. Accompaniment, as a means of exercising the virtue of justice, assists the faithful to do the will of God by being grounded in what is most important to God. In other words, what is primary to the Lord is our willingness to do his will and to make outreach to the poor among us. Friendliness, as a virtue, enables us to do so.

II. The Role of Holy Scripture, the Medieval Period, the Reformation, and Modern Church History and Affability

Holy Scripture

Chapter Three of this book presents both Old and New Testament proof of affability and friendliness in action. In this chapter, I discuss some key phrases in scripture which demonstrate affability. In Chapter Three these sections and verses of scripture depict how God's people respond and act in accordance with the commandments through the action of the Holy Spirit in guiding his people to recognize the importance of exercising justice in our culture. From biblical times throughout the history of the Church, this moral virtue has been both needed and implemented.

Definitions of Affability

In reflecting on the origins of affability, one must go to definitions particularly the English, Latin, Hebrew, and Greek definitions.

Before delving into to Holy Scripture, below are the various definitions from each of these languages:

English definition of *affability*:

"The state or quality of having a pleasant or agreeable manner in socializing with others."[25]

Latin definition *affabilité* (Old French).

"Approachable, courteous, or kind," and literally means "can be easily spoken to."[26]

Hebrew definition of *afə 'bilədē*:

"סֵבֶר פָּנִים: affability, cordiality, kindness, geniality. Example: "It cannot unfold with such elegance, tranquility, and delicacy or with sweetness, *affability*, courtesy, restraint and generosity."[27]

---

[25] Merriam-Webster.com: https://www.merriam-webster.com/thesaurus/affability

[26] Vocabulary.com: https://www.vocabulary.com/dictionary/affability#:~:text=In%20the%20Old%20French%2C%20it,Definitions%20of%20affability

[27] Context.Reverso.net: https://context.reverso.net/translation/english-hebrew/affability

Chapter One: Demeanor and Sincerity of Action

Greek definition of *ευγενικός* (affable):

"Friendly, good-natured, or easy to talk to; an affable and agreeable companion."[28]

All four of the above definitions indicate that affability is an attitude and behavior of openness, pleasantness, and of friendliness. Depending on how a sentence is being used and the context of what is being communicated, there may be slight variations of each interpretation; however, the consensus translates a commonality indicative of general openness in communication style.

In the chapters related to Holy Scripture, Chapter Three, I expand on the related terms keeping in mind the proper biblical definitions of the verses selected. I present various chapters of both the Old and New Testaments centering on the moral virtue of affability. These examples are meant to demonstrate God's plan for holiness of life through living out friendliness and in developing lasting bonds through interpersonal relationships which are ordained through the Holy Spirit.

The Medieval Period, The Reformation and Modern Times

In this book, I discuss a timeline associated with the moral virtue of affability and when it is evident. The time periods presented are biblical times up to the medieval period from 476-1500. In addition, I discuss saints who lived during the reformation and modern times,

---

[28] En.Bab.La: https://en.bab.la/dictionary/english/affable

which is any time after the 16th century. In fourth century, I discuss the Cappadocians[29]: St. Basil the Great, St. Gregory Nazianzus, St. Gregory Nyssa, and other early Church fathers.

Before medieval times, I present Aristotle[30] since St. Thomas Aquinas refers to him often in his writings related to moral justice. I discuss Cicero,[31] an ancient philosopher, and Aelred of Rievaulx[32] who lived in the twelfth century.

In the current era I cover popes of modern times, namely: St. Pope John Paul II, Pope Emeritus Benedict XVI, and of course, Pope Francis. I extract from their writings those elements which pertain to the moral virtue of affability and its relevance in modern evangelization. The combination of both biblical analysis, Church fathers,

---

[29] The Cappadocians lived in the fourth century, and they consist of: St. Basil the Great, St. Gregory Nazianzus, and St. Gregory of Nyssa. Catholic Apologetics: http://www.catholicapologetics.info/apologetics/general/cappadocians.htm

[30] Aristotle (384 BCE – 322 BCE). "Aristotle is a towering figure in ancient Greek philosophy who made important contributions to logic, criticism, rhetoric, physics, biology, psychology, mathematics, metaphysics, ethics, and politics. He was a student of Plato for twenty years but is famous for rejecting Plato's theory of forms. He was more empirically minded than both Plato and Plato's teacher, Socrates." Internet Encyclopedia of Philosophy: https://iep.utm.edu/aristotle/

[31] Cicero (106-43 BCE). Cicero was an orator, a lawyer, a politician, and a philosopher known to be one of the greatest orators Rome ever produced. Internet Encyclopedia of Philosophy: https://iep.utm.edu/cicero-roman-philosopher/

[32] Aelred of Rievaulx (1110-1167) was an English Cistercian monk, a homilist, and historian. New Advent: https://www.newadvent.org/cathen/01172b.htm

and particular periods of the history of the Church, I present a thorough analysis of affability and time-tested wisdom on the pertinence of this valuable virtue.

III. The Universal Call to Holiness and Friendliness

The universal call to holiness[33] is God's call to us as faithful Catholics to live out this primary mission. Holiness[34] consists in identification with Christ, our savior, and acceptance of his will for our lives. It is in living and imitating the virtues of faith each day which have a profound influence on the world. Holiness is never a "once and done" experience, rather as faithful Catholics, it is in living, loving, and obeying Christ commands as he taught in the Gospels. God's graces are available to us as Catholics through the sacraments of the church as we strive for sainthood in the little ways of love each day[35]. This

---

[33] CCC, 2013.

[34] "The way of perfection passes by the way of the Cross. There is no holiness without renunciation and spiritual battle. Spiritual battle entails the ascesis and mortification that gradually leads to living in the peace and joy of the Beatitudes." CCC, 2015. (As stated in the Catechism, holiness comes by Way of the Cross in our lives. The cross comes in various forms to each individual person. One example is in accepting the changes that happen to each person as life continues to old age such as the loss of a loved one, difficult familial or financial situations, and a variety of other examples. In accepting the will of God, we can be assured of his presence during all of the challenging times of life presented in life. Through prayer and the gifts of the Holy Spirit and by his grace, we can be made holy through lives of love and charity.)

[35] Pope Francis. General Audience. https://www.vatican.va (June 7, 2023).

call to holiness is also about listening to God. Being attentive to God involves reading the scriptures, meditating on them, and getting to know the heart of Jesus' teachings which are focused on caring for our brothers in sisters, especially those in need.

The universal call to holiness includes a certain receptivity to those in our communities. The first people within communities are those within our own families. Husbands, wives, children, parents, and others make up those people who are often times closest. Evangelization efforts must include members of one's own domestic church in making outreach. Friendliness and affability are keyways to show love and care within the family unit. Acting upon the virtues of faith such as charity, kindness, patience, gentleness, and the other virtues help to accompany family members in the distresses of life which happen to all communities and families of faith.

Pope Francis speaks of the reciprocal gifts[36] which can be offered in friendship. These offerings are ways to present mutual gifts of love and respect, especially those who may not live or think as we do. This is part of exercising the virtue of affability as we, the faithful, encounter new people and new cultures. It is part of the universal call to holiness in respecting and admiring those people and communities unlike us and who deserve utmost respect and love. The love given in these circumstances is monumental for healing. This type of universal friendship and love is necessary in evangelization in conducting God's will to do good and avoid evil. We are called to practice love in all interpersonal relationships. Sharing reciprocal gifts of kindness *always* involves exercising affability. It helps one to live in

---

[36] *Fratelli Tutti*, p. 80.

Christian duty to see the face of Christ in everyone. This is always done with a smile in seeing Jesus at work and in daily life.

Catechesis indicates that exercising the faith includes knowledge of the truth and in living it out. The truths of the faith can be found in its teachings and in reading and meditating on Holy Scripture in attempting to follow Christ. The highest truths of the faith are in charity and love since *God is love.* Pope Francis writes about the aspects of love[37] in *Amoris Laetitia* pertaining to marriage and family and in evangelization. Each area of love is valuable, and aids in bringing hope to those who suffer. The aspects of love[38] include patience, service to others, in not being jealous, not boastful, and more. Patience helps one to exercise acceptance of others and in not demanding one's own way. In fully trusting the Lord, we can learn to be patient with our families and those around us. We learn that the things which are important to us may not necessarily be of the same importance to others. We, God's people, also learn to bend in terms of having things done our own way. This is all part of having a patient attitude.

Service of others[39] is in giving without the need to repay. Service is at the heart of what it means to live and be active in Christian life. It is a constant but healthy outpouring of ourselves through the gifts that God has given us. Of those gifts of service is having a positive demeanor and pleasant smile toward others, especially those who need a friend. This act of service is easy to give and makes a

---

[37] *Amoris Laetitia*, p. 74.
[38] I Corinthians 13, NOAB.
[39] Ibid., p.78.

tremendous difference in all evangelization efforts. When done in a spirit of love, service to others is not a burden. Love is also not jealous. This type of love propels us to want justice for those who may be oppressed in some way. We wish to share a deeply rooted sense of happiness so that they may enjoy the same sense of joy and peace. Since affability is an offshoot of justice, it makes sense that love and the desire to love would not be jealous in nature. Avoiding jealousy is often a lifelong battle for many, even those who are religious in nature and who may be well-educated and intelligent in faith matters are subject to becoming jealous of others.

Love is also not boastful.[40] Boastfulness reminds us, Christ's followers, that in speaking too much about ourselves and in being obsessed with our own needs is an immoral and sinful behavior. When we allow our pride to be healed and let our humanity come forth, it helps to gives others the opportunity to share the things that matter to them. It is the Lord's will in exercising this kind of giving by allowing family and friends to fully experience love through being an active listener in conversations. Exercising active listening is a major piece of this writing since it is a primary method of being an affable person. Additionally, love should not be rude, it should be generous, and it should not be resentful according to Francis[41]. All these aspects tie together with the universal call to holiness and affability. Learning to listen, to be generous with our time and talents, and in not allowing for moodiness or resentfulness to rule the day is monumental. Not only are these points of action good for the soul in

---

[40] Ibid., p. 78.
[41] *Amoris Laetitia*, p. 82.

Chapter One: Demeanor and Sincerity of Action

taking the positive road instead of the negative, but they also have psychological ramifications when wrong paths are chosen. Rudeness is commonplace in the 21st century and educating the faithful on affability is a way to combat the evil of unkindness in society.

At the top of the list of how love is fostered in our hearts is when we bear all things, believe all things, and do all of this in hope and in love[42]. Francis alludes that in all we do we should bear it with a cheerful outlook[43]. This is endurance when the faithful trust the Lord during times of crisis knowing that through patience and perseverance, the path of peace will open up. Evangelization takes place when people of faith decide to help a brother or sister who is going through a tragic time. Those who suffer need to know that in the end things will be fine with God's help. This is where affability and friendliness make a tremendous difference for both for the giver and the receiver.

The universal call to holiness and friendliness calls the faithful to lifelong sharing with one another. This kind of sharing often begins within the family unit extending to all those we encounter. Francis states in relations to love in marriage:

> Yet promising love for ever is possible when we perceive a plan bigger than our own ideas and undertakings, a plan which sustains us to surrender our future entirely to the one we love.[44]

---

[42] I Corinthians: 13:7. NOAB.
[43] *Amoris Laetitia*, p. 91.
[44] *Amoris Laetitia*, p. 95-96.

This "plan bigger than our own"[45] includes the concept of sharing ourselves in love with family, friends, and contacts. In this way, the universal call to holiness of followers of Christ is expressed and matured over a lifetime. From the gifts of the vocation of marriage springs forth this lifelong sharing of self through tenderness which is permeated through a lifetime of love. It is a bond in conjunction and imitation of the relationship between Christ and the Church, which is inseparable, life-giving, and sustaining. This call to holiness is initially expressed through the virtue of affability and cheerfulness[46] opens the door to those who feel left-out and abandoned by the world.[47]

Friendliness is a virtue which intensely engages the other with true care. It has the power to demonstrate in a more profound way the virtue of charity, the greatest of all virtues. Since the universal call to holiness begins within the family dynamic, love is at the core of the marital bond and in every relationship connected to it. The domestic church cannot live and grow[48] without positive experiences of life through a living charity expressed by virtue. Joy and beauty[49] come together to bring this growth into its maturity. This call includes those of all vocations: priests, religious, those called the consecrated life, mothers, fathers, and children. Each day gives new

---

[45] Ibid., p. 95.

[46] *Evangelii Gaudium*, p. 1

[47] *Fratelli Tutti*, p. 9.

[48] Gerard O'Collins, S.J. "The Joy of Love (Amoris Laetitia) the Papal Exhortation in its Context. *Sage Theological Studies*. Vol. 77(4), p. 909. 2016.

[49] *Amoris Laetitia*, p. 97.

opportunities[50] to encounter the poor and marginalized to be welcomed through the bonds of charity. Being a good shepherd in imitation of the Lord and offering healing and accompaniment to forsaken offers those opportunities in the encounters of life. When the poor experience the initial kindly gaze of a follower of Christ, it is an invitation to join in the community of love. This can be accomplished through genuine friendliness. Affability is a virtue of truth, beauty, and goodness.

Those who have experienced various tragedies of life need to know the love of God more deeply, and it will only come via the modern disciples of Christ, his domestic church. One of those areas of pain are those affected by various scandals of life and the gossip and judgement[51] of others. This type of alienation is very real to countless people both inside and outside the church, and as Christ's followers, we are encouraged to seek out the marginalized and to befriend them. It is a blasphemy of our faith to reject those who feel outside the boundaries of love as exercised by those who claim to be Christians following the faith. The universal call to holiness encompasses the whole of our lives in attempting to walk with Christ in finding those people who need to know that not only does God love them, but so do we. This can come to realization through genuine friendly dialogue which offers authentic care and lasting friendship.

This call to holiness encompasses friendship that is not done just for the sake of evangelization, but it is done in oneness as Christians

---

[50] Pope Francis, *I Ask You, Be Shepherds. Reflections on Pastoral Ministry*, Crossroads Publishing. 2015, p. 38.

[51] Ibid., p. 39.

in going forth[52] in virtue and charity because of our profound love of God and others. Francis states:

> Each Christian and every community must discern the path that the Lord points out, but all of us are asked to obey his call and to reach all the peripheries in need of the light of the Gospel.[53]

Occasionally, those "peripheries" are ones that we place in blockage of those who are in most need of our friendship and care. Pope Francis invites all the faithful to examine our hearts so that we can be a church which goes forth[54] in joy to love and serve every member of the worldwide community of the human family. Not only is this an obligation, but it is also an honor and privilege to serve God's people.

IV. The Effects to Society When Affability is Neglected

There are monumental effects to society when the virtue of affability is disregarded in daily life. People can become faceless to others, and the focus often follows the path of self-centered behavior. As stated in examining the call to holiness, living out our baptismal call as Catholics is done through exercising the Spiritual and Corporal Works of Mercy[55] of our faith.

---

[52] *Evangelii Gaudium*, p. 11.
[53] Ibid., p. 11.
[54] Ibid., p. 11.
[55] CCC, 2247.

Chapter One: Demeanor and Sincerity of Action

Pope Franics suggests that faithful followers of Christ need a "healthy dose of self-criticism"[56] in terms of meeting the needs of both the family and of the problems and situations of our world. He recommends that the answers to those problems must be concrete and understood well by the receiver, which are individuals and families who struggle in some way. The Church is called to offer listening ears and an open heart in accompanying one another. This openness should not be overly abstract or theological to the point of not being understood by the average person. One does not have to have a doctorate in theology to grasp these simple concepts of love and care. In analyzing our behavior toward family and peers daily, we must remember the rudimentary basics of love and charity. Pope Francis states, "We have been called to form consciences, not to replace them."[57] In this way, the primary goal is love toward others. The catechesis and educational pieces are prime, but the bridge is a desire to acquire more knowledge about the faith through charity. Affability is often the initial step in that direction. Friendliness is an intelligent way to be faithful and well-catechized in combination with knowledge of the faith.

All age groups have been affected by lack of faith and a falling-away from the Catholic Church in modern times. With this lack of faith often comes the absence of charity[58] toward others as life's focus often becomes self-concerned with a lack of mission. "Lack of

---

[56] *Amoris Laetitia*, p. 31. Pope Francis is referring to the fact that as faithful followers of Christ we need to always be keenly aware of our intentions and have a desire to do the will of God in all things.

[57] Ibid., p.32

[58] *Evangelii Gaudium*, p. 27.

respect for others and violence are on the rise"[59] causes chaos in our world. This chaos spreads as disrespect and fear grips the hearts of both the young, old, and those in between. Kindness, which is exercised through daily affable interactions, is replaced by barriers of hatred and indifference. This indifference is visible in the expressions between human beings as they fail to see the dignity of those who may be different from them in some way.

It is true that the numbers of those who choose to be Catholic are dwindling year by year and this is a fact in terms of trends[60]. With that in mind, just as Francis suggests we must be self-critical in our faith journey; to be invitational people, we must be open to others and their struggles along the journey of life. The tie between affability and the decline in the number of practicing Catholics are the possibilities of how this virtue offers a bridge to those who have fallen away. Open dialogue blended with genuine care and outreach to a suffering world is a mission which cannot be deferred[61] any longer. These concepts may appear to be too rudimentary, but if put into practice in a tangible way, they could save the Church from–additional decline in the future.

In an examination of what is currently happening throughout the world related to this decline, we witness suffering brought about by attitudes of mediocrity of mission. Francis calls the faithful to be a real part of daily evangelization since the only way the Church will prevail in this way is when everyone takes responsibility and does

---

[59] Ibid., p. 27.

[60] Pew Research Center. "Leaving Catholicism." February 2011. https://www.pewresearch.org/religion/2009/04/27/faith-in-flux3/

[61] *Evangelii Gaudium*, p. 15.

their part. There must be an earnest desire to go forth "to elicit a positive response from all those whom Jesus summons to friendship with him."[62] This positive response we expect from others is not gained through force; it happens through an authentic encounter with the other. The interaction must be affable, kind, and caring and through the spirit of God.

Economic injustices are part of the equation in exercising the virtue of friendliness as a justice due to others in daily interactions. Strangers along the road come in many forms during life's pilgrimage. As members of the Church, we interact with the rich, the poor, and those who are somewhere in the middle in terms of social class and diversified dynamics. Injustices affect each person in a variety of ways as some may have resources but lack friendship and support. In a more visible way to the world, the poor suffer because of economic injustices and deal with a lack of the basics. Oftentimes, they have been shunned by the world and are left marginalized. As Christ's followers, we must be a ray of light guiding all toward tangible love and compassion so that their burdens may be lightened, and life can be lived in joy.

The effects to society when affability is not a part of evangelization efforts are evident in the numbers[63][64] themselves but mostly through what is witnessed in daily living. Pope Francis calls for

---

[62] Ibid., p. 15.

[63] Pew Research Center. "Leaving Catholicism." February 2011. https://www.pewresearch.org/religion/2009/04/27/faith-in-flux3/

[64] Jeffrey Jones, "Church Attendance Has Declined in Most U.S. Religious Groups." Gallup. March 25, 2024. https://news.gallup.com/poll/642548/church-attendance-declined-religious-groups.aspx

missional conversion of the entire human family as the antidote in evangelization efforts. "The poor are the most concrete manifestation of the face of God in history."[65] We must step into the chaos of confusion in other people's lives to help them be guided by the light of Christ's love. Friendliness, although a small seeming attribute, offers care as we strive to understand the complexities in the lives of the alienated, offering them solidarity and kindness.

Tenderness goes together with friendliness in the efforts of missional conversion. The effects of sin in our world include lack of empathy and compassion for others. Often in our efforts to educate the faithful on what it means to be a "good Catholic" we can fall into the practice of looking for results in terms of this definition and in what it means to be a follower of Christ. Occasionally, those devoted to the faith who are active and looking to evangelize, offer book-knowledge catechesis with a "truth-only" view[66] excluding efforts to be a part of this missional effort to love and outreach for the marginalized. Those who feel abandoned by the Church may feel judged by those who have good intentions but who fail to love[67]. Tenderness combined with a non-judgmental listening ear can help to guide the

---

[65] Stan Chu Ilo, "Poverty and the Economic Justice of Pope Francis." Bulletin of Mission Research. DePaul University. Vol. 43. Issue 1. 2019, p. 39. https://doi.org/10.1177/239699318810698

[66] A "truth only" view in this context refers to a mindset which is not all inclusive of the complete deposit of faith and which also may ignore the social teachings of the Church. Affability encompasses all aspects of truth, beauty, and goodness.

[67] "Failing to love" in this context refers to those who may be well-educated in the faith but who fail to practice what the Church teaches on loving others in imitation of Christ.

Chapter One: Demeanor and Sincerity of Action

lost back to the love of God through simple efforts of friendliness and charity. We must learn to not only laugh together on our life journey, but to also cry together[68] to show empathy and true concern for those who feel neglected by the Church. Since affability encompasses all aspects of truth, beauty and goodness, truths related to affability tie together the valuable teachings of the Church on genuine and sincere love.

One aspect of division both inside the church and outside is the idea of traditional versus progressives. Some may argue that this distinction is an issue of economics and other factors. This is where the notion of inserting affability as a treasured virtue brings back the idea of politeness, kindness, and the ability to hear the "other side" of a disagreement. Whatever we believe in terms of the political spectrum, in whatever the sphere of discussion or belief, affability builds a bridge of oneness as members of the human family. There are currently divisions in the church similar to the political systems of our world. We will always have cause and reason to disagree on matters, but this call for a new direction[69] of understanding is necessary in evangelical efforts. The efforts help us to gain back our priorities in terms of the missional call to make outreach to the alienated.

It is never too late to partake in the missional efforts of the Church. The invitation is infinitely open to all to follow Christ and to be a part of the solution and not of the problem. The issue is in the understanding and in the decision to not only know the faith but to

---

[68] Ibid., p. 41.
[69] Ibid., p. 40.

live it. Graciousness[70] toward others is another avenue to accomplish this in order to diminish the neglect that a vast amount of people experience related to rejection and isolation. Through graciousness, love is given without expecting anything in return. We are called to exercise graciousness with those who may feel misplaced and not part of community. When the faithful do not exercise virtues such as friendliness, the effects of this disconnect in society manifests itself in the escalation of violence, war, poverty, and disregard for human life. This indifference is the outcome of not partaking in the broader vision of the Church which is a greater awareness of and care for the complexities which arise out of marriage and family life. The Church has the responsibility to respond to the doctrinal, moral, spiritual, and pastoral[71] questions of the faithful. The goal is to find greater clarity of mission, and this is a job for all members of the Church.

In pondering the effects of where the Church has missed the mark in exercising affability in a more tangible way, there may be reason to feel a sense of loss considering all of the missed opportunities. Although this may be true in terms of those failures, Pope Francis alludes[72] to the fact that there is reason for great hope because dialogue and discussion in these matters offers Godly solutions which can transform our world as we know it. At the root of it is the desire to pass on the faith to our children[73]. The effects of lack of love and charity will not deter God's love to work in the hearts of all who

---

[70] *Fratelli Tutti*, p. 86. Graciousness is the act or feeling of being thankful toward others and to God for the gifts he bestows on all of his children.

[71] *Amoris Laetitia*, p. 9.

[72] Ibid., p. 12.

[73] Ibid., p. 216.

love him so that the truths of the faith can be passed down and exercised to the next generation. When we, as members of the Church, have compassion for the complex situations of families throughout the world, we begin to foster healing through active listening and care. This listening helps to bridge the sadness often experienced in family life when tragedy occurs and when the practice of faith becomes a chore.

An overall view of the effects of lack of affable dialogue with others, which exercises love and listening, suggests that the Church has much work to do. There is, however, great hope when the human family and the domestic church come together to make the necessary efforts needed to bridge the gap. This cannot be done without a recognition of the importance of the family as the basic unit of society. We must recognize that in every aspect each member of the family is needed and has immense value by God. Francis states:

> The family is important, and it is necessary for the survival of humanity. Without the family, the cultural survival of the human race would be at risk. The family, whether we like it or not, is the foundation.[74]

Families and individuals who open their hearts to the will of God in exercising friendliness especially to those who feel abandoned by the Church can make a difference in the future effects of affability in our culture. Accepting the missional invitation to partake in the

---

[74] USCCB. *Pope Francis and the Family*, Libreria Editrice Vaticana, 2014, p. 4.

restoration of social bonds both at home and globally will assist in making this imperative work part of the foundation of society now and in the future.

Chapter Two

Church Teachings on Human Interaction, Community, and the Desire of Love

I. Church Teachings on Love of God and Neighbor

The teachings of the Church[1] on love of God and neighbor point to an active relationship with Christ knowing no bounds in love and charity for the other. "Love does no wrong to a neighbor; therefore, love is the fulfilling of the law."[2] Since love knows no bounds, the same can be said on the willingness to exercise the virtues of the faith. These teachings are offered as positive guidance to living a more grace-filled life in following the commands of God in loving best our Father and our neighbor. The family is always at the heart of this mission as the domestic church is the gateway for involvement in missionary activities to those who are away from the Church.

Moving beyond oneself is a primary way to say "yes" to the call to missional undertakings and in the universal call to holiness. We, as members of the Church, must not be closed in upon ourselves both individually and within family life. We must embrace the cross put before us and make outreach to those people God has placed within reach who feel neglected and abandoned. Love of God and of neighbor reminds us that the baptismal call encourages the faithful

---

[1] CCC, 2196.
[2] Ibid.

to live the commission we were given at the time of our baptism and at confirmation.

With this call, missional love requires us to remove boundaries such as prejudice, bias, and exclusion. We must face the challenges and fix what we lack with God's grace and help. Pope Francis states:

> Closed groups and self-absorbed couples that define themselves in opposition to others tend to be expressions of selfishness and mere self-preservation.[3]

This idea of "self-preservation" is in opposition to the teachings of the Church in terms of how we, Christ's followers, may be a part of the worldwide community of faith in exercising love and virtue. A love more open[4] impels us to universal communities out of love for the marginalized. In pondering where the family fits into the grand scheme of this landscape; it is in breaking the chains of the limitations which societies have placed on themselves in not being open to the good of the other. Affability and friendliness fit into these evangelization efforts as an initial step to making tangible what was once intangible. Friendliness and kindness are the opposite of the "self-preservation" mentality which isolates communities and the world.

Liberty, equality, and fraternity[5] which is taught by the Catholic Church are necessary attributes which enhance freedom for all. There can be the tendency toward a shallow understanding of what

---

[3] *Fratelli Tutti*, p.58.
[4] Ibid., p.60.
[5] Ibid., p. 64.

these words encompass in pondering more fully. Pope Francis reminds us that in thinking through their meanings, we must remember that our brothers and sisters are not "associates"[6] they are children of God deserving of love and care not just by God *but by us too*. It is important to distinguish this as the faithful sometimes may fall into the mentality that once a person understands and knows the love of God in evangelizing efforts, life will be perfectly transformed. Although this, at times, is partially correct, God acts through his followers and through our living the faith. We must not only wish and *desire* for people to experience and know God's love solely. We must partake in missional action and be a part of their experiences of love and care when we are able. The charity given toward our world collectively is part of the mission. In leaving ourselves out of this picture of "love" is incorrect theology[7]. Love of God includes our own "yes" in imitating him and in being a part of both the smaller and larger pictures of evangelization. In only desiring for others to be loved by God, which they already are, is just a piece of this dynamic. Followers of Christ are to make tangible which may appear to be almost impossible.

This is a universal love that promotes persons since everyone has the right to live with dignity given by God. This dignity is never based on circumstances but on the intrinsic worth they have from the Father. We are partakers in this mission, and we are called to love and imitate Christ by actions and through love of him and of neighbor. These are the teachings of the Church which guide the faithful

---

[6] Ibid., p.65.
[7] CCC, 1823.

to care deeply through words, activity, and charity toward others. Misunderstandings[8] exist in terms of judgements and biases toward the poor and those in need. This call to universal love invites Christ's followers to promote moral good and to see the value of each person encountered every day and at each moment.

Pastoral accompaniment is relevant to the modern church. Pope Francis speaks of the "logic of mercy"[9] as the means to make pastoral outreach to those who feel alone and rejected by society. This mercy is available through the gifts of the Holy Spirit in direct response to God's call to the faithful to walk alongside those who need to know both God's love and the love we have to offer in tactile ways. "Acting in accordance with the logic of mercy, the Church bears witness to her fidelity to God and makes a significant contribution to building a more human world."[10] Building a more human world requires patience and charity. Exercising the virtue of affability is a stepping-stone in helping to build and rebuild a world based on the love of God and others.

The logic of mercy must also consider that misunderstandings can and will happen both in family life in smaller ways and within the larger scale of the universal church. The reason it is important to take a step back and evaluate, discuss, and most of all to pray is because it is integral in finding healing. Francis writes:

---

[8] *Fratelli Tutti*, p. 66.

[9] Ryszard Hajduk, "Pope Francis, Renewal of Pastoral Care in the Logic of Mercy." University of Warmia and Mazury in Olyzlyn. 2021, p. 301. https://doi.org/10.31648/sw.6378

[10] Ibid., p. 301.

To show understanding in the face of exceptional situations never implies dimming the light of the fuller ideal, or proposing less than what Jesus offers to the human being.[11]

In marriage and family, there are various exceptional situations which occur in the world today which challenge families and tempt them to give up on their faith journeys. This is where the Church steps forth to encourage, care for, and invite back. True evangelization happens when Church teachings on marriage and family are acknowledged and grasped. It is never a one-size fits all approach in terms of pastoral ministry. We, as the faithful, must listen and care about each situation that occurs and offer the guidance and love of God in the process so that healing can take place over time.

Love of God and of neighbor is established and solidified as we come together as a Church in understanding the logic of mercy and how this reasoning can transform not only our own lives but all those around us. It is a love which encompasses all the virtues of faith, and considering this discussion, also affability which is exercised through sincere kindness and a willingness to befriend those who need help and accompaniment. Mercy is at the heart of how we express love and compassion for our neighbors. Mercy impels the faithful to proclaim the Gospel to all the corners of the world in making real the teachings of the Church and the universal call to holiness as disciples of Christ. Pope Francis writes:

---

[11] *Amoris Laetitia*, p. 239.

Evangelization is the task of the Church. The Church are the agents of evangelization, is more than an organic and hierarchical institution. She is first and foremost a people advancing on the way its pilgrim way toward God.[12]

As pilgrims journeying toward God, we walk the path Christ did in carrying his cross and in following the will of his Father, our Father. Mercy toward others and evangelization combine in assisting the faithful to do God's will and in announcing and living the Gospel in daily life. This expression of love is mercy in action accompanying individuals and families through times of challenge and adversity.

The salvation of the world is not just about the salvation of others in exclusion of ourselves. It has to do with conversion of heart that affects "me" in my daily path toward heaven. The way of the cross is the road to heaven. Church teachings and scripture proclaim that we are to "go and make disciples of all nations."[13] In moving forward in the process to make disciples, we love God with our whole hearts and minds and others as much as we love ourselves. As Francis writes:

> God has found a way to unite himself to every human being in every age. He has chosen to call them together as a people not as isolated individuals.[14]

---

[12] *Evangelii Gaudium*, p. 56.
[13] Matthew 28:19, NOAB.
[14] *Evangelii Gaudium*, p. 57.

The theme of calling us out of isolation comes forth again from Pope Francis, and this is in union with the teachings of the Church on love of God and of neighbor. As we are called out the isolation of selfishness, self-preservation, and prejudice toward the marginalized, we find ourselves in the love of God prepared to go forward in faith. The Church cannot be changed for the good without the hard work of the faithful. The Lord needs every member to come forth to make a conscious decision to exercise the teachings of the Church on love of God and neighbor in a sincere way and in being friendly and loving toward others in the process.

II. Communio Theology

Communio theology stems from the goal of living a life filled with the life of Christ, walking with him and in living in the three persons of the Trinity, Father, Son, and Holy Spirit. This life willingly draws itself to Christ through the Paschal Mystery of faith and draws on the love of God, our Creator. In developing our relationship with God to the highest level, we can then learn how to be a friend to others in communion with the Lord on the deepest plane. This relates to affability since authentic friendship calls us, as Christ's followers, out of ourselves and into sacrificial love for others. In moving away from self-interest we find fulfillment in giving ourselves to those around us.

> The self moves forth from itself in the ecstasis of love and knowledge not in order to subjugate or subdue, but to encounter being that is 'separate and external.' Aristotle says

very clearly that philoi are 'the greatest of the external goods.' This unassailable separateness of the other, notwithstanding my involvement in his life, is part of what makes friendship an apprenticeship in virtue; through my discernment of his separateness; my respect for it, my reticence before it, I learn to see my friend as another subject, another center of freedom and personhood; not, despite the affinity that has drawn us together, as an equivalent centre of self.[15]

The "apprenticeship in virtue" is a lesson in treating the other with kindness, dignity, and respect as we learn that friends are indeed separate from us, however the freedom given to the other is what joins friends in Christ. The freedom to be oneself and to allow a friend to do the same creates space for growth and for virtue to blossom within the relationship. The nature and demeanor of this freedom is pleasant and affable since it is justice given to the other through the gifts of the spirit.

In adhering to virtue in friendship and in communion with the Lord in all things, relationships begin to flourish, and selfishness becomes less prevalent in daily interactions. Being called out of oneself through a "discernment of separateness"[16], we can appreciate a friend as a true and valued gift from God in living and being together in communion. Although this depiction of friendship is of one friend to another, it is multiplied when friends invite more people into this communion, and the result is growth in the domestic church at large.

---

[15] Communio, International Catholic Review, p. 255.
[16] Ibid., p. 255.

Chapter Two: Human Interaction, Community, and the Desire of Love 57

Sympathy and Common Interests

In further thought and discussion on the communion of friendship, there are different bonds that form both in friendship and in love. There are a variety of ways that relationships develop, where they begin, and where they end up. When virtue is a grand part of this equation, and when Christ is at the heart of this participation, sympathy, develops. In addition to sympathy, feelings are developed which often guide the spirit in varying directions in matters of the heart.

To these bonds of sympathy and interest, however, there is added a quality of excitement that typically characterizes two forms of human relationships; that of people who are, in the mysterious phase, "in love;" and the no less mysterious encounter between 'mind and delighted mind" (Yeates words), which is a feature of certain intellectual friendships. By intellectual friendships I do not simply mean friendships based on 'common interests,' such as we might find between two chess players, but rather, a commingling of ideas between people for whom the life of the mind is as real as the life of the feelings, who as Eliot famously has it in one of the great essays of our time, 'feel their thought,' for whom, 'a thought it an experience, modifying their sensibility. Such friends will typically talk about books, and ideas, dispassionately and without any explicit or embarrassing self-disclosure, yet speaking obliquely out of their deep impassioned quest for truth, for a just perception of the whole reality, a quest so constitutive for their inner life.[17]

Friendships vary in terms of how and why we feel connected to another person. We may begin a friendship with true sympathy and compassion for another, and as the relationship progresses the nature of the bond becomes more comfortable over time. Common interests have a great deal to do with some of the initial attractions in a friendship, and the camaraderie developed may lead to various discussions related to pastimes and activities which are shared together. Although the conversations may surround upon familiar topics, the associations which are formed have less to do with those amusements and more to do with the deeper bonds being formed in communion with one another. *Where does affability fit into this picture?* The nature of these "intellectual friendships" and connections are also based in the heart. These ties, when rooted in virtue, are affable and just since the spirit is at work in the souls of people who allow the Holy Spirit to live and breathe in dialogue with one another.

The quest for truth in friendship leads in a positive direction for all involved in the daily living out of deep, and virtuous friendship. Friends learn to care about the "little things" of life and of the most valuable parts of the relationship between both the giver and the receiver. In the self-disclosure and freedom granted to all members of a genuine familiarity with one another in a close-knit bond, there is a warm and sympathetic openness which allows each person the space to be who they are. This leads to even deeper communion with

---

[17] Ibid., p. 263-264.

one another and with God as the spirit dwells. Sympathy and common interests often lead to immeasurable attachments which are affable and virtuous.

Wisdom is Needed in this Age

St. Pope John Paul II in his Apostolic Exhortation, *Familiaris Consortio* wrote about the need for wisdom in the modern age. In his piece he mentions the dignity of both the human person and of marriage. The domestic church consists of "communio," the relationships which make up the universal Church and the presence of the Holy Spirit and the guidance he instills to his people. This is not an automatic happening, as wisdom is needed in order to mature as families and as a Church worldwide.

> It becomes necessary, therefore, on the part of all, to recover an awareness of the primacy of moral values, which are the values of the human person as such. The great task that has to be faced today for the renewal of society is that of recapturing the ultimate meaning of life and its fundamental values. Only an awareness of the primacy of these values enables man to use the immense possibilities given him by science in such a way as to bring about the true advancement of the human person in his or her whole truth, in his or her freedom and dignity. Science is called to ally itself with wisdom.[18]

---

[18] Pope John Paul II. *Familiaris Consortio. Apostolic Exhortation.* Vatican.va. November 22, 1981, No. 8.

Pope John Paul calls upon the faithful to seek wisdom and the "primacy of moral values" one of which is the virtues of justice. Affability, of course, being a virtue of justice is one of those values we as God's people are called upon to pursue. Doing so enables us to have deeper communion with others and the Church at large. He also says "science is called to ally itself with wisdom" which is a call to use the tools that science has given the world to create and foster greater care of family life and of God's children. Making science an ally reveals that as Catholics we can learn from fields of science including human development and psychology to better understand how to build bridges of hope in the world through the wisdom given us in Church teachings. This is a call to communion in creating a more just society which includes affability.

Communio Draws Us Toward God

In Pope Emeritus Benedict XVI's encyclical, *Deus Caritas Est.*, he speaks about this communion of love between the Creator and his creation. He states that through love of God and of neighbor we can be truly united:

> Here we need to consider yet another aspect: this sacramental 'mysticism' is social in character, for in sacramental communion I become one with the Lord, like all the other communicants. As Saint Paul says, 'Because there is one bread, we who are many are one body, for we all partake of the one bread' (1 Cor 10:17). Union with Christ is also union with all those to whom he gives himself. I cannot possess Christ just

for myself; I can belong to him only in union with l those who have become, or who will become, his own. Communion draws me out of myself towards him, and thus also towards unity with all Christians. We become 'one body,' completely joined in a single existence. Love of God and love of neighbour are now truly united: God incarnate draws us all to himself.[19]

He states we become "completely joined by a single existence," which is the true definition of what communion means in terms of the connection with both God those around us. Communio theology which is often centered around the teachings of St. Pope John Paul II and Pope Emeritus Benedict XVI coincides with the theories presented in this book. Moral virtues, including affability, lead to deeper communion with God, the domestic church, and the universal Church. "Communion" draws me out of myself towards him, and thus also towards unity with all Christians."[20] The essence of communion calls each of us to imitate the Lord through kindness in offering ourselves to others in solidarity.

III. Ecclesiology and Soteriology in Relation to Communal Outreach

On the topic of Church teachings on human interaction, community, and the desire to love there are also the ecclesial and

---

[19] Pope Benedict XVI. *Deus Caritas Est. God is Love.* Liberia Editrice Vaticana. Kindle Version. December 25, 2005, Location 245-255.
[20] Ibid.

soteriology aspects relative to this discussion. Ecclesiology is the theological study of the Catholic Church as an organization, and its progressive development over the course of years. Pope Emeritus Benedict XVI has written a great deal on the topic of ecclesiology, and his theories have been adopted and implanted by many parishes and dioceses throughout the world in modern times. Soteriology is the study of salvation. Soteriology has much to say on the topic of how human actions and virtues have much to do with salvation questions related to it. In looking at both ecclesiology and soteriology and modern-day effects on evangelization, we can grasp more fully how the Church can grow in making outreach to the marginalized.

Ecclesiology

Knowing that ecclesiology is the study of the Church as an organization, we turn to intelligent and trusted theologians to understand the relevance and importance of the mission of the Catholic Church on a whole. With the study comes the meaning of "theology" itself. Pope Emeritus Benedict XVI writes:

Scripture, the Word we have been given, with which theology concerns itself, does not, on the basis of its own nature exist as a book alone. Its the human author, the People of God, alive and through all the ages has its own consistent identity.[21]

---

[21] Joseph Ratzinger, *Pilgrim Fellowship of Faith*. Ignatius Press. 2005, p. 47.

God is the divine author of Sacred Scripture, working through human authors who were inspired by the Holy Spirit. In a similar way, the Catechism of the Catholic Church is authored by the Church under the guidance of the Holy Spirit. "Theology" likewise seeks to be guided by God, though it always requires careful discernment.

We cannot speak of the Church and its ecclesial mission without mention of the Holy Spirit and of the Holy Eucharist. Benedict speaks of the Holy Spirit as love. In this way the Holy Spirit is also a gift given by God as the Lord's way of nourishing his children during the earthly pilgrimage in the quest to live for God and to do good. In reflecting upon the concepts presented in this book on the relevance of affability in the evangelical efforts of the Church, we learn that openness to others and a friendly spirit enables one to exercise charity toward the less fortunate in all encounters. We cannot do this alone, as the Holy Spirit is the means to love others best, especially those who have been rejected. Benedict writes:

> He and he alone is, at the profound level, the fresh water without which there is no life. In the image of a spring, of the water that irrigates and transforms a desert, that man meets like a secret promise, the mystery of the Spirit becomes visible in an ineffable fashion that no rational meditation can encompass.[22]

---

[22] Ibid., p. 47.

Jesus is that water that refreshes the soul, and he comes to the faithful through his spirit in prayer and through the sacramental gifts of the Catholic Church. These gifts are life-giving, and they offer all we need in terms of the direction of our lives in living out the Beatitudes.[23] Without the spirit of God living in us and in exercising these virtues of faith, there would be no life within us. This is the ecclesial mission of the Church in loving and accepting Christ's teachings in order to bring true peace in knowing the heart of God in daily existence.

Additionally, a discussion on the ecclesial mission of the Church cannot be had without prayer and the daily communication with God that is necessary for salvation and for the pilgrim journey on earth. Prayer enables us, his followers, to open our hearts to the Lord's will and to those who feel apart from God. It should always be our mission as disciples of Christ to care about the ways in which we can love and serve. In this journey of faith, the poor should always be close to our hearts. The poor are those who may be defined as "poor" such as those who do not have adequate food, shelter, clothing, or support. In addition, the poor are people we know well. Family, friends, acquaintances, co-workers, neighbors, those at church, and strangers we meet along the way may also be "poor," as previously mentioned. Those who are poor need to know someone cares, is praying, and is with them on the path of life. This is where affability can make a profound impact in the ecclesial mission of the church in striving to do good in making a difference to alleviate suffering. Pope Francis writes on the topic of the poor:

---

[23] Matthew 5:7, NOAB.

We are called to be poor, to strip ourselves; and do this we must learn how to be with the poor, to share with those who lack basic necessities, to touch the flesh of Christ. The Christian is not one who speaks about the poor, no! He is one who encounters them, who looks them in the eye, and who touches them.[24]

Learning "how to be with the poor" involves pastoral care and accompaniment. It is not a verification-list activity; is much more than this. It involves prayer, time, effort, and love. This is an active love that desires to be close to God and to others at the same time. It involves removing selfishness and desires from our minds and hearts to exercise God's will in loving and caring for the rejected of the world. This is the ecclesial mission of the Church that we, the faithful, make a conscience effort and a decision to be part of the solution and not a part of the problem by remaining inactive in these efforts. This mission can also involve family members who need to know the love of God in a tangible way.

The ecclesial actions of the Church would not be complete without further discussion of the Holy Eucharist and in being lovers of the bread of life in all aspects of our lives. The Holy Spirit is alive and active in trying to live this mission each day. In conjunction to receiving the Eucharist and in prayer to our heavenly Father, Pope Benedict writes on the topic:

He is 'our bread' – ours as what is not ours, as what is entirely

---

[24] Pope Francis. General Audience. www.vatican.va. October 4, 2013.

wholly given. 'Our' Spirit is not our spirit."[25]

The bread of life we receive enables us, his followers, to live as Jesus did, which is part of the ecclesial mission of the Church. The spirit of God is not accomplished on our own as Benedict writes, it is the Lord's. This gift restores our relationship with God and the bonds of love which formed and created humanity. We must strive always to recognize the Eucharist as the true body, blood, soul, and divinity of Christ and let others know the real presence of Christ is alive on earth and in our hearts. The Eucharist enables us, Christ's followers, to be able to love God to a higher degree and to live in deeper communion with him.

Lumen Gentium,[26] the Dogmatic Constitution of the Church has much to say in terms of the ecclesial mission of the Catholic Church. Pope Benedict contributed to the writing of this document of the Church, and he reflects that all the teachings of the Church come from God himself through the Holy Spirit as gift. He states:

> Fellowship with God is mediated by the fellowship of God with man, which is Christ in person; the encounter with Christ brings about fellowship with him and, thus, with the Father in the Holy Spirit; on this basis it unites men with one another.[27]

---

[25] Joseph Ratzinger, *Pilgrim Fellowship of Faith*. Ignatius Press. 2005, p. 49.

[26] Pope Paul VI. *Lumen Gentium*. The Dogmatic Constitutions of the Church. 1964. This book will refer to this Church document as: *LG*.

[27] Ibid., p. 130.

This is at the heart of the ecclesial mission of the universal church as the goal is the relationship between God the Father and that of all his children through the Holy Spirit and the gift of the Eucharist. The Holy Spirit will unite these efforts to create a culture of encounter within the Church and toward the world. The Eucharist and the Mass is the nucleus of this work. This mission is essential as we live the faith in higher levels of communion with the Lord.

Soteriology

Since soteriology is the study of the salvation of the Church, this book would not be fully accomplished without mentioning how it affects the mission in evangelization efforts. Salvation is attained by the grace of God by the power of the Holy Spirit to justify us[28]. The Catholic Church teaches and believes that salvation comes by virtue of God's grace and by the Paschal Mystery[29] of the faith which is the life, death resurrection, and ascension of our Lord Jesus Christ. We cannot accomplish this on our own, it is given by God, through the gift of his son. Catholics believe that the offering of an affirmative "yes" to God as an acceptance of salvation is something we do not just once but each day of our lives.

When the Blessed Mother Mary, gave her fiat to God in being the Mother of God, this was the beginning of the salvific journey of the Church. Without this "yes" by Mary, the work of salvation would not have occurred. For this reason, Our Lady has a crucial role in the

---

[28] CCC, 1987.
[29] Ibid., 1085.

salvation of the world as Christ's mother and our mother. Praying and interceding to Mary is a beautiful way Catholics enhance their faith, come closer to Christ, and unite to the Lord. Interceding to Mary for all of the Church's missional efforts is imperative and for the salvation of the world.

The Church and her presence are part of the salvation efforts of the Church. When a person falls away from the faith or decides to leave, it impacts the entire body of Christ. Pope Emeritus Benedict states:

> The Church is not there for her own sake but should be the instrument of God for gathering men to him, so as to prepare for the moment when God shall be everything to everyone.[30]

It is a true statement to reflect in prayer that the Church's *presence* alone continues to make an impact in terms of the salvation of the faithful and of the human family. The doors are open to all. A question we may ask ourselves is: *Does everyone feel welcome?* In respect to the topic of affability, it is a gateway to continuing to build bridges of love and respect as in invitation for all to join in the mission of the Church and be an active member.

---

[30] Joseph Ratzinger, *Pilgrim Fellowship of Faith*. Ignatius Press. 2005, p. 129.

IV. The Desire to Love is Expressed within Community

The desire within our hearts to be loved and to love comes from God. This is expressed within community beginning in the domestic church, to smaller communities and in parishes, and to the entire universal Church. With this aspiration also comes a thirst to help the poor. To be genuinely happy in this world is a desire to bless and care for those who suffer, those who go without, and those who do not feel loved. This inclination to love ignites our hearts to service and to live out the works of mercy each day. We must hear the call of the poor, those who the Church instructs us to not only pray for but also to tangibly help, when able. On the topic of friendliness and sincerity, we begin to walk that path by being affable to those with whom we meet whether family, friends, or strangers. Pope Francis writes:

> Each individual Christian and every community is called to be an instrument for God for the liberation and promotion of the poor and for enabling them to be fully part of society. This demands that we be docile and attentive to the cry of the poor and to come to their aid.[31]

This is a serious calling for the faithful to jump into mission and partake by acting. Each individual and community is called, and it is a gift from God to not only receive the call but to make a conscience decision to do it, as well. We, as members of the Church, recognize this call through prayer to the Holy Spirit. Acting on this mission

---

[31] *Evangelii Gaudium*, p. 94.

fulfills the desire of the heart to serve, and it brings a certain closeness to the Lord in walking side by side with him in the daily missional activities of the Catholic Church. We live in a world which has lost the meaning of the importance of this calling which brings lightness of heart to life and brings joy to those who say "yes" to God in ministering to the poor.

How is all this accomplished? It is accomplished through an openness of spirit and through courage of heart. Courage, which is accomplished by acting on the good, comes through prayer and perseverance and through a desire to do the will God in all circumstances especially those related to caring and loving the ostracized and in offering them friendship. Mary, our Mother, is the greatest saint of the Church and one to intercede along the path of life in gaining courage to partake in ministry. Through her prayerful guidance and in modeling her life of submission to God in all things, we can do the same when it comes to the desire of heart to participate in community and to serve. In doing so, members of the church can model after Mary and the saints who loved the Lord with all their hearts, souls, and minds.

Many times, these desires to act for others begin at home but branch out to parishes and communities. There is much wisdom to gain in listening and reflecting on the teachings of the Church in making this special outreach to the poor and forsaken. We, the faithful, must have a certain air of faith to accomplish this for God and for others. Pope Francis writes:

> Let us become bold in exploring new ways with which our communities can be homes where the door is always open.

And open door! And it is important that the welcome is followed by a clear proposal of the faith; many times a proposal of the faith may not be explicit but is conveyed by attitude, by witness. In the institution called the Church, in the institution called the parish; one breathes the air of faith because one believes in the Lord Jesus.[32]

The image of the open door in community is one of warmth and welcome. We can ponder this image both in terms of the domestic church, the home, and of the parish community. In addition, the image of the universal Church as being open to newcomers and those who are not practicing the faith comes to mind, as well. The breath of fresh air guiding us through the Holy Spirit enables us, his followers, to reach the unreachable. In the same way the image of opening a door to breathe fresh air, we can be guided to pursue the virtue of friendliness. As basic as it may sound, affability helps to open the doors wider for inclusion. It offers strangers who may be afraid to enter the doors a chance to feel welcomed and included.

We, as members of the Church, can remind all those we encounter that they do not need to be perfect to come back to the Church. What is needed is a desire to learn, to grow, and to pray for conversion of heart as a first step. After initial steps of faith are taken, being formally introduced to either becoming a Catholic or in coming back to the faith could follow. All these activities can and must be guided in charity in walking alongside those who feel as an outcast in

---

[32] Pope Francis. General Audience. www.Vatican.va. June 16, 2014.

accompanying them to the Lord and his Church. This is a job not just for some. This is the ecclesial mission of the Church.

The desire to seek community springs a joy like no other in the decision to follow Christ for the good of the other. In family life, when a mission is formed and acted on, members of the family find their place in the world. Fulfillment is found aside from worldly desires which often bombard the minds of many. This fulfillment is about service, and in imitation of Christ. Christian families can find a peace like no other being guided by the spirit. Francis writes:

> …It represents an invitation to Christian families to value the gifts of marriage and family, and to persevere in a love strengthened by the virtues of generosity, commitment, fidelity, and patience.[33]

This perseverance of the heart is one that takes on the burdens within that family unit enabling everyone to love and to serve together. The same idea is brought forth in this service at the parish level and the entire Church at large. A daily decision of service is to consider the less fortunate in helping to restore their dignity through friendship. We live in a world centered on the things apart from God such as power, money, honor, and various vices. Unfortunately, this is the path of destruction as it leaves out those who feel rejected and who do not have the support they deserve. In partaking in the family mission of evangelization, we, his followers, make the decision to put

---

[33] *Amoris Laetitia*, p. 11.

aside sinful habits such as selfishness and self-centeredness and instead direct our hearts and minds to love of the poor.

In these efforts to discover this mission and in moving ahead in reaching those who are cast aside by our world, we express and fulfill the desire to love at the highest level. Peace and love build bridges which last a lifetime. It is the will of God that we, the faithful, continue this path of charity. In evangelization, the Church must never forget that we must meet people where they are and not where we feel they should be in terms of faith and spirituality.

Chapter Three

Biblical Sources that Demonstrate Friendliness is an Integral Part of the Call to Holiness

I. The Old Testament and the Virtue of Friendliness

There are hundreds of verses in the Old Testament which allude to the fact that friendliness and affability are integral in the faith life. Proverbs and the Psalms are prevalent chapters in the bible which offer wisdom on these topics. I will explore *a small sampling* of the evidence which suggests that affability is a predominant theme in the Old Testament toward those who wish to live a better life and make greater outreach to the poor and less fortunate. Verses and passages were chosen based on the fact that the moral virtue of affability is present in these biblical stories. There are a variety of other verses which are not presented in this book.

Genesis

Kindness and affability go hand in hand in terms of interactions and reactions to others. When one demonstrates love for others and God's creation, it is also a way show an open spirit ready to help with delight. This is affability. God's love is demonstrated in varied ways throughout Genesis and the Old Testament which in turn shows justice toward his children. As the Old Testament timeline proceeds, in chapter twenty-four of Genesis, Abraham prayed to the Lord for his son Isaac to find a wife. Verse fourteen speaks of the prayer of Abraham's heart in this regard:

> Let the girl to whom I shall say, 'Please offer your jar that I may drink and who shall say 'Drink' and I will water your camels'—let her be the one whom you have appointed[1] for your servant Isaac. By this I shall know that you have shown steadfast love to my master.[2]

Abraham's plea to God was that his son would find a virtuous wife who displayed affability and kindness. He prayed God would reveal her upright character upon being asked the favor of doing a good deed as presented. In the proceeding verses of that section of scripture, Rebekah[3] appears coming out with the water jar on her shoulders.[4] The story continues with all its twists, but the voice of God is clear in the outcome. The lesson to be learned is that Abraham's prayer was not solely for his son to find a beautiful, attractive wife but that kindness would be the most prevalent piece of her

---

[1] The word "appointed" in Hebrew translates to nominate or designate. In Latin, it also translates to designate or define. In Greek, to depute or name. Paul A. Boer, Sr. *A Catholic Interlinear Bible. Old Testament Polyglot. Vol. 1. Genesis, Exodus, and Leviticus in English, Latin, and Transliterated Greek and Hebrew.* Kindle Edition. Veritatis Splendor Publications. 2013, Location 5600.

[2] Genesis 24:14, NOAB.

[3] Rebekah will eventually become the wife of Isaac and the mother of Jacob and Esau.

[4] Ibid., p. 43.

personality. This is evident in her reaction to meeting someone new and in need.

Later in the book of Genesis, the story of Joseph and his brother demonstrates that in holding fast to virtue despite all troubling circumstances, God has the final say in our lives. Joseph displays great faith during times of alienation from the rest of his family when he is threatened, placed in exile, and in danger of death. God sent Joseph to Egypt to preserve the lives of his entire family and others from the threat of dying from a seven-year famine. In Genesis, Joseph lays down his life to save his people[5]. He brings the blessing of God to all the nations. He forgave his brothers for leaving him for dead and for trying to kill him. Joseph repays good for evil toward his family. In the last chapter of Genesis, chapter fifty, Joseph, and his family make full reconciliation when Joseph proclaims:

> "Do not be afraid! Am I in the place of God? Even though you intended to do harm to me, God intended it for good, in order to preserve a numerous people, as he is doing today. So have no fear; I myself will provide for you and your little ones." In this way, he assured them, speaking kindly[6] to them.[7]

---

[5] Joseph saved his people by providing bread for Israel and saved them from dying, all without cost.

[6] The word "kindly" in Hebrew translates to soft-hearted or compassionate. In Latin, to misericordiam or graciously. In Greek, to warm-heartedness or willingness. Paul A. Boer, Sr. *A Catholic Interlinear Bible. Old Testament Polyglot. Vol. 1. Genesis, Exodus, and Leviticus in English, Latin, and Transliterated Greek and Hebrew.* Kindle Edition. Veritatis Splendor Publications. 2013, Location 12080-12094.

[7] Genesis 50:19-21, NOAB.

The last verse of the scripture above speaks loudly of the significance of affability. Notice that Joseph speaks kindly to them. In other words, it was *not* just about the message he was giving. In speaking kindly, he demonstrated that being friendly and affable is a valuable virtue. For those who have gone through similar trials such as betrayal, back-stabbing, and suffering deep alienation, the way that we speak and communicate is not just about the message itself. It is about the way it is said, and the love put into it. Joseph's story is a testament to this point.

Exodus

God himself is the divine image of mercy and of kindness toward all, and the Old Testament demonstrates this repeatedly. In the book of Exodus, God spoke to Moses on Mount Sinai as Moses presents the tablets to the Lord:

> The Lord, the Lord, a God merciful[8] and gracious, slow to anger and abounding in steadfast love and faithfulness, keeping standfast love for the thousandth generation, forgiving inequity and transgression and sin, yet by no means clearing the guilty, but visiting the inequity of the parents upon the

---

[8] The word "merciful" in Hebrew translates to soft-hearted or tender-hearted. In Latin, to misericors or compassionate. In Greek, to pitiful or ruthful. Paul A. Boer, Sr. *A Catholic Interlinear Bible. Old Testament Polyglot. Vol. 1. Genesis, Exodus, and Leviticus in English, Latin, and Transliterated Greek and Hebrew.* Kindle Edition. Veritatis Splendor Publications. 2013, Location 21246-21264.

children and the children's children, to the third and fourth generation."[9]

God displays his very nature as affable not only toward Moses but to all generations. By mentioning the third and fourth generations in the verses above, God's love prevails as he promises to exercise steadfast love in the years to come. Affability is a smaller piece of the picture of God's love and charity toward all his children, but nonetheless, the nature of God in these verses and others in the Old Testament suggest his kind and friendly nature in being "slow to anger." Holding back anger is a virtue when there is good reason to act on justified cruelty in the world. However, God demonstrates that even in these kinds of circumstances, he chooses to act in love which includes an affable and kind spirit.

Job

The age-old story of Job in the Old Testament is another example of how the virtue of affability is prevalent. The theme of the book is on the prevalence of suffering endured by Job, a man who attempted to understand the hardships that engulfed his life. Job is the righteous servant of God who faithfully prayed to God during the most challenging of life's adventures and adversities. By continuing his prayers and by staying silent before the Lord, the tapestry of Job's life displays that following the will of God has its end in the love of the Lord. In chapter six, Job's prayer to the Lord speaks of the noteworthiness of kindness and affability toward others:

---

[9] Exodus 34:6-7, NOAB.

Those who withhold kindness from a friend[10] forsake the fear of the almighty.[11]

Forsaking the fear of the almighty suggests that those who do not display kindness and goodness toward others are making an omission. Since kindness and friendliness go together, it suggests that despite the most burdensome circumstances of Job's life, it is recognized that withholding a kind and affable spirit is a wrongdoing to be avoided. Job suffered much in terms of his interactions with family and losing his loved ones and livelihood. This caused immense pain in his life. His cry to the Lord was that of asking God to guide him even despite heart-wrenching moments of life. He chooses to wait on God's providence, which saved him from overwhelming despair, and it brought him toward eternal life.

Psalms

The Book of Psalms demonstrates the prime essentiality of prayer but also in acknowledgement of the challenges and trials of life humans experience. The Psalms offer lessons to live a better life for God as a prayer book for those who read and meditate on offering one's heart, pain, and suffering to the Lord. In Psalm 133, there is a

---

[10] The word "friend" in Hebrew translates to associate or colleague. In Latin, to amica or familiaris. In Greek, to philoi or reciprocal. Paul A. Boer, Sr. *A Catholic Interlinear Bible. Old Testament Polyglot. Vol. VII. Job & Psalms in Latin, English, Greek, and Hebrew.* Kindle Edition. Veritatis Splendor Publications, 2013, Location 1119.

[11] Job 6:14, NOAB.

suggestion that affability and friendliness are integral in healthy living and society:

> How very good and pleasant it is when kindred[12] live together in unity. It is like the precious oil on the head, running down upon the beard of Aaron, running down over the collar of the robes."[13]

The imagery of the oil running down Aaron's beard is also symbolic of the protection of God and of his great blessing upon the people It is pleasant to the Lord when people live together in complete unity as verse one states. It seems evident that happy demeanor and affability have a place in the scheme of salvation history when it is understood that God desires society to live in harmony with one another in loving and serving him. Friendly demeanor and kindness make societies more just, and affability is a way to exercise justice in a practical way.

Proverbs

The Book of Proverbs are lessons in gaining wisdom from the reproofs of God himself and how to gain knowledge and wisdom in living a life for God alone. Proverbs suggest that this is done through

---

[12] The word "kindred" in Hebrew translates to brother or of the same tribe. In Latin, to cognatio or related. In Greek, to syngenis or kin. Paul A. Boer, Sr. *A Catholic Interlinear Bible. Old Testament Polyglot. Vol. VII. Job & Psalms in Latin, English, Greek, and Hebrew.* Kindle Edition. Veritatis Splendor Publications, 2013, Location 20953.

[13] Psalms 133:1-2, NOAB.

prayer and obedience to the Lord in all things. An overarching theme in Proverbs is of justice, and affability is an offshoot of this virtue. Proverbs has themes related to various areas of justice throughout. Proverbs fourteen speaks of the primality of kindness:

> Those who despise[14] their neighbors are sinners, but happy are those who are kind to the poor.[15]

This verse speaks of happiness as something to strive for. The type of happiness which is alluded to is joy in being good to the poor, in fulfilling the will of God, and in creating a better world. The advice states that those who "despise neighbors are sinners" suggests that hateful feelings as desires are always sinful and indicative of wrong behaviors. When followers of God's law consciously and joyfully show kindness to the neglected and poor, the Lord is happy. Additionally, the happiness of God boils over to societies as they practice charity and love. The use of the word "happiness" also suggests a blessed and a positive spirit which is associated with affability in terms of emotional joy which is given away for the good of the other.

---

[14] The word "despise" in Hebrew translates to scorn or distain. In Latin, to despicere or to look down on. In Greek, to perifrono or spurn. Paul A. Boer, Sr. *A Catholic Interlinear Bible. Old Testament Polyglot. Vol. VIII. Proverbs, Ecclesiastes, and Song of Soloman in Latin, English, Greek, and Hebrew*. Kindle Edition. Veritatis Splendor Publications, 2013, Location 7839.

[15] Proverbs 14:21, NOAB.

Isaiah

The Book of Isaiah has references to kindness in terms of God's relationship with us and our relationship with him. Isaiah teaches lessons on trusting in God's strength instead of our own, and in waiting on his providence and love. The book also contains prophesy on the atonement of the coming of a savior[16], which is, of course, Jesus. The heart of the book delves into the fact that the Messiah would one day come and save the people from their sins[17]. Chapter fifty-four of Isaiah speaks of God's steadfast love:

For the mountains may depart and the hills be removed, but my steadfast love shall not depart from you, and my covenant of peace[18] shall not be removed, says the Lord who has compassion on you.[19]

The very nature of God suggests in the verse above that even if the mountains are departed from each other, his love will last forever. God speaks to us today through this verse since his love is everlasting and filled with goodness and charity for all. We are called in our actions to imitate the behavior of God which is demonstrated through

---

[16] Isaiah 9:6-7, NOAB.

[17] Isaiah 53:6, NOAB.

[18] The word "peace" in Hebrew translates to pes or tranquility. In Latin, to pes or pax. In Greek, to eirini or concord. Paul A. Boer, Sr. *A Catholic Interlinear Bible. Old Testament Polyglot. Vol. X. Isaiah, Jeremiah, Lamentations and Baruch in Latin, English, Greek, and Hebrew.* Kindle Edition. Veritatis Splendor Publications, 2013, Location 18395.

[19] Isaiah 54:10, NOAB.

kindness and charity toward us. This type of love cannot disconnect itself from affability and friendliness as it is God's nature to be cheerful and caring. We cannot separate the notion of charity and affability of spirit since they go together as they are performed. God has compassion on us. Compassion is never an emotionless activity when given to the poor and marginalized. It is something offered with a kind and cheerful heart to those in need.

The Old Testament scriptural verses noted in this book are just a piece of the biblical references to affability and on the nature of God's kind spirit, which we as believers can imitate. Thorough scaling of scripture, it presents even more evidence that affability and kindness go together as it is God's command to the faithful to live better lives. Doing so enables us, the faithful, to offer genuine care to our brothers and sisters in imitation of his own spirit of generosity and charity. God *does not* present himself as emotionless in Old Testament teachings. He is always compassionate and wishes the best for our lives in a sincere and fatherly way. We should do the same for others.

II. The New Testament and Affability

Just as in the Old Testament, there are numerous mentions of the intense significance of affability and friendliness in living out the Christian life. The New Testament is about Jesus and the Paschal Mystery of salvation given by God as gift. Jesus sets the ultimate example of kindness, goodness, and having an affable spirit to those around him. His teachings remind his followers throughout the New Testament that being loving, charitable, and kind in spirit is the way to follow the command of God to love others[20]. This type of love does not end at just being kind; it is a sacrificial love in imitation of Christ's love for us since he gave himself for the salvation of souls.[21] Let us explore just some of the verses which speak of the correlation between kindness and affability.

Matthew

In chapter five of the Book of Matthew, Jesus speaks of love of neighbor and love of our enemies. Jesus states:

You have heard that it was said, "You shall love your neighbor and hate your enemy."[22] But I say to you, love your enemies and pray for those who persecute you so that you may be children of your Father in heaven; for he makes his sun rise on the evil, and on the good, and sends rain on the righteous and one the unrighteous.[23]

This is a call on how to obey the second commandment of God. To be children of our Father we, as members of the Church, must imitate Christ and love our enemies. This is a demanding mission for

---

[20] Leviticus 19:17, NOAB.

[21] CCC, 161.

[22] In Hebrew, the word "enemy" translates to hostile or foe. In Latin, to inimicus or antagonistic. In Greek, to exopoc or foe. Paul A. Boer, Sr. *A Catholic Interlinear New Testament. Volume I. The Four Gospels and the Acts of the Apostles in Latin, English, and Greek.* Kindle Edition. Veritatis Splendor Publications. 2012, Location 6382-6403.

[23] Matthew 22:37-40, NOAB.

Christians who take their faith seriously. Forgiving an enemy does not necessarily entail the virtue of affability per se. However, the love of neighbor, although not a "feeling," can be exercised with an affable spirit of charity through genuine acts of love. When the giver of good does so in combination with an emotion of openness, the receiver can feel the goodness and is apt to respond in joy. It is a goal of life to do this with a spirit of cheerfulness which shows the love of God.

Mark

In Mark chapter ten, the topic of "who is the greatest"[24] amongst us is a topic of discussion between the disciples. Jesus challenges them by instructing his disciples that the path to fulfillment in life comes through service of others in doing God's will. He states:

> You know that among the Gentiles those whom they recognize as their rulers lord it over them, and their great one and tyrants over them. But it is not so among you; but whoever wishes to become great[25] among you is your servant, and whoever wishes to be first among you must be slave of all" (Mark 10:35-44).[26]

---

[24] Mark 10:35-44, NOAB.

[25] In Hebrew, the word "great" translates to great or large. In Latin, to great or magnus. In Greek, to exairetiki or big. Paul A. Boer, Sr. *A Catholic Interlinear New Testament. Volume I. The Four Gospels and the Acts of the Apostles in Latin, English, and Greek.* Kindle Edition. Veritatis Splendor Publications. 2012, Location 11293-11342.

[26] Ibid., p. 1812.

Chapter Three: Biblical Sources that Demonstrate Friendliness

Jesus clearly communicates to the disciples that the path of humility is the correct one in terms of acting for and with God. One may ask, *how does this relate to affability?* The affable spirit is one that is pliable in doing God's will and in acting in charity toward others. The proud turn away to do their own will and ignore the whisper of God to serve. The spirit of affability demonstrated in these verses is a willingness to become little for the sake of others, which is evidence of the kind of heart ready to follow the Lord. Those who have this type of heart are docile to God's will.

Luke

One of the best demonstrations of kindness and affable spirit is the Parable of the Good Samaritan in Luke ten. In this story, Jesus talks about a man who is attacked by robbers, stripped, and beaten. In the parable, a priest, and a Levite pass by the man as he calls for help. Neither of them acknowledge the man, and they continue their path. Finally, a Samaritan, stops by and cares for the man taking him to an inn for care. It is a story of kindness and true charity toward those in need. When Jesus is challenged with the question "Who is my neighbor?"[27] by a lawyer probing to understand discipleship, Jesus gives the following response toward the end of the interaction:

"Which of these three do you think was neighbor was neighbor to the man who fell into the hands of robbers?" He said,

---

[27] Luke 10:29, NOAB.

"The one who showed him mercy." Jesus said, "Go and do[28] likewise." (Luke 10:36-37)[29]

These final words of this passage reveal much on what is key in the life of a disciple. The first two witnesses had no openness of spirit to the man who fell victim to thieves. Each made a conscious decision not to be bothered with helping someone, especially a man considered an enemy. Jesus' advice to the lawyer expresses the need to have not only a compassionate heart but also an affable spirit. This entails keeping one's eyes open to the needs of others. We, as members of the Church, can imitate Christ by being kind and affable especially when a person is presented to us who has been rejected and cast aside by the world. As Christians, this is one of the greatest callings in living out the baptismal call.

John

The Book of John in holy scripture points to the way to find eternal life. This, of course, comes through faith in Jesus Christ and in following him in our daily lives. God works in us through his spirit which is alive. John states at the beginning of the Book of John that Jesus is God incarnate and that all creation came to be through him.[30]

---

[28] In Hebrew, the word "do" translates to do or perform. In Latin, to give or offer. In Greek, to kano or commit. Paul A. Boer, Sr. *A Catholic Interlinear New Testament. Volume I. The Four Gospels and the Acts of the Apostles in Latin, English, and Greek.* Kindle Edition. Veritatis Splendor Publications. 2012, Location 16353-16373.

[29] Luke 10:36-37, NOAB.

[30] John 1:3, NOAB.

In chapter thirteen, Jesus talks about a new commandment which is to love one another. He states:

> I give you a new commandment, that you love one another. Just as I have loved you; you should also love one another. By this everyone[31] will know that you are my disciples if you have love for one another.[32]

The way that a person recognizes the goodness of others is through their actions toward people. In these actions, which are recognizable to the world at large, visibility takes place through the demeanor portrayed in helping those in need. In taking the time to do excellent work in kindness and love, and not out of sheer obligation, it becomes not just a matter of the will but of the heart. This is the will of God that we do acts of charity with complete love and cheerfulness[33] toward the receiver. Jesus gives this new commandment to love others, and he states that it will be known in the way we love one another. This also translates to those daily actions which involve a friendly and kind spirit. Of course, there are those times when doing the right thing is difficult, and feelings will not always be positive. It is then we must ask God for the grace to become more affable in order to show others their worth and dignity.

---

[31] The Hebrew translation of the word "everyone" is everybody or everything. In Latin, omnis or whosoever. In Greek, olio or everybody. Paul A. Boer, Sr. *A Catholic Interlinear New Testament. Volume I. The Four Gospels and the Acts of the Apostles in Latin, English, and Greek.* Kindle Edition. Veritatis Splendor Publications. 2012, Location 24222.

[32] John 13:34-35, NOAB.

[33] Proverbs 12:22, NOAB.

Acts

It is more blessed to give than to receive says the Lord[34]. The Book of Acts was written after Jesus' death and resurrection, and when the Holy Spirit was sent down to continue his work on earth. The Book of Acts recounts the story of St. Paul beginning after the resurrection of the Lord. The Holy Spirit was at work in Christ's disciples as they suffered great hardships to preach the Gospel to the ends of the earth. Acts twenty has something relevant to say regarding making outreach to the marginalized of the world:

> In all of this I have given you an example that by such work we must support[35] the weak, remembering the words of the Lord Jesus, for he himself said, 'It is more blessed to give than to receive.'[36]

The blessing of giving more than we receive involves affability of spirit since we must possess a willingness of heart to help the weak. If we, as his followers, do not possess this spirit, we can certainly pray for it to be able to exercise the will of God. When friendliness of heart is coupled with the resignation to do God's work by helping those

---

[34] Acts: 20:35, NOAB.

[35] The Hebrew translation of the word "support" in Hebrew is assistance or aid. In Latin, auxilium or help. In Greek, ypostirixi or countenance. Paul A. Boer, Sr. *A Catholic Interlinear New Testament. Volume I. The Four Gospels and the Acts of the Apostles in Latin, English, and Greek.* Kindle Edition. Veritatis Splendor Publications. 2012, Location 31128.

[36] Ibid.

who have been rejected by society, we partake in the mission of the Lord.

Romans

In St. Paul's Letter to the Romans, the main message is a geared toward the salvation given to us in Christ and in his teachings. Key points discuss the sinfulness of humankind, union with Christ and sanctification through him.[37] St. Paul teaches that by faith in Christ, salvation[38] is granted through him. As Catholics we further understand that not only is this made possible through Christ, but the task of being a disciple is never a once and done concept. This sanctification is made *daily* through carrying the cross[39] and living the mission given to us by God. Romans 12 speaks of the love we must demonstrate toward our brothers and sisters:

Let love be genuine, hate what is evil, hold fast to what is good; love one another with mutual[40] affection; outdo one another in showing honor.[41]

---

[37] Romans 8:12-14. NOAB.
[38] Romans 8:1, NOAB.
[39] CCC, 618.
[40] The Hebrew translation of the word "mutual" is reciprocal or shared. In Latin, mutuus or done in exchange. In Greek, amoivaios or reciprocating. Paul A. Boer, Sr. *A Catholic Interlinear New Testament. Volume II. The Epistles of St. Paul the Apostle in Latin, English, and Greek.* Kindle Edition. Veritatis Splendor Publications. 2012, Location 2881-2902.
[41] Romans 12:9-10, NOAB.

The mutual "affection" referred to in this verse additionally points to the friendly and affable spirit we are to have which demonstrates the love of Christ. Not only does Christ instruct his followers to do this, but he says we should also be "genuine" in the matter we communicate. Genuineness is another form of sincerity in the heart. A sincere person is often kind, friendly, and caring. This is excellent advice, and again, it points to the fact that affability is integral in daily interactions with the uncared for of the world.

Ephesians

Ephesians focuses on teachings on salvation[42] and the nature of God's family which are important aspects to study and understand. In this letter, St. Paul emphasizes the Church as one body[43], and key understandings in terms of harmony and mutual love amongst the followers of Christ. In speaking on how we should treat one another, St. Paul writes:

> Put away[44] from you all bitterness and wrath and anger and wrangling and slander, together with malice, and be kind to one another, as God in Christ has forgiven you.[45]

---

[42] Ephesians 2:8-9, NOAB.

[43] Ephesians 4:4-6, NOAB.

[44] The Hebrew translation of the words "put away" is hide or conceal. In Latin, it is auferte or remove. In Greek, apotamievo or set free. Paul A. Boer, Sr. *A Catholic Interlinear New Testament. Volume II. The Epistles of St. Paul the Apostle in Latin, English, and Greek.* Kindle Edition. Veritatis Splendor Publications. 2012, Location 10772-10794.

[45] Ephesians 4:31-32, NOAB.

After instructing followers to put away all bitterness, the next instruction is to be "kind to one another." This is done so because Christ has forgiven us. This verse speaks of the fact that the way we speak to one another is of prime importance in terms of the way we use our voices, facial expressions, and in carrying a message to another person. In communication, it is normally not about using a monotone-like voice with a message or instruction in order to convey a thought. Emotions generally do accompany messages and how they are relayed. In following Christ, the verse points to having an affable spirit which is loving, forgiving, and sincere.

There are countless other scriptural references in both the New and Old Testaments giving witness to the fact that the love we give, and show is also a demonstration of friendliness to the downtrodden and uncared for. The life of Christ, himself, is a prime way to see love demonstrated, to observe his care, and his affability in action toward others. In taking the time to read and reflect on the scriptures, countless instances of the friendly spirit come forth. The examples given in this chapter are meant to whet the appetite to learn more about how affability is present throughout Holy Scripture. As stated, there are many more references in Holy Scripture alluding to affability as not only important but integral; however the purpose of these chapters dedicated to scripture is to reflect on a small sampling of the verses and sections of the bible which point to affability as valuable.

III. The Church Fathers

The Cappadocian Fathers

The Cappadocian Fathers[46] consist of: St. Basil the Great (330–379), St. Gregory Nyssa (332-395), and St. Gregory Nazianzus (329-389). St. Basil and St. Gregory of Nyssa were brothers, and St. Gregory Nazianzus was a friend of both brothers. Basil and Gregory of Nazianzus knew each other through their studies as they were both theologians, and they had met numerous times in Athens. Later, Basil became the bishop of Caesarea, and his brother Gregory later became bishop of Nyssa. The three Cappadocians together made significant contributions to the development of the doctrine of the Trinity[47] and of Christology.

In 325, there was the council at Nicaea, and after this time, various bishops drifted away from the Nicene Creed. There were a significant number of bishops at the time who rejected that Jesus Christ is truly God and truly man. Soon after, another council, the council of Constantinople, came about in 381. At this council, the Nicene Creed[48] was affirmed and reestablished. The Cappadocian Fathers clarified Trinitarian doctrine by teaching that the one God of one essence (ousia), exists eternally as three distinct divine persons (hypostases): the Father, the Son, and the Holy Spirit. This language

---

[46] Patrick Whitworth, *Three Wise Men from the East, the Cappadocian Fathers and the Struggle for Orthodoxy*. Sacristy Press. 2005, Location 304-326.

[47] Ibid., Location 1038.

[48] CCC, 198. The Nicene Creed is the profession of faith as Catholics or *Credo*.

Chapter Three: Biblical Sources that Demonstrate Friendliness   95

became more widely used in the Church because of the influence of the Cappadocians. All three, St. Basil, St. Gregory Nyssa, and St. Gregory Nazianzus had varied personalities, but they worked together well and experienced true and lasting friendship. The early church fathers helped the church tremendously at a crucial moment in history in the Church. They aided in shaping early Christianity and the Monastic tradition and advanced the doctrine of the trinity as we know it today.

> For Gregory Nyssa, it would develop of love of speculative theology; for Basil, a groundwork for defending stages of development, and for Greogory of Nazianzus, this hybrid education led to an unresolved tension between advocating with great elegance the Nicene faith and fleeing to follow an uninterrupted philosophic life far from the intrusions of pastoral responsibilities and ecclesiastical dispute.[49]

Their lives remained in sync through difficulties, and God had a unique and specific plan for each of them in their missions for the Church. Throughout this time period, Gregory of Nyssa was known to give sermons related to the sick and homeless and love of the poor; Basil on famine, wealth, and divestment. The tensions of pastoral life led them to a greater care for God's people and in preaching in imitating of Christ. What can we learn about affability from these three men? They lived and preached during a time when there was great

---

[49] Patrick Whitworth, *Three Wise Men from the East, the Cappadocian Fathers and the Struggle for Orthodoxy*. Sacristy Press. 2005, Location 358-368.

misunderstandings in the Church related to the doctrine of the Trinity, which was a critical time in history when "red martyrdom" [50] was commonplace and a daily reality for many. The bonds of friendship and openness to the spirit of the Cappadocian fathers steered the Catholic Church in the right direction through turbulent times.

St. Augustine

St. Augustine of Hippo[51] was born in 354 at Tagaste, Algeria and died in 430 in Hippo, and he is known as one of the most influential of the Church fathers in the history of the Church. His well-known writings are: *The Confessions* and *The City of God* along with hundreds of other writings, and he is the patron saint of brewers, printers, theologians, and several diocese and cities. At an early age, Augustine possessed an inquisitive mind, and he set his sights on fame and wealth. His parents supported his goals at the time, as they wanted only the best for him in pursuit of his educational and career goals.

Sins of pride and impurity darkened his heart in early life, and he began to live life as a pagan for years before coming to faith. St. Monica, his holy mother, famously prayed for her son's conversion which happened after St. Augustine finally became convinced that Christianity was the one true religion. He was baptized at age thirty-

---

[50] "Red martyrdom" refers to death through violence or torture related to religious persecution.

[51] Joe Aaron Gafford, "The Life and Conversion of Augustine of Hippo." Harding University. *Tenor of Our Times*. Vol. 4. Article 4. Spring 2015, pp. 12-23.

three and became a priest three years later. He then became a writer and founded an order and became one of the greatest and most influential fathers of the Church. In ministry, Augustine traveled from city to city and encountered opportunities for evangelization wherever he went.

As bishop, he chose a life of solitude and contemplation where he didn't have to concern himself with the day-to-day worldly aspects. He traveled to church councils in Northern Africa as bishop, which he did numerous times throughout his life. Although travel was a part of his daily life, his main focus was on his writing, and he authored more than two hundred books and 1,000 sermons. As his life ended, he prayed the prayers of the psalms which were written on the wall of his room. Following his death, his body was laid to rest in Hippo. His body now rests in Pavia, Italy where hundreds of thousands visit each year. In his legacy, he is known as being loving, empathetic, and servant of the Lord. He treated others as they wished to be treated, and he valued community, and spreading the Gospel wherever he went. Various religious orders around the world are dedicated the Rule of St. Augustine[52] following the footsteps of this great spiritual master and man of deep faith and prayer.

Which aspects of St. Augustine's life demonstrate affability and openness with others? After his baptism and conversion to the faith, he made a steadfast and decisive move to do all that he could to love and follow the Lord in all of his ways. Although he had struggles with vice including chastity, he constantly questioned himself in order to make himself accountable with God in all of his activities of life even

---

[52] The Rule of St. Augustine was written in the year 400, and it is an outline for religious life as lived in Community.

after being consecrated as a bishop. Justice to him, was a valuable virtue to emulate and live by.

> But how do they know what faith is, of which it is the prime and greatest function that the true God may be believed in? But why has not virtue suffered? Does it not include faith also? Forasmuch as they have thought proper to distribute virtue into four divisions – prudence, justice, fortitude, and temperance – and as each of these divisions has its own virtues, faith among the parts of justice, and has the chief place with as many of us as know what that saying means. 'The just shall live by faith.'[53]

Justice has value and was obviously an integral part of both his intellectual and spiritual life as Augustine described justice as having a "chief place" in terms of living the faith life. He mentions the other cardinal virtues in the above statement from *City of God*[54], those being prudence, fortitude, and temperance in addition to justice. Justice as a moral virtue is guided by prudence, the intellectual virtue, in the way that human reason seeks to conform itself to concupiscence[55]. For one who is of a pagan[56] mindset, prudence is the highest of human virtues. For those who are baptized, they receive the

---

[53] Paul A. Boer, Sr. (Editor). St. Augustine of Hippo. *City of God*. June 24, 2012, Location 5567.

[54] Ibid., Location 5567.

[55] CCC, 2515.

[56] A "pagan" refers to one who in the broadest sense includes all religions other than the one true revealed God. In a narrower sense, all except Christianity, Judaism, and Mohammedanism.

Chapter Three: Biblical Sources that Demonstrate Friendliness   99

theological virtues of faith, hope, and charity. Prudence is perfected by charity. Prudence then guides justice through a theological anthropology[57] based on salvific grace[58]. It is then that affability partakes in sanctifying grace. This aspect is not only part of St. Augustine's way of thinking, but it is a major part of this book in terms of the thesis itself. St. Augustine understood well the pagan mindset and also where justice fit into daily life and within the spiritual life. Justice and affability had a place in his preaching and teaching, and he deeply understood its relevance in living a good and moral life.

St. Bernard of Clairvaux

St. Bernard of Clairvaux[59] was born in 1090 at Fontaines, France, and died in Clairvaux on August 21, 1153. In Bernard's life story[60], he is known as a great saint, unifier, theologian, and Doctor of the Church. He had an intense desire to love God, to have union with Christ, and to bring people to the Lord surrendering all to him for his glory. St. Bernard was the third of seven children, and the member of a wealthy family with high social status. Faith was instilled in him at a young age, and he studied scripture, theology, poetry, and literature. He had a heartfelt devotion to the Blessed Virgin Mary

---

[57] Anthropology is the study of human societies and their development.

[58] CCC, 2000.

[59] Julian Hasseldine, "Friends, Friendship, and Networks in the Letter of St. Bernard of Clairvaux." University of Hull. Department of History. Academia.edu. 2006, p. 1-49.

[60] St. Bernard of Clairvaux, *Collection of 8 Books Life and Works of Saint Bernard*. Aeterna Press. Volume One. September 22, 2016, p. 133-140.

throughout his life. At a young age, he entered a Cistercian[61] monastery in Citeaux which is known as the Abbey of Notre Dame. Thirty other young men joined him at the abbey, although he had endured resistance in its growth. Eventually, all of his brothers but one also joined the abbey, and his sister became a Benedictine nun.

During that time period of his entering, the Benedictine rule became deviated, and it was Benedict who helped in its restoration. He prescribed a balance of prayer, with less time at labor, and more time dedicated to study and chapel time. He spent twenty-five years as an abbot, and during his time he was responsible for establishing a great many new monasteries. He earned respect for his sermons and is known for his "Song of Songs" which was a series of eighty-six sermons on the topic. These sermons delve deeply into the soul's longing for God's love. He also wrote a treatise called, "Oh Loving God" which articulates why we, as humans, should love God with all of our hearts, minds, and souls. He founded many monasteries, assisted popes, and was an eloquent defender against heresies and spoke in defense of persecuted Jews. He is also known as a unifier and a peacemaker. His writings continue to have a major impact on Monastic life to this day, and he saw Mary, our Mother, as the Mediatrix who guides us through the challenges of life. He exhibited profound understanding that wisdom of God and his Church leads to practicing virtue.

---

[61] The Cistercian Religious Order are a Catholic religious order of nuns and monks that follow the Rule of St. Augustine. They are also known as the Benedictines.

Wisdom is the power whereby he recognizes this dignity, and perceives also that it is no accomplishment of his own, and virtue impels man to seek eagerly Him who is man's source, and to lay fast hold on him when he has been found.[62]

In terms of affability, this great doctor of the Church preached on not only love of God but love of neighbor. This is the definition of affability as these two facets of living out the Gospel message must always go together. St. Bernard taught that humility is knowledge of the self, and confronting our sinfulness with the Lord leads to true knowledge of God. He did not separate the two great commandments of loving God and others throughout his life and ministry. He had a variety of types of friendships in all of his dealings which is evident in the countless letters he wrote during his lifetime. His openness, prayerfulness, and affability is proven in respect to his life's mission and in the fruits of his labor for others.

St. Thomas Aquinas

This book features St. Thomas Aquinas[63] a major contributor to the theological study of virtue as it pertains to affability. This Italian Dominican friar was an influential philosopher, and jurist is a prominent doctor of the Church, and his countless works have contributed greatly to the teaching of the Catholic Church as we know them

---

[62] St. Bernard of Clairvaux. *On Loving God*. Chapter II. Fordham University. June 11, 2009, Location 68.

[63] Saint Thomas Aquinas Collection (22 Books). Aeterna Press. September 16, 2016, p. 4.

today. This book discusses his life and mission throughout the discussion on affability, but a chapter dedicated to the doctors of the Church cannot conclude without a mention of St. Thomas Aquinas and his influences. Born in 1225, he is the patron saint of Catholic schools, apologists, philosophers, theologians, and of chastity. Pope John XXII canonized him[64] on July 18, 1323. He joined the Dominicans[65] at the age of nineteen, although his family wanted him to become the Abbot of Monte Cassino as this title would have been more noble. His family did all they could to detract him from moving ahead with his plan to become a Dominican, however their plans failed, and Thomas refused to become a Benedictine. The famous story of how Thomas' mother abducted and locked him into a family castle for a year and how some family members attempted to lure him by sending a prostitute to his cell is well-known in terms of his perseverance in doing the will of God and in avoiding sin. Eventually, his mother permitted him to escape the castle as a way of saving the family from any further disgrace related to these matters.

After enduring this trial, he continued his journey as a Dominican and became a student of Brother Albert the Great (St. Albert the Great)[66], and he studied under him for several years. He was quiet and studious, and he was misunderstood as being unintelligent by

---

[64] Pope John XXII was head of the Catholic Church from August 7, 1316, until his death in December of 1334.

[65] The Dominican Order is an order of priests founded by St. Dominic in the year 1215. Its members included friars, active sisters, nuns, and lay Dominicans.

[66] St. Albert the Great, OP, was born in 1200 and died in 1280. A German Dominican friar, he is known as a great medieval philosopher, scientist, and bishop.

his peers being a called a "Dumb Ox." Soon after, and through endurance, his peers began to see his brilliance shine through, and everyone around him recognized that he would one day blossom into a major theologian contributing greatly to the writings of the Church. His writings of the *Summa Theologica*[67] and the *Summa Contra Gentiles*[68] along with countless other pieces continue to have a massive impact on all of the Church's teachings.

Perhaps no other doctor of the Catholic Church has addressed friendliness quite like St. Thomas Aquinas, as he made it a point to include it in his most famous writing the *Summa Theologica*. He states:

> Therefore affability, which is what we mean by friendship, is a special virtue. I answer that, as stated above, since virtue is directed to good. There must be a special kind of virtue. Now good consists in order, as stated above. And it behooves man to be maintained in a becoming order towards other men as regard their mutual relations with one another, in point of both deeds and words, so that they behave towards one another in a becoming manner. Hence, the need of a special virtue that maintains the becomingness of this order: and this is friendship.[69]

---

[67] The *Summa Theologica* is the best-known writing of St. Thomas Aquinas written in 1265-1274. It is one of the most important documents in the history of Christianity.

[68] The *Summa Contra Gentiles* is one the most well-known treatises written by St. Thomas Aquinas. It was written between 1259-1265.

[69] Saint Thomas Aquinas Collection (22 Books). Aeterna Press. September 30, 2016, Location 13050-13051.

Affability is indeed a "special virtue" as recognized by St. Thomas Aquinas. There is a need for this virtue and as he states, it translates into friendship. To him, being affable and open toward others is directed toward the good, which is virtue. In this book, we will further explore the teachings of St. Thomas, and discover why his teachings were precious then, and why they will continue to have value in bringing the Gospel of Christ to the entire world.

IV. The Life of Christ and Outreach to the Marginalized

Jesus' life in and of itself is the perfect model of sacrificial love for the sake of the eternal salvation of souls and out of deep love for them. His sacrifice which is the Paschal Mystery of our salvation, is the ultimate way he not only gave us life for us, but he gave us the gifts of the Church such as the Mass, the Eucharist, and the gift of heaven to those who follow his path and commit their lives fully to him. His life consisted of teaching people, healing the sick, taking care of widows, and in defending the marginalized at every stage of life. We are called to do the same and follow him each day of our lives.

Luke Chapter 22

In Luke Chapter 22, Jesus is betrayed by Judas with a kiss (Luke 22:49).[70]. Jesus is clearly hurt by the actions of Judas which will eventually lead to his death on the cross. Even at a moment of utter despair and sadness upon this happening, Jesus heals the ear of the slave

---

[70] Luke 22:49, NOAB.

of the high priest in the presence of others. Despite his fear, sadness, and pain, he heals another person which shows the heart of God through his actions. He questions what is happening at that moment but still chooses to do good, and he is affable to the situation at hand by continuing to follow God's will no matter what.

The Crucifixion

Jesus is condemned to death[71], and he suffers greatly at the hands of his enemies. His pain is unimaginable as he carries his cross, bears the pain of crucifixion, and dies for the salvation of humankind. In thinking deeply upon his suffering, the question at hand may arise related to how an affable spirit in Christ is present during this devasting time of his life on earth. The answer comes through the observance of his willing spirit[72] to freely give himself up to death for the eternal salvation of the world. In a human sense, Jesus could have responded with utter hate, anger, and a refusal to do the will of the Father. He could have refused to move ahead with God's plan, but he did not. This would have shown a spirit of defiance to God's will should he have defied his Father. Jesus chose to submit to the plan God had chosen to die for the salvation of the world through his death and resurrection. Although Jesus did not display a "happy" spirit during this time of suffering, his affability was demonstrated and a determination to move ahead even though he knew it would involve tremendous suffering. This determination indicates the virtue of affability in Jesus' spirit in a time of devastation and trial. In

---

[71] Mark 15:24; Luke 22:33; John 19:18, NOAB.
[72] Matthew 26:39, NOAB.

looking back at his life before this point, we see a pattern of love and charity in all that he did. When he healed a leper[73] and the sick, when he dined with sinners,[74] when he preached, and when he forgave his enemies, he was obedient to his Father[75]. This receptiveness of spirit is the openness of affability of heart.

The greatest lessons of Jesus life is revealed by meditating on Holy Scripture, and most profoundly, every time we receive the Eucharist, the eternal gift given by Christ as a reminder of his presence until the end of time. This gift remains part of our observation of his life since through the Paschal Mystery he accomplished the will of the Father. This enables us, as his followers, to partake in this co-redemption through daily lives of charity and love in the mission of salvation. This includes those daily interactions which calls us to be kind, caring, sacrificial, and doing so with an affable spirit open to the direction of God's will.

---

[73] Matthew 8:1-4, NOAB.
[74] Luke 19:1-10, NOAB.
[75] Luke 22:42: NOAB.

Chapter Four

Evangelization and Friendliness through Faith

I. Human Development and Affability

Human development[1] is the study of the life span and core development. Psychology has long studied the stages of all aspects of development since it brings about a broader understanding of areas of growth as they occur throughout life. The twentieth century saw many theories from prominent psychologists[2] which came forth, perhaps too many to mention in this book. Aspects such as behavior, mental and physical capabilities, cognitive abilities, and changes that happen as we age are arenas of discussion and study. Psychologists continue to study these spheres as they reveal more of the variables[3] which affect human life. For this book, we will explore a small sampling of variables.

As Catholics and as people of faith, we should not only care about what psychology says about human development, but we, the faithful, should also have a core grasp of it. This pertains to spirituality, growth, and ultimately our relationship with God and others. Affability fits into this picture since openness and friendliness have a major impact on evangelization and on creating a kinder and gentler

---

[1] Barbara M. Newman and Phillip R. Newman, *Development Through Life. Psychosocial Approach*. Brooks/Cole Publishing. 1995, p. 4.

[2] Ibid., p. 39.

[3] Ibid., p. 42.

world overall. Learning more about how affability fosters healing is an integral aspect for greater awareness in this book.

Psychologists have offered concentrated studies related to emotional interpretation in both the young and the old. These studies, although too varied and vast to list, suggest that positive interactions, which foster trust and wholeness, have a major imprint on growth and human development. A study done on infants clearly demonstrates the impact of a smile below:

> Social smiles begin to be observed at the age of about five weeks. These smiles are first produced in response to a wide range of stimuli: familiar faces and voices (especially the mother's, strangers, and non-human objects.) After about twenty weeks, the smiling response becomes differentiated. Infants continue to smile broadly and frequently at familiar people and objects, but they no longer smile readily at strangers or unfamiliar objects. The social smile conveys both the recognition of familiarity and an invitation to further communication of interaction.[4]

While there is much more data available to present within the world of psychology, the above example speaks of how happy and positive feelings produce smiles in infants. This may lead to the question, when does this begin to occur inside the womb? Whatever the answer may be to questions such as this and other ponderings, one of the most influential factors of what produces overall "good feelings" from the beginning of early life is when the subject has

---

[4] Ibid., p. 225.

experienced a certain trust[5] factor in the closest relationships. This trust factor is influential not only in infanthood, but through life. Knowing this we can surmise that positivity, trust, and safe feelings of the overall surroundings produces happiness. As Catholics, we believe that happiness is not the end goal of life, rather true happiness comes from living in union with God, and knowing, loving, and serving him which produces joy. This joy is not dependent on outward circumstances. While learning more about human development and its relationship to happiness is beneficial, it does not discount the aspect of the experience of Christian joy.

When we, God's people, witness the suffering of many people, through circumstances such as trauma, poor familial bonds from the beginning of life, lack of support, health crisis, loss of a loved one, and more, we can take knowledge from the world of psychology related to human emotions and apply it to our lives. Happiness is *key to survival* for many because of traumatic experiences of early life and beyond. The Church must take a stand in comprehending these human experiences to meet people where they are through the trials and challenges of life. Just as when a baby smiles in seeing his/her mother, this reaction of happiness has something to do with the relevance of affability and friendliness as a virtue worth striving for. One of the goals of this book is to bring these factors to light to help create a kinder world for all, but especially for the marginalized.

Another aspect of this discussion is the fostering of emotional and cognitive development[6]. Cognitive growth levels are determined in an examination of the progression of stages. A great deal of

---

[5] Ibid., p. 227.
[6] Ibid., p. 234.

nurturing and positive interaction is needed to proceed to the next stages. When traumatic experiences happen or when the relationship between the child and the primary caretaker(s) are not positive experiences, delays may happen that can threaten future maturation. In addition to threatening development, experts feel it can also cause lifelong battles[7] with sadness, anxiety, and other areas of growth.

Given what we know about human development and about the seriousness of those extremely principal bonds formed between mother, father, and child[8] and between other core relationships in a child's life, we learn that affability is a key factor in our lives. Affability, as a virtue, is the openness displayed in daily life interactions with others which gives love to those who need it most. As God's children, we have the responsibility to act on this virtue by showing a friendly smile which in turn says the words, "You are accepted.," "You are loved," "You are respected." Daily interactions with people showing respect and gratitude for who they are as human beings are life giving.

Some in the Church may believe that affability or friendliness does not have a relevant impact in evangelization as much as I hold to in this book. There are those who consider the "doctrine only" or "truth only"[9] view of the Church without including the human elements of affability, tangible acts of kindness, and sincerity into real action. The true elements and roots of our Catholic faith are eternal

---

[7] Ibid., p. 239.

[8] Ibid., p. 237.

[9] The "truth only" view refers to Catholics who may subscribe to the idea that the social justice issues of the Church are not as integral to Catholic teachings compared to moral teachings. Affability encompasses all aspects of truth, goodness, and beauty.

Chapter Four: Evangelization and Friendliness through Faith

and will never change. Devout Catholics, theologians, and churchgoers must develop a greater level of understanding of the whole picture of the principality of this concept. This notion is related to putting affability at the core of the Church's mission in reaching those who are abandoned in some capacity. If we are to reach those margins, evangelization efforts need to be directed at teaching the faithful the monumental impact of being a friendlier people toward all. Affability consists in living and being full of truth, goodness, and beauty, and these truths are monumental in the evangelical efforts of the Church.

Neuroscience studies on human behavior and emotions have recently sparked interest amongst psychologists in making a concerted effort to understand the neuroscience of emotion and the ways that friendliness and affability have a positive impact on human behavior. Of particular interest is how much control we have over our emotions:

> Another area of common intense interdisciplinary interest is the self-regulation of emotion. Affect regulation is usually defined as the set of control processes by which we influence, consciously and voluntarily, our emotions, and how we experience and behaviorally express them.[10]

The control processes involve consciousness and the controlling of emotions. This vastly depends on life experiences, level of

---

[10] Diana Fosha, Daniel J. Siegel, Marion F. Solomon, *The Healing Power of Emotion. Affective Neuroscience, Development and Clinical Practice* (New York: W.W. Norton and Company, 2009), p. 115.

understanding, and maturity levels. The degree to which one has undergone trauma and the ability to cope greatly affect the outcomes.

Early childhood trauma and its effects have a major impact on an individual's ability to deal with stress, pain, and any ongoing trauma. *Emotion is integration*, and exploring this area of neuroscience helps to bring understanding. When a person is raised with ongoing traumas in childhood, it affects every aspect of their being: mental, emotional, and physical.

> Though science and subjectivity narrate the story of emotion in very different ways, we can see that the consilient scientific view may be indeed that emotion is integrative. What this means, literally, is that emotion, emotional process, emotional experiences, emotional meaningful events, emotional development, and emotional well-being each involve integration.[11]

The above statement from *The Healing Power of Emotion* suggests that emotions affect every aspect of human development and wholeness. There is a definite tie to emotions and integration in terms of feeling a sense of well-being and security, especially for those who have suffered psychological injury in early life. Integration happens in the right circumstances over time when a person has positive experiences involving their emotions guiding them in the direction of healing. The neuroscience of emotion helps to bring wholeness through developing positive interactions.

---

[11] Ibid., p. 149.

Chapter Four: Evangelization and Friendliness through Faith 113

> Psychologists speak of positive emotional experiences as pathways for people who need finding healing to live a happier life in the future: "Healing is integration; psychotherapy is facilitated integration catalyzed by the relationship between two people. As we shall soon see, integration is the heart of a coherent mind and living a harmonious life."[12]

The relationship between two people has proven to be more intimate and this kind of one-to-one interaction aids in healing. Whether in therapy or in family or friend relationships, the intimate settings of listening and caring help the person who has been traumatized to experience an emotional relationship that fosters better pathways for the future. Pondering these facts help Catholics to better understand affability as an extremely valuable virtue.

In this discussion on emotion, there is no doubt that friendliness and affability is an integral part in aiding marginalized people who have experienced traumatic situations in life to be able to experience God's love in a dynamic way. Just as an infant may smile in response to positive stimuli in the early weeks of life, the smile and positive emotional response of a person who has suffered in the past is a sign of healing and hope. Psychology and the neuroscience of emotions solidify the fact that affability is needed to help to create a gentler atmosphere for hurts and distresses of our world.

There is much to be said about the effects of upbringing, parental relationships, and how trauma plays a part in the ways that personalities are developed starting at birth and through life. There are attachments and emotional tendencies for all of us, and psychologists

---

[12] Ibid., p. 155.

work hard to find answers on how to best serve and help those people who have had to deal with extensive challenges making day-to-day life difficult. Knowing that the goal is integration and that positive emotional experiences[13] are a key in finding needed healing, friendly and caring interactions can help bridge the gap so they can experience integration in the world for better relationships and experiences in the future.

In a deeper exploration, one may ask the question: "Can friendliness be a learned behavior if one is not naturally outgoing or empathetic to others?" Some people are naturally more introverted and less responsive to the needs of other people, at least what appears on the outside, which is their reactions and interactions with others. There are those people who, because of "self-awareness" on matters such as their physical appearance, or how they appear to others in various facets, become closed off. Closed off personalities can occur in both those who are outgoing or introverted and those in between. Narcissistic[14] and passive aggressive[15] personalities may be more apt to live life with "blinders" on toward the marginalized, creating disconnect and alienation with those who suffer, are rejected, or cast aside by peer groups. Can empathy be taught? This is a good question to ask in terms of teaching others about affability and its significance in evangelization.

---

[13] Diana Fosha, Daniel J. Siegel, Marion F. Solomon, *The Healing Power of Emotion: Affective Neuroscience, Development and Clinical Practice* (New York: W.W. Norton and Company. 2009), p. 218.

[14] Narcissistic Personality is when a person has an inflated sense of self-importance.

[15] Passive aggressive behavior is a pattern of indirectly expressing negative feelings instead of openly addressing them.

Chapter Four: Evangelization and Friendliness through Faith

The first step in teaching friendliness is to learn to actively listen. Active listening does not include judging. Good listeners are to be in receiving mode. This is not an easy task especially for those who do not have the natural tools to foster friendship with those people who are outside their comfort zones. As Catholics we are called to reach out and befriend the outcasts and those who suffer. Teaching affability would involve an awareness of ourselves and our behavior toward others. It would especially involve our openness to those who are different from us in a variety of ways to be friendly and welcoming. Being affable is an openness of heart especially in situations of fear or isolation. Educating[16] the faithful to the fact that even if our own peer groups include seemingly "holy" and faithful people we may fellowship with in camaraderie within church communities, we should never be exclusive. Cohorts with others are called to be *inclusive* especially toward those who do not have the love and support they well deserve. Those who have experienced trauma in any form can find hope and healing when a sense of confidence is gained through emotional attachment with other people:

> Secure attachment complements self-confidence, and autonomy. Secure dependence and autonomy are two sides of the same coin, rather dichotomies as often presented in couples and family literature. Security is associated with a more coherent, articulated, and positive sense of self. The more

---

[16] Rick Hanson, Ph.D. "Be Friendly. Friendliness is a down-to-earth approach that is welcoming and positive." *Psychology Today.* November 7, 2012.

securely connected we are, the more separate and different we can be.[17]

Confidence is a goal when it comes to working with those severely affected by trauma. As people of faith, we can help foster healing in offering tender care and friendship. When we learn[18] to become affable and open with others, bridges are built in terms of creating a kinder world which preaches "the truth" in an effective yet compassionate way. Psychologists[19] would tend to agree that avenues can be opened in a greater capacity when the virtue of affability is accepted on a larger scale by societies.

Science and faith blend together in terms of these concepts on the relevance of affability to the marginalized of our world in evangelization efforts. For these theories to be shared to the world, education is necessary; the Church teaches that we are to be kind, charitable, and loving toward all and these concepts must be communicated widely. Education entails getting to know Church teachings and acting on them. When we, as a church, move forward in becoming friendlier people as a learned effort, we will be able to create a more caring and compassionate outreach worldwide. The goal of this book is to educate the Church and the world that the matters presented in this chapter on affability and human development have a massive impact on creating a better world for the future in all aspects of existence.

---

[17] Ibid., p. 263.

[18] Ibid.

[19] Suzanne Degges-White, Ph.D. "Friendology: The Science of Friendship." *Psychology Today*. May 29, 2018.

II. Happiness Through a Living Faith

Pastoral ministry brings joy to the heart in spreading the Gospel. There is an exultation which comes with spreading the good news of the faith to the world; it is the joy of the Spirit. When we, as members of the Church, live the faith as Christ commands, we do it in an uncomplicated way, which is out of love for God and others. Pope Francis speaks of pastoral ministry which produces joy and happiness as not something which is done in an obsessive way. It is exercised in true happiness and in a spirit of complete trust:

> Pastoral ministry style is not obsessed with the disjoined transmission of a multitude of doctrines to be insistently imposed. When we adopt a pastoral goal and a missionary style which would actually reach everyone without exception or exclusion, the message has to concentrate on the essentials, on what is most beautiful, most grand most appealing and at the same time most necessary. The message is simplified, while losing none of its depth and truth, and thus becomes all the more forceful and convincing.[20]

A key phrase to note is: "reach everyone without exception or exclusion." This alludes to the fact that putting God at the center of evangelization efforts and not doing anything out of compulsion or obsessiveness is essential to these efforts. When friendliness and a relaxed way of communicating is part of daily living in missionary efforts, the Holy Spirit works in monumental ways in pastoral

---

[20] *Evangelii Gaudium*, p. 19.

outreach for accompaniment. Pope Francis highlights the need for simplicity in conducting missionary discipleship out of love for all people individually and on a global level. This creates both joy and happiness in life. Pope Francis states it is important to build a culture of encounter:

> Building happiness also means that we build a culture of encounter. We must know how to meet each other. We must build, create, construct a culture of encounter. How many differences, how many problems in the family there always are! Problems in the neighborhood, problems at work, problems everywhere. And differences don't help. The culture of encounter. Going out to meet each other.[21]

A culture of encounter builds jubilation which surpasses understanding. It also fosters love and genuine happiness in life. It is something to strive for when we build this kind of culture. A culture of encounter means that wherever we go and whomever we meet, we are ready to share God's love with everyone. Not only does this attitude build joy which surpasses understanding, but it also fosters love and genuine happiness in life. It is something to strive for when we, the faithful, build this kind of culture.

In the quote above, Pope Francis is speaking of affability as well because none of the above is done without this virtue. People can see through inauthenticity quite easily. They know when someone is authentic about their faith and about their love of God and when they

---

[21] United States Conference of Catholic Bishops. *Pope Francis and the Family*. Libreria Editrice Vaticana. 2014, p. 25.

are not. Franics proclaims that there will always be problems, but when we meet each other to talk and dialogue, this is how we, God's people, build a culture of care and of real love. This is what people desire. They hunger for love and acceptance for who they are before God. Friendliness and openness lead to genuine happiness.

What creates "happiness" in life? According to the teachings of our Church and of the writings of Pope Francis it is service to others. Through service, we find our Christian calling which is love of neighbor and care especially for suffering. Those people are remarkably close to our lives, often within families. Pope Francis writes:

> Interpersonal relationships within families are not always easy, yet they should be characterized by: The law of love, love for God and love for neighbor according to the new commandment that the Lord left to us. It is a love, however, that is not sterile sentimentality or something vague, but the acknowledgement of God as the one Lord of life and, at the same time, the acceptance of the other as my true brother, overcoming division, rivalry, misunderstanding, selfishness; these two things go together. Oh, how much of the journey do we have to make in order to actually live the new law – the law of the Holy Spirit who acts in us, the law of charity, of love! Even within the family itself, there are so many internal wars.[22]

Interpersonal relationships are places to exercise the greatest charity since Christ dwells within the human spirit. Not giving in to

---

[22] Ibid., p. 29.

selfishness is part of the journey of virtue which leads to joy of spirit in following and imitating Christ. Vice prevails when we, his followers, decide to do things our own way, and as Pope Francis has stated "internal wars" begin within family life and often extends outward into society. In moving beyond feelings of self-pity and misunderstanding toward others, we can work toward engaging with those who suffer. Those people are close by; they are immediate family members and various others. Through prayer and careful discernment, the will of God can be done in all circumstances. Although there may be doubts, we, the Church, must persist in doing good.

Questions of faith will always arise in terms of why terrible things happen to good people and to societies. In his own humility, Pope Francis shares his thoughts:

> I sometimes wonder why, in light of this, it took so long for the Church unequivocally to condemn slavery and various forms of violence. Today, with our developed spirituality and theology, we have no excuse.[23]

Pope Franics alludes the above comment toward the well-educated within the Church in reference to the above quote related to why slavery and forms of violence were ever accepted. The same concept can be said of affability in evangelization. Unless theologians and those who are deliberate about their faith agree and promote the truth of affability's relevance, it will remain *only as a concept*. The concept refers to materializing missionary discipleship to the

---

[23] *Fratelli Tutti*, p. 54.

marginalized. To manifest affability in the world, we are obligated to teach others to partake as evangelizers in creating a kinder world.

We can also look at these concepts on a global scale in terms of how they affect the entire world and evangelization. The ideas at hand are related to putting affability into action in the world. The open dialogue that Francis speaks of is an "unmasking" in the way that we communicate with those who are different from us in ways of thinking and culture. We, as members of the Church, must analyze the methods used in the past and pray to the Lord for his guidance to reveal better avenues to meet people where they are now and in the future. Francis states:

> We need to learn how to unmask the various ways that the truth is manipulated, distorted, and concealed in public and private discourse. What we call "truth" is not only reporting of facts and events, such as we find in the daily papers. It is primarily the search for the solid foundations sustaining our decisions and our laws.[24]

The truth can also be manipulated by the faithful of the Church, and this has been done for centuries. There is no doubt that this virtue helps to build a stronger world of faith, and this truth must be taught and communicated better to all followers of Christ and to all Catholics. Truth teaches us that although happiness is not an end-goal of life, it is a byproduct of living service to others. There is a tie to affability and following the truths of the faith. This is all part of truth, beauty, and goodness.

---

[24] Ibid., p. 120.

Happiness is found in mission and in participating as a disciple of Christ in the modern world. Not only is happiness found, but as stated earlier, so is joy. Along with joy comes peace which the world cannot give but only God can offer. As we implement the virtue of affability, not just those we are "comfortable" with, it can be shared on a larger scale which is a goal of the Church in evangelization. Pope Francis addresses the issue of Christian spirituality and the relevance of not becoming obsessed with things and materialistic goods:

> Christian spirituality proposes and alternatives understanding of the quality of life, and encourages a prophetic and contemplative lifestyle, one capable of deep enjoyment free of obsession and consumption. We need to take up on an ancient lesson, found in different religious traditions and also in the Bible. It is the conviction that less is more.[25]

In evangelization, efforts to gain understanding of the experiences and religious practices of those we encounter is of utmost importance. There must be a deep respect for all aspects of the human person, and this is what Pope Francis is expressing. He speaks of a kind of openness and affability toward others which is not compulsive. Sometimes within specific circles of evangelization of serious-minded Catholics, there is a sense of obsessional prayer and evangelization that is unhealthy and ineffective. These individuals are often described as scrupulous about their faith to a point of unhealthy

---

[25] *Laudato Si*, p. 144.

Chapter Four: Evangelization and Friendliness through Faith

anxiety for the salvation of others, but with little effort to befriend or reach out to those who are marginalized and friendless.

Evangelization efforts become open and truly human when the overly obsessional sense of urgency is not part of the overall picture. Affability requires good listening efforts, friendly interaction, and genuine kindness. It is devoid of a check-box mentality of evangelization similar to a math equation or completed grocery list. Compulsive and obsessional ways of thinking about faith do not aide in communicating deep care about the traumas and trials that others have undergone. This kind of irrational thinking focused only on the afterlife and "salvation" after death does not aide people in experiencing God's love in the present moment in finding hope and healing.

Francis also speaks of the attitudes of our hearts, which is one of the most prime aspects of human interactions and evangelization in the Church. The happiness of heart that comes from developing real friendships with those who feel rejected and uncared for is a result of a closeness with the Holy Spirit, which is Christ's spirit alive in us. Francis states:

> We are speaking of an attitude of the heart, one which approaches life with serene attentiveness, which is capable of being fully present to someone without thinking of what comes next, which accepts each moment as a gift from God to be lived to the full.[26]

---

[26] Ibid., p. 146-147.

The attentiveness we, the faithful, give to others is a sincere gift from the heart, as Pope Francis states. It is one that not only do we treasure, but the other person will hold in immense value, as well. The gift of time and of genuine concern is greater than any material gift we may offer to someone. The time we, Christ's followers, take to actively listen and demonstrate love in the ways that matter to another person is where it comes to life. Collectively, these are the avenues in which happiness is lived through faith. Happiness is a key component in evangelization in consideration of psychology, human care and interactions, and the teachings of the Catholic Church to reach the those who are on the fringes of society. It is time for theologians and the Church at large to recognize that happiness is not only a positive aspect of life but also of faith since it brings restoration to the weary.

III. The Teachings of St. Teresa of Calcutta

The teachings of St. Teresa of Calcutta (Mother Teresa) also suggest the importance of affability as one of the most effective ways to show love and tenderness to those who feel cast aside and do not have the support of others. "We shall never know all the good a smile can do."[27] Never underestimate the profound impact the power of a smile can make in our daily lives in living out our mission. On the topic of the relevance of affability in evangelization, this is a monumental discovery that is simple yet true. With this must come sincerity; for without sincerity of heart, a smile has zero value; it is

---

[27] Sarah Mett, "The Church's Mission: Evangelizing like Mother Teresa in the Year of Mercy." Catholic Exchange. January 21, 2016.

Chapter Four: Evangelization and Friendliness through Faith

meaningless. When done only to "evangelize" for the sake of saving souls as a "duty" without the care of a person, there is much less value. These are valid points to consider in the Church that we must be sincere of heart in efforts to reach the rejected and vulnerable.

St. Teresa of Calcutta spoke often about how imperative it is to offer outreach to the poor and those who do not have family or friends to support them during challenging times. The genuine love shown to others in a spirit of care and charity makes a profound difference. Offering a genuine smile and openness to is a step in the right direction for the process of creating a warmer, caring culture. Another quote comes from Mother Teresa specifically on happiness and the importance of fostering love and joy to all we encounter. She said: "Spread love wherever you go. Let no one ever come to you without leaving happier."[28] We can take this thought seriously in the expansion of evangelization. It is putting love into action.

This idea of letting no one leave our conversations unhappy has a direct correlation to affability. Leaving oneself open to others in active listening and compassion opens the doors to being able to hear the stories of those who do not have support. This is the pathway to evangelization by being open to new people, new situations, and new encounters with others in order to help them. The help offered creates an environment for happiness, fosters joy and healing, and can help others experience God in various ways. St. Teresa of Calcutta also spoke of never judging others, as we do not know the suffering they have endured in life. We, as followers of Christ, have never walked in their shoes or had to face the difficult choices they have had to make. Some of these "choices" may have involved sinful

---

[28] Ibid.

behaviors, hence they are poor choices. Unless there is dialogue with the marginalized to find out more about their life stories, it will be hard to fully understand the traumas they have experienced. Mother Teresa also writes: "If you judge people, you have no time to love them." [29]

It is true that if we judge others, we will not have time to love them. It is a fallen world, and the sin of judgement affects all of us. It is prudent to take the advice of Mother Teresa on judging others. In the modern world, there are a variety of areas which separate, including: culture, religion, race, ethnicity, sexuality, living situations, and other factors. No matter what divides, evangelization begins in opening our ears, eyes, and hearts to those who suffer. Listening to stories and exercising compassion, we, members of the Church, can show them a better way of life and introduce them to the Catholic faith. In a suffering world in need of friendship and affability, the first step must be that of genuine care in a non-judgmental way for those who are ostracized.

An examination of the life of St. Teresa of Calcutta also makes it clear that not only did she know suffering, but she experienced it daily. She committed herself to others through her vocation with the Missionaries of Charity[30]. The Missionaries of Charity continue her mission to this day in love of the poorest of the poor. Mother Teresa, in her missionary work in Calcutta and in the surrounding areas came face to face with pronounced suffering with people who had

---

[29] Ibid.

[30] The Missionaries of Charity are a Catholic religious institute of consecrated life of Pontifical right for women founded by St. Teresa of Calcutta in 1950.

Chapter Four: Evangelization and Friendliness through Faith

no one. Often those same people had no shelter, food, family, or love from others. She ministered with love to people of all ages, offering her hands, her feet, and her deepest care.

Mother Teresa constantly invited others, namely the faithful, to join her in the mission. She was not afraid to speak of the suffering she witnessed, and she fervently called out to Catholics and people of good will to help in efforts to reach the forsaken. She often spoke that to be marginalized, one does not have to live in a third world country. Oftentimes, people who feel alone, uncared for, and without support live in prospering countries. They are not always homeless or poor. She said that some of the loneliest people are those who are unloved by others, regardless of their status in life. This is a calling to us to make outreach to people who need deeper care and outreach. By offering active listening and a pro-active way of encountering, we, the faithful, can make a difference.

Mother Teresa was a small-framed woman with a big heart and a deep faith. She loved God with all her heart, and she desired that all of people could join more closely together to work to alleviate the suffering of the poor:

> Time and time again this tiny woman, almost fragile looking from the outside, displayed an inner strength and drive that no one could stop. She often asked us not to praise her but to take part in her mission in some small way. She often said that "God doesn't ask us to do great things. He asks us to do small things with great love.[31]

---

[31] Pete Socks, "Mother Teresa. Carrier of God's Mercy," *Operando*. October 19, 2016, p. 79.

Doing small things with great love has much to do with affability. The openness of an affable spirit helps Christ's followers to find those people who need support. Oftentimes, they are immediate family members, neighbors, or extended family, as previously stated. They are also those with whom we worship at church in our parishes. Getting involved in the work of one's local parish enables the faithful to find those who lack care and support. We, Christ's followers, can imitate St. Teresa of Calcutta and Jesus by being more aware of those who are uncared for and lonely.

The suffering of the soul is often more painful than physical suffering, however, this does not discount the effects of physical suffering which can be enormous, and we, as people of faith, should always pray for and support those who have physical limitations, disease, and anything that affects the health of the body. For whatever affects the body can sometimes affect the soul. We need to be mindful of this fact and to care for our brothers and sisters who have gone through tragedies and ailments which affects their lives and those around them.

St. Teresa of Calcutta says we should be aware of those who suffer inside their hearts day in and day out. The greatest suffering comes from those who have little support and love from others. This is the greatest tragedy:

> Mother also recognized a second level of suffering. The unseen suffering that television and still photos cannot see. Physical pain and suffering are not the only ailments we can

be faced with. There is the hunger of the soul. The thirsting that one may have for the love of God.[32]

This is a hunger that is invisible to the world at times. Mother Teresa experienced this agonizing separation from God in prayer in specific times of her life, and it caused her immense mental and spiritual pain. The agony of soul she experienced helped her to empathize with the ache we all feel in life in seeing and experiencing dreadful things happening to good people. This is always terrible to observe. There is a pain of the soul in witnessing this suffering. We may ask ourselves, "What can I do to help?" Mother Teresa experienced immense pain and suffering in her own life. She had questions of faith. She didn't find "answers" to all of life's questions, but she did experience the peace of God which carried her through her entire life. This is a monumental life lesson for us, as Catholics.

In a deeper examination of St. Teresa of Calcutta's ministry and teachings, we can be assured that she lived an affable spirit of friendliness and love toward others. She understood that to preach justice, affability must go along with that. The smile given to those in need goes a much longer way than we may realize; and we must understand that the rejected of the world are close by. The places we live and breathe are where we find ostracized people of the world. St. Teresa of Calcutta's life is the perfect example of affability. We, the faithful, must carry her message of compassion, gentleness, perseverance, and love to everyone. This invitation of Mother's is not just for committed Catholics; she invited the human family to partake in the mission. For this reason, she must be taken seriously. Her life and work

---

[32] Ibid., p. 92.

are evidence that affability is essential in today's world and in all evangelical efforts of the Catholic Church. Let us live this mission.

IV. St. Francis Cabrini: A Life of Compassion

St. Francis Xavier Cabrini[33] was born on July 15, 1850, in the village of Sant'Angelo Lodigiano near Milan, Italy. At an early age, she decided her future goal would be to join a religious order, but because of poor health she was not permitted to join the Daughters of the Sacred Heart[34] who were her instructors and mentors pertaining to her teaching certificate which she had previously earned. In 1880, with seven women alongside, she founded the Institute of the Missionary Sisters of the Sacred Heart of Jesus[35]. St. Francis Cabrini was not only spiritual and prayerful, but she was also resourceful in finding the financial help necessary for her projects including religious communities, hospitals, and orphanages. She obtained and audience with Pope Leo XIII[36] asking him directly about becoming a missionary in China, which was a dream of hers to minister in the east. Pope Leo's response to her request was, "not to the east but to the west."

---

[33] Fr. Vincent X. Veneration, *St. Francis Cabrini Novena, Detailed Biography, Novena and Devotion to St. Francis Xavier Cabrini.* Amazon Kindle Book. November 3, 2023, Locations 21-107.

[34] The Daughters of the Sacred Heart is a Roman Catholic religious institute for women founded By Mother Teresa Nuzzo in 1903.

[35] The Institute of the Missionaries of the Sacred Heart of Jesus is an international missionary Congregation of women religious present in six continents and in sixteen countries.

[36] Pope Leo XIII was head of the Catholic Church from February 20, 1878, until his death on July 20, 1903.

Chapter Four: Evangelization and Friendliness through Faith

Her assignment led her to the heart of New York City where thousands of needy Italian immigrants were living in sometimes horrid conditions. It would be her and the sisters' job to minister to the immigrants.

In 1889, in New York, Mother Cabrini and her sister companions stepped into a world of strife and poverty in their quest to bring tangible help to the poor Italian immigrants at that time. They offered catechism classes and education to the orphans in that area despite great odds in gathering the funds and resources necessary to bring aid. As time progressed, Mother began to receive requests from different parts of the world to open schools and to repeat the mission she began in New York. Her travels brought her to Central and South America, to Europe, and to twenty-three trans-Atlantic trips. She established a total of sixty-seven institutions including schools, hospitals, and orphanages.

St. Francis Cabrini worked hard and tirelessly until her death in Chicago on December 22, 1917. Pope Pius XII canonized her[37] in recognition for her holiness and care for humankind on July 7, 1946. She is the patron saint of immigrants, and the Missionary Sisters and lay collaborators are in seventeen countries and on six continents. In 2024, a movie was produced by Angel Studios called "Cabrini"[38] on the life of St. Francis Cabrini, bringing greater awareness of her life and mission. She stated the following, "The most valuable gift we can provide is not material possessions but the gift of ourselves. It is

---

[37] Pope Pius XII was head of the Catholic Church from March 2, 1939, until his death on October 9, 1958.

[38] "Cabrini" is a 2024 movie directed by Alexjandro Gomez Monteverde on the life, faith, and mission of St. Francis Xavier Cabrini.

through our love and service that we truly all make a difference in the world."[39]

Her life story indicates an openness that points to affability as an integral part of her personality and charism. She dedicated her life to those in need especially the marginalized who were immigrants, orphans, and outcasts. She persisted to do good against great odds for the sake of those who did not have adequate love and support. She cared deeply for the everyday needs of the people, especially children.

> Mother Cabrini placed the education of the learned at the disposal of the uneducated, turned kindness to the relief of misery, and brought fresh air and sunlight for the destruction of typhoid and tuberculosis.

The kindness she displayed toward others, especially to those most in need, is a further demonstration of her affable disposition and great virtue. The choices she made to show genuine concern and mercy are a perfect, saintly example of justice given to those who suffer and search for love. Her life story points directly to the moral virtue of affability, and she is a modern-day example to all on giving one's life to others in charity and in deep love and care.

---

[39] Fr. Vincent X. Veneration, *St. Francis Cabrini Novena, Detailed Biography, Novena And Devotion to St. Francis Xavier Cabrini.* Amazon Kindle Book. November 3, 2023, Location 67.

Chapter Five

Teachings on Living a Virtuous Life

I. What is a Virtuous Life According to the Church?

In this discussion on affability and its relevance in evangelization, we turn to the Church and its teachings on virtue. The virtues are the vehicle we, the faithful, facilitate to follow the commands of Christ in our daily lives:

> Human virtues are firm attitudes, stable dispositions, habitual perfections of intellect and will that govern our actions, order our passions, and guide our conduct according to reason and faith. They make possible ease, self-mastery, and joy in leading a morally good life. The virtuous man is he who freely practices the good.[1]

In practicing virtue, we, as members of the Church, must be firm and create good habits to be guided by the spirit of Christ in all that we say in do. As stated earlier in this book, this does not have to do with obsessive thinking or actions in terms of being perfect to the point of not being able live a normal life. It refers to a complete trust in God and in being guided by good and avoiding evil in actions, thoughts, and in conversations with others. Virtue becomes habitual in striving to not only walk with Christ, but to be taught by him in

---

[1] CCC, 1803.

reading Holy Scripture in order to practice charity in imitation of his life.

The Cardinal Virtues of our Faith

The Church teaches that the cardinal virtues are prudence[2], justice[3], fortitude[4], and temperance[5]. Through these four virtues springs every other virtue. Affability falls under the category of justice as explored and written about through St. Thomas Aquinas in the *Summa Theologica*. The definition of justice is as follows:

> Justice is the moral virtue that consists in the constant and firm will to give their due to God and neighbor. Justice toward God is called the virtue of religion. Justice toward men disposes one to respect the rights of each and to establish in human relationships the harmony that promotes equity with man, often mentioned in the Sacred Scriptures, is distinguished by habitual right thinking and the uprightness of his conduct toward his neighbor. You shall not be partial to the poor and defer to the great, but in his righteousness you shall

---

[2] CCC, 1806. (Prudence is the virtue that disposes practical reason to discern our true good in every circumstance and to choose the right means of achieving it.)

[3] Ibid., 1807. (Justice is the moral virtue that consists in the constant and firm will to give their due to God and neighbor.)

[4] Ibid., 1808. (Fortitude or courage is the moral virtue that ensures firmness in difficulties and constancy in the pursuit of good.)

[5] Ibid., 1809. (Temperance is the moral virtue that moderates the attraction of pleasures and provides balance in the use of created goods.)

judge your neighbor. Master's treat your slaves justly and fairly, knowing that you also have a Master in heaven.[6]

There is a constancy in giving due to our neighbor. This constancy includes the justice of affability and the way we treat and interact with those around us. We, God's people, have a responsibility to recognize the human dignity of another. There should also be no partiality in how justice is expressed and acted upon. In terms of affability, this refers to the fact that in expressions of friendliness and openness to others, faithful followers of Christ should not ignore or snub people. Snubbing and showing partiality are the opposite action of affability.

Another aspect of these teachings which are along the same line has to do with acting in respect for people regardless of race, religion, ethnicity, or sexuality, or socio-economic status. The respect given is justice due since we are children of God, and the Lord commands his followers to act in justice toward one another. This human respect for each person and for their struggles helps the faithful to live justice to the fullest. It promotes equality in human relationships regardless of any worldly aspects which separates families and communities.

St. Thomas Aquinas

St. Thomas Aquinas and his teachings in the *Summa Theologica* will be explored in this book in depth. In looking at the overall teachings of the Church on justice, Aquinas is one of the primary saints to have taught affability by including it in his writings making it stand

---

[6] Ibid., 1807.

out to be respected and followed. His methodology of using questions and answers to explore and reveal important truths of faith was how this accomplished. Over the years, countless authors and theologians have chosen to study and instruct what Aquinas communicated so that it could be digested more easily by those who are not schooled in theological studies.

In the world of theology and of academia, we search for proof which cannot be debated or questioned, but in Aquinas' methodology, there is an understanding that there will always be critics for every statement or research theory presented. This does not change the fact that understanding the teachings on justice which are related to affability are both essential and needed in our world. We present these findings as facts but understand that in Aquinas' time *there were critics*. Most importantly, we, the Church, accept these teachings in faith, guided by the Holy Spirit. St. Thomas Aquinas' insights have great relevance for outreach to the marginalized in the realm of justice.

In Summa Theologica Part Two, Question 114, St. Thomas Aquinas teaches about affability, and he makes it a point that each relationship has a certain level of intimacy. Some relationships are close such as spouses, children, and relatives; others are friends: neighbors, co-workers, and others in the community. Despite the closeness of these bonds, affability is a justice to be given to others:

> The friendliness which is called affability governs relationships between people because it behooves man to be maintained in a becoming order towards other men as regards their mutual relationships with one another, in point of both

Chapter Five: Teachings on Living a Virtuous Life

deeds and words, so they behave towards one another in a becoming manner.[7]

Behaving toward one another in a "becoming matter" may sound as a proper term for treating each other with the utmost respect. Language used at the time of publication of the *Summa* was far from twenty-first century linguistics, but it nonetheless indicated the momentousness of having good and upright relationships. Behaving properly and with love is not just a "justice;" it is also charity at the deepest level. When kindness is offered in true sincerity, it surpasses the idea of being nice or sweet to a person just because we ought. It is justice given in a spirit of deep care. St. Thomas talks of mutual relationships which are part of everyday life. The affable and open spirit of friendship is proper to all, and this virtue needs to be communicated as prime in evangelization efforts. There is virtue in having a good relationship with others. The Church teaches that this falls under the umbrella of justice[8]. Justice should be a constant in our lives of faith and so should affability and friendliness. The Church instructs that human virtues are acquired by effort. They do not come automatically without prayer and without the will to execute them. When the fruit and seeds of good acts are brought forth, this communion produces divine love in the soul. Therefore, when affability is practiced and attained as a virtue of our faith, the Holy Spirit will bring forth a beautiful gift of charity which makes a difference

---

[7] Antony Augustine Cherian, O.P., "The Friendliness Called Affability." The Dominican Friars. February 3, 2023. *Quoted from the Summa Theologica, St. Thomas Aquinas. Vol. Two, Question 113.

[8] CCC, 1807.

in the lives of those who feel apart from the Church and from other people.

II. The Effects of Bullying and Gossip on the Human Person

In this discussion the relevance of affability, it would not be complete without mention of the effects of bullying and of gossip on the human person. Pope Francis has made it a point over the years to mention how damaging it is to human relations and in building peace since kindness fosters justice, and it helps in avoiding bullying or gossip. He speaks of gossip as a weapon:

> Gossip is a weapon, and it threatens the human community every day; it sows envy, jealousy, and power struggles. It has even caused murder. Therefore discussing peace must take into account that evil that can be done with one's tongue.[9]

Pope Francis has made this discussion one of the forefront issues of his pontificate, which speaks loudly on the importance of striving to be kind and affable. In saying that gossip sows envy, jealousy, and power struggles, and can even cause murder, is a wake-up call to the faithful to exercise charity and justice in daily interactions. As people of faith and especially to those who fully understand the teachings of the Church, we must not only discuss these issues, but we must also actively get rid of gossip from our lives. Those who feel abandoned by others and the Church have often experienced gossip and

---

[9] Pope Francis, *"The Threat of Gossip."* Morning Meditation in the Chapel of Domus Sanctae Marthae. www.vatican.va. September 2, 2013.

bullying, and they often exhibit feelings of unacceptance of despair. Tight knit circles of holy and devout Catholics in parishes need to be aware that even within Christian settings, these vices can fester and grow. They can create a structure of sin on a social level within a community. Pope Francis goes into detail:

> This isn't just about 2,000 years ago. It happens every day. In our heart, in our communities. We might welcome someone and speak well of him the first day but little by little that worm eats away at our minds until our gossip banishes him from good opinion. That person is in a community who gossips against his or her neighbor, is in a sense, killing him.[10]

When we think of our own communities at large, there are a vast number of groups we are associated with in daily living. As stated, those communities are within our own homes, neighborhoods, churches, and elsewhere. Pope Francis offers an example: when we first meet a person, perhaps they charm us for whatever reason. He then says the worm eats away at our minds, and gossip creeps into our hearts, which is a serious vice. Gossip alienates and assumes the worst of a person or family, creating disharmony, sadness, and rejection. The results can be devasting since people often lose relationships, social standing, and their sense of community. Youth and young adults are affected, as well, since gossip and bullying often happens in school settings where they are forced to be in the presence of their persecutors.

---

[10] Ibid.

Gossip is evil, and Pope Francis speaks of the importance of the faithful to fully recognizing it. Gossip can often lead to bullying which is a threatening and divisive behavior coupled with cruel action that often leaves victims hurt both mentally, physically, and emotionally. Pope Francis goes on to speak of how the evil one works in this regard pertaining to the evils of gossip and bullying:

> The devil came into the world through envy. A community, a family, is destroyed by this envy that the devil teaches in the heart and causes one to speak ill of the other. We must think of our own daily weapons: the tongue, gossip, tittle-tattle. In order that there may be peace in a community, in a family, in a country, in the world, we must start by being with the Lord; never to kill our neighbor with our tongue, and to be with the Lord just as we shall be in heaven.[11]

We all have our "daily weapons" in terms of speaking ill of others. Many a parish priest in a homily has referred to the fact that this sin is one that affects all of us even if we don't realize we are doing it. These weapons can deeply hurt and even kill all confidence within a person who has been affected by gossip and bullying. Unfortunately, even within the theological world where intelligent scholars of the faith teach others the deposits of faith are partakers in this serious sin. The effects of sin have no boundaries regardless of educational levels or anything else that separates.

Bullying takes gossip to the next level as it reaches the height of sin when a person is ridiculed, excluded, and often even hurt

---

[11] Ibid.

physically. It happens in schools, neighborhoods, workplaces, families, and sadly even with the walls of parish communities. Bullying is a serious offense, and the world is beginning to understand its profound impact in terms of its effects on the human person.

> Bullying is a form of aggressive behavior in which someone intentionally and repeatedly causes another person injury and discomfort. Bullying can take the form of physical contact, words, or more subtle actions.[12]

Notice that bullying can take form not only in an outward or physical way but also subtly. The subtle ways of bullying may be more difficult to detect, making it even harder for those who suffer from being bullied by others. For this reason, as a Church, we must be fully aware of the impact of bullying since there are many who suffer in silence by the aggressive actions and behaviors of the perpetrators. The Church can recognize and respond to bullying by becoming educated on it and in taking steps teach Church leaders to spread greater awareness to minimize its impact. This needs to be accomplished through a top-down approach starting with the hierarchy of the Church, to bishops, priests, and deacons, and the lay faithful.

Ignoring someone who needs friendship and care can also be a form of bullying since as Catholics we are called to love and care for those who suffer and who are abandoned and alone without support. By not being congenial in social settings, we may be without realizing, adding to their hurt, stress, and emotional pain. Simple steps

---

[12] American Psychological Association, "Bullying." Adapted from APA Dictionary of Psychology, 2023.

that we can do daily in becoming more loving and kinder can make a world of difference for those who have been affected by both gossip and bullying. Bullying is on the rise in our culture since cyber-bullying is an issue with both the young and old and those who are in between. All too often in the news we may hear of incidents where a young person is bullied to the point of committing suicide or of having serious mental and emotional complications due to it. This happens across numerous platforms and venues on social media and online, perhaps too vast to detail. We, as a Church, must not only be aware of the ill effects of bullying but be on guard of it for ourselves and for those close to us.

> Life other evils, bullying is a product of sin, bad choices, and a broken society. But the apathy that allows it to continue is also a product of those same things.[13]

One of the most vital aspects of bullying awareness is putting forth the effort to know the signs and to report it to the authorities at hand when it happens. Keeping track and finding the proper help and resources to find help, counseling, and protection is first. As people of faith, we can offer prayers and sacrifices for those who are affected by letting them know they have our love and support during a time of crisis. Sadly, one outcome of the times we are living in related to social media is that comments can be made publicly about people with little to no repercussions. This is where deeper awareness of the issues at hand are integral. To make a difference we must

---

[13] Susan Ciancio, "The Reality of Bullying: A Pro-life Perspective." *The Catholic World Report* (August 11, 2023).

accept the fact that is happening and do something about it. Through prayer, education, and implementation; this is how it will be accomplished.

Listening and Being Attentive is a Key

In all these matters pertaining to both gossip and bullying, learning to be a good listener is a key to opening doors. People affected by these vices can become alienated and even further marginalized once they have suffered the effects of gossip and bullying. As a worldwide community of faith, it is all our responsibility to make outreach to those around us, especially those who may seem awkward within a group setting and those who do not have family, friends, or support. As people of faith, it is easy to get distracted by our surroundings, our own family, and friends, and not to keep the door open for others to partake in friendship with us. Pope Francis message from a homily is below:

> Listen to Jesus: But, Father, I do listen to Jesus, I listen a lot! Yes! What do you listen to? I listen to the radio. I listen to the television, I listen to people gossip. We listen to so many things throughout the day, so many things. But I ask you a question. Do we take a little time each day to listen to Jesus, to listen to Jesus' word? Do we have the Gospels at home? And do we listen to the Gospel? I suggest that each day you take a few minutes and read a nice passage of the Gospel and hear what happens there.[14]

---

[14] Pope Francis. General Audience. www.vatican.va. March 16, 2014.

The above may sound effortless, but it is far-reaching in terms of how we, the faithful, can do something to help prevent the evil of gossip and bullying. Pope Francis suggests for us to listen to Christ in the Gospels and through Jesus' life. We should not just be listening to radio, or watching TV, social media, or online sources to be enlightened on these matters, although the virtual world does have numerous benefits. If we wish to grow in love of God and others, we need to go directly to the source which is through the teachings of the life of Christ and Paschal Mystery.

Taking just a few minutes throughout the day is a place to begin to learn to love and to listen closely to Jesus. When in a social setting whether at home, in community, or other places, the time taken to reflect, pray, and be open to the spirit can be life changing. Openness creates a space to love others and to care about the matters which are important to them. It is especially integral to be aware in social situations to walk over to a person who may seem unhappy or in pain. Those people are all around within communities; we, the faithful, must open our eyes to them. Simple actions can help to foster compassion, empathy, and deep concern for those who have been affected by gossip and bullying in the past.

Nothing can be done in terms of making an impact without the help of the Holy Spirit. We, as members of the Church, know that gossiping and bullying go against what we believe as faithful Catholics. The next step is to act to make the proper outreach to spread the mission of mercy to the world. Listening and deeper care create a bridge to bring healing to those wounded by gossip. The key is active listening which is a skill involving full attentiveness and compassion in the moment. Being attentive to Holy Spirit calls us to conversion

Chapter Five: Teachings on Living a Virtuous Life

of heart in stepping out of a comfort zones. We, Christ's followers, can then be willing to befriend the marginalized *not out of obligation* but because it is a joy to love and serve:

> The Holy Spirit lets us speak in the act of faith. Without the Holy Spirit, none of us is able to say, 'Jesus is Lord.' It is the Spirit who lets us speak with people in fraternal dialogue. He lets us speak with others, recognizing them as brother and sisters, to speak with friendship, with tenderness, with compassion, understanding the heartaches and hopes, the sorrows and joys of others.[15]

In allowing the Holy Spirit to help to speak in outreach to the forsaken, this is the right direction. According to Pope Francis, this fraternal dialogue is one that enables members of the Church to speak with tenderness. This is the goal of our lives to alleviate the pain and suffering of people; Christ did the same thing in his earthly mission. He helped to bring hope and healing to those in need by offering his love and healing touch. Dialogue and openness demonstrate affability in action. These actions help to show those who feel downtrodden and sad that God cares deeply and loves them. We, the faithful, can share the joys and pains of their lives in unison. On the topic of gossip and bullying, we exercise great mercy and tenderness by offering listening and genuine friendship. This kind of friendship is not simply to say to oneself, "I did the right thing. Now I can move on with my life." It is not about this. It is about accepting the mission

---

[15] Pope Francis. Homily. www.vatican.va. June 14, 2014.

of friendship as a deep honor given by God. We, the Church, make this outreach because it is a beautiful treasure and ministry to befriend those who suffer and have been betrayed.

III. Illuminations from St. John Paul II and Pope Emeritus Benedict XVI

Pope John Paul II

Pope John Paul II, the 264th Pope in succession of St. Peter was elected pope on October 16, 1978, after the sudden passing of Pope John Paul I. He chose his name in honor of his successor, and he was the youngest pope elected in over a century. He was also the first non-Italian pope in over 455 years, and the first from a Slavic country. He was the first globally oriented pope, and his list of accomplishments during his twenty-seven years as pope is outstanding. St. John Paul II was canonized on April 27, 2014, by Pope Francis. A major part of his accomplishments as pope were his numerous writings. In his writings, he covered a large range of topics including virtue, justice, and occasionally subjects related to affability in some form.

Love of God and Others

When Pope John Paul II wrote the apostolic exhortation *Familiaris Consortio* in November of 1981, he was writing to an audience geared toward the family. This piece focuses on the challenges of marriage and family life, and it offers the great wisdom of the Church through the lens of St. John Paul II. He speaks about the conflict people can experience between love of God and love of self:

> This shows that history is not simply a fixed progression towards what is better, but rather an event of freedom, and even a struggle between freedoms that are in mutual conflict, that is according to the well-known expression of St. Augustine, a conflict between two loves: the love of God to the point of disregarding self, and the love of self to the point of disregarding God.[16]

The struggle between loving God and of honoring and loving the self is very real, and something that affects families since within the home life there will always be challenges between choosing what is good and what is not. His recognizing this conflict and addressing it offers wisdom in leading the faithful to seek after virtue. This is also a recognition of justice and of moral virtues. He continues through his apostolic exhortation to educate his readers on their dignity as creations of God and of members of the human family. Part of this education includes various realms of justice including the importance of treating one another with kindness, dignity, and respect.

Additionally, at the very beginning of his pontificate in March of 1979, he wrote the encyclical letter *Redemptor Hominis*. This was his first piece of writing as pope. He discusses various topics in the letter, and there is a definite focus on discussing love of God and love of others.

---

[16] Pope John Paul II, *Familiaris Consortio. Apostolic Exhortation.* Libreria Editrice Vaticana. November 22, 1981, Location 285-295.

> Man cannot live without love. He remains a being that is incomprehensible for himself, his life is senseless, if love is not revealed to him, if he does not encounter love, if he does not experience it and make it his own, if he does not participate intimately in it.[17]

Of course, throughout his pontificate, Pope John Paull II spoke and wrote on numerous occasions on topics related to how-to-live in God's love which was also deeply revealed in his famous writing the *Theology of the Body*[18]. His recognition in communicating that "man cannot live without love" also relates to the fact that man cannot live without giving love, as well. Giving love translates into how well we give of ourselves to others including those who are less fortunate and those who are marginalized. Additionally, opening oneself to others is in offering justice and also affability. It is all part of love. St. John Paul says that "if he doesn't encounter love, if he doesn't participate in it intimately." He is referring to the fact that when people do not have that experience of giving and receiving love, it is an unfortunate circumstance. In offering friendliness and openness, this is another way that love is fully expressed.

Both St. John Paul II and Pope Emeritus Benedict XVI have made numerous references that one of the definitions of God is of

---

[17] Pope John Paul II, *Redemptor Hominis. Encyclical Letter.* Liberia Editrice Vaticana. March 4, 1979, Location 343.

[18] *Theology of the Body* is a series of lectures given by St. John Paul II during his pontificate between September 5, 1979, and November 28, 1984. The topics of the lectures are an anthropology in which the human body reveals God. He gave a total of 129 lectures on the topic. The topics were later expanded upon in his encyclicals, letters, and exhortations.

him being "love"[19]. Although there are various other correct theological definitions of God and of love, these two great popes of modern times confess that one of the simple, yet profound definitions is this: "God is love."

> God is love and Himself, He lives a mystery of personal loving communion. Creating the human race in His own image and continually keeping it in being, God inscribed in the humanity of man and woman the vocation and responsibility, of love and communion. Love is therefore fundamental and innate vocation of every human being.[20]

John Paul explains perfectly that the communion of God is the love that is his being. He also explains it as a "mystery" which is something that we as humans may never fully grasp one hundred percent. The love between the Father, and the Son, and the Holy Spirit, which consists of the Trinity is also a *great mystery*, but it also refers to the love generated between them, which is inscribed in every human being, as he states. This concept of love also points to the *action* of love that we as God's people offer both to God and to others. To reiterate, the openness displayed to others through virtue, justice, and affability is a participation in love. Therefore, what St.

---

[19] Pope John Paul II refers to God as love throughout his writings especially in the *Theology of the Body* and many other of his writings. Pope Emeritus Benedict XVI did the same and also wrote The encyclical *Deus Caritas Est* which translates to *God is Love* on December 25, 2005.

[20] Pope John Paul II, *Familiaris Consortio. Apostolic Exhortation*. Libreria Editrice Vaticana. November 22, 1981, Location 418.

John Paul II presents in his writings on the love of God relate to the importance of affability as an integral piece of making outreach to our brothers and sisters, especially the suffering. Based on his pontificate, his life, and all of his writings, St. John Paul II understood well the meaning and relevance of affability as a virtue.

Pope Emeritus Benedict XVI

The late Cardinal Joseph Ratzinger, Pope Emeritus Benedict XVI was elected pope on April 19, 2005, and his papacy ended on February 28, 2013. He is the 265th pope and is known as a brilliant scholar and contributor to the teachings of the Church especially the Catechism of the Catholic Church. Like his predecessor Pope John Paul II, he had much to say on the subject of God's love, virtue, and of living a good, moral life as a Christian. Some of his most well-known writings are *Deus Caritas Est (God is Love)*[21] written in 2005; *Spe Salvi (In Hope we are Saved)*[22] written in 2007; *Caritas in Veritate (Charity in Truth)*[23] written in 2009. Through his life as a priest, cardinal, and as pope, he made a focused effort to educate the faithful on what he felt to be the most integral matters of the Church namely

---

[21] *Deus Caritas Est (God is Love)* by Pope Benedict XVI is a book about the levels and depths of human and divine love written in 2005.

[22] *Spe Salvi (In Hope we are Saved)* by Pope Benedict XVI is a book about the challenges of faith lived out in light of the virtue of hope. It was written in 2007.

[23] *Caritas in Veritate (Charity in Truth)* by Pope Benedict XVI is a book about the relationship between humans and environmental ecologies, justice, the common good, and human development. It was written in 2009.

creating a greater awareness and appreciation of the moral truths of the Church and in living them out.

Pope Benedict and the Virtue of Justice

In speaking on the topic of love and justice, in Pope Benedict's first encyclical *Deus Caritas Est*, he discusses the love of God and of neighbor which is pertinent in an investigation on justice, as well.

Having reflected on the nature of love and its meaning in biblical faith, we are left with two questions concerning our own attitude: can we love God without seeing him? And can love be commanded? Against the double commandments raise a double objection. No one will ever see God, so how could we love him? Moreover, love cannot be commanded; it is ultimately a feeling that is either there or not, nor can it be produced by the will. Scripture seems to reinforce the first objection when it states: "If anyone says, 'I love God,' and hates his is brother, he is a liar; for he who does not love his brother whom he has seen, cannot love God whom he has not seen" (1 Jn 4:20). But this text hardly excludes the love of God as something impossible. On the contrary, context of the passage quoted from the First Letter of John shows that such love is explicitly demanded. The unbreakable bond between love of God and love of neighbor is emphasized. One is so closely connected to the other that to say that we love God becomes a lie if we are closed to our neighbor or hate him altogether. Saint John's words should rather be interpreted to mean that love of neighbor is a path that leads to the encounter with God, and that closing our eyes to our neighbor also blinds us to God.[24]

Pope Benedict speaks of the verse in the I John 4:20, "If anyone says, 'I love God,' and hates his brother, he is a liar; for he who does not have his brother whom he has seen, cannot love his brother whom he has seen, cannot love God whom he has not seen." His reflection on the above is a direct correlation to the moral justice given in affability, which is openness of spirit. He also states, "that closing our eyes to our neighbor also blinds us to God." As this book has repeated over and over is the fact that affability as a moral virtue is necessary in order to bring the love of God to one's peers and especially to those who have faced challenges and family crises. Additionally, Pope Benedict XVI makes it clear that love of God and of neighbor are intricately linked in terms of doing the will of God and giving justice to others.

Pope Benedict also spoke of justice in his encyclical *Caritas in Veritate*. He mentioned the parallels between justice and charity, and how the two should never be separated as they are in essence inseparable:

> Not only is justice not extraneous in charity, not only is it not an alternative or parallel path to charity; justice is inseparable from charity, and intrinsic to it. Justice is the primary way to charity or, in Paul IV's words 'the minimum measure of it, an

---

[24] Pope Benedict XVI, *Deus Caritas Est. God is Love.* Liberia Editrice Vaticana. Kindle Edition. December 25, 2005, Location 275-284.

integral part of love 'in deed and truth' (I Jn 3:18), to which Saint exhorts us.[25]

The piece that refers to "in deed and truth" is interesting to note since any justice given must be in deed and not just in truth, as Benedict states. This would also indicate that the action of justice which would include the moral virtue of affability is something that is due to our neighbor just as any truth is integral pertaining to God's laws. He writes that offering justice is "intrinsic to charity," which stresses the fact that charity and truth are as one. Therefore, the acts of kindness given to the poor, marginalized, and forsaken are equal to truth and justice.

As a final example to share, Pope Emeritus Benedict XVI also speaks of justice as imperative in his encyclical *Spe Salvi*.

> Truth and justice must stand above my comfort and physical well-being, or else my life itself becomes a lie in the end, even the "yes" to love is a source of suffering because love always requires expropriations of my "I," in which I allow myself to be pruned and wounded. Love simply cannot exist without this painful renunciation of myself, for otherwise it becomes pure selfishness and thereby ceases to be love.[26]

---

[25] Pope Benedict XVI, *Caritas in Veritate. Charity in Truth*. Liberia Editrice Vaticana. June 29, 2009, p. 9.

[26] Pope Benedict XVI, *Spe Salvi. Saved in Hope*. Liberia Editrice Vaticana. November 30, 2009, No. 38.

The statement that "love simply cannot exist" in regard to the renunciation of self draws a picture which clarifies the fact that truth and justice involve giving of oneself. Truth is much more that doctrine or a definition, it must be combined with justice and love to have the full meaning of the teachings of Christ especially related to carry the cross and giving of ourselves. Benedict is solidifying the fact that truth, justice, and love go together hand-in-hand in living daily life. This self-renunciation is part of becoming affable and open to other people each day in all interactions. Pope Emeritus Benedict knew and understood that all of the forms of justice are not only important but *absolutely essential*, and this includes friendliness and kindness to everyone.

IV. Pope Francis Teachings on Holiness of Life

Pope Francis has much to say on what constitutes a holy life in terms of living it out day by day. He often points to the most significant gifts of our faith, which are the sacraments and specifically the Eucharist, and in leading a life dedicated to Christ in every way. He believes in going to Confession regularly and in entrusting the Lord for his forgiveness so that we, the faithful, can move on after dealing with the effects of sin in our own lives.

> The Church offers the possibility of follow a path of holiness, that is a path of the Christian; she brings us to encounter Jesus Christ in the sacraments, especially in confession and in the Eucharist; she communicates the Word of God to us, she

lets us live in charity, in the love of God for all. Let us ask ourselves then, will we let ourselves be sanctified?[27]

In the above statement by Pope Francis, he asks the question "will we let ourselves be sanctified?" This is an exceptionally good and relevant question in terms of what it means to be holy. Allowing ourselves to be sanctified means to entrust God with our whole selves including sins and the mistakes made in the past. Once this is accomplished, the slate is wiped clean through the Sacrament of Confession, and we move forward to a new life in Christ. Of course, this concept is never a "once and done" as the sacramental life includes continually taking sins and failings to the Lord for absolution and to be restored to a full communion relationship with both the Jesus and others.

Pope Francis has included similar thoughts on the prime importance of living close to the Lord in honoring the sacraments of faith. He challenges the faithful with the invitation to get to know Jesus better through prayer, dialogue, and in staying close to the sacramental life of the Church. The same sentiments he shares on Confession, he also shares on the Eucharist in receiving the body, blood, soul, and divinity of our faith. He understands the imperative nature of allowing ourselves to partake in the sacramental life of the Church to transform our hearts and minds.

---

[27] Pope Francis, General Audience. www.vatican.va. October 2, 2013.

The Eucharist

As the source and summit[28] of the Catholic faith, the Eucharistic gifts enables God's people to experience the beauty of a life in Christ. Pope Francis constantly points to the Eucharist as the main avenue in growing closer to Jesus:

> The road to Emmaus thus becomes a symbol of our journey of faith: the Scriptures and the Eucharist are the indispensable elements for encountering the Lord. We too often go to Sunday Mass with our worries, difficulties, and disappointments. Life sometimes wounds us, and we go away feeling sad toward our 'Emmaus' turning our backs and God's plan. We distance ourselves from God. But the Liturgy of the Word welcomes us.[29]

In the quote above, Pope Francis acknowledges those worries and difficulties that every person encounters in life at some point. Despite life's challenges, Christ's invitation remains. When we, his followers, come to the Lord in trust, we can be healed through reception of the Eucharist and in meditating on the scriptures. This kind of healing is often not an immediate feeling; it is an encounter with the Lord which fulfills deepest longings. There is life-changing holiness in this Eucharistic experience. In combination with the gift of the Sacrament of Confession and in allowing the Holy Spirit to manifest, happiness and joy can be experienced. This is a holiness of

---

[28] CCC, 1324.

[29] Pope Francis, Regina Caeli Audience. May 4, 2014.

Chapter Five: Teachings on Living a Virtuous Life

life in which opens the doors to God in a definitive way. It also entails deciding to slow our lives down enough to experience a real kind of faith. This is an invitation to the world.

What does Pope Francis teachings on holiness of life and the Eucharist have to do with affability? Francis continues to communicate that the outcome of living a Eucharistic lifestyle includes every interaction of daily life. This lifestyle consists in keeping the spirit of Christ in one's heart in daily interactions and in imitating Jesus. Since we, the faithful, are in union with Christ, he is ever-present. He invites the faithful to receive the Eucharist as a gift to others out of love. He speaks about the spiritual nourishment provided in receiving the body and blood of Christ to be able to spread God's love in greater ways:

> The Eucharist communicates God's love for us; a love so great that it nourishes us with himself; a freely given love, always available to every person who hungers and needs to regenerate his own strength. To live the experience of faith means to allow oneself to be nourished by the Lord and to build one's own existence not with material goods but with the reality that does not perish; the gifts of God, his Word, and his Body.[30]

The communication between God and the one who is receiving him is life changing. Francis speaks of how we, modern disciples of Christ, can regenerate strength in life when we are spiritually nourished. This nourishment enables God's people to be fed not with the

---

[30] Pope Francis, General Audience. www.vatican.va. June 19, 2014.

material goods of the world which in the end does not bring joy. We find that joy, as Pope Francis states, in the reality of receiving his Word and his Body which will not perish. This is where we draw strength in living out the Christian life. In addition, in receiving these divine gifts, we can ask the Lord for strength to live out justice and the other virtues. Under the virtue of justice is affability, which is openness to others and befriending them out of love and charity. We draw strength from the Eucharist and in receiving Christ *fully* which enables members of the Church to live in full communion with others.

The Joy of Holiness

One of the most intense lessons of Pope Francis on holiness of life is related to living the joy of holiness in daily life. As stated above, the Eucharist is the source of joy since Christ remains with us on earth through all the sacraments and most profoundly at the Eucharistic table. This jubilation can and should radiate in the belief of the Real Presence of Christ. We, Christ's followers, cannot help but be happy knowing that Jesus will never leave us. Pope Francis communicates with his flock that living in joy is a gift given by Christ and received by us. Pope Francis states:

> And so let us ask ourselves: How is it possible to live the joy which comes from faith, in the family, today? But I ask you also: It is possible to live this joy, or is it not possible? A saying

of Jesus in the Gospel of Matthew speaks to us: "Come to me, all who labor and are heavily laden, and I will give you rest."[31]

In a homily for his general audience in the statement above, Pope Francis tells members of the Church that is it not possible to lose joy if we trust and rest with Jesus. The gifts of the Catholic faith give us, Christ's followers, all that we need to live lives of holiness and exultation. This is an exciting reality to ponder since with the Lord we can find the strength to proceed in the journey of life. We can pursue living for others by being disciples of Jesus in the modern world.

Moving Forward in Holiness

Pope Francis' theories on holiness may seem rather simplistic on the outset, for his style of communication is uncomplicated and easy to understand. For Pope Francis, holiness comes in obedience in loving God, neighbor, and in doing God's will each day. When we fail, we thankfully have the Church and the sacramental life to enable us to continue strong in virtue. In living a life of holiness, we, Christ's disciples, are impelled to remember that this includes living the virtues of affability and kindness. Those who love and follow Christ must be open to the pain and suffering of the world and be willing to lay down our lives for the good of others.

---

[31] Pope Francis, Address to Pilgrimage of Families. www.vatican.va. October 26, 2013.

Chapter Six

St. Thomas Aquinas on Friendliness

I. The Virtue of Affability According to St. Thomas Aquinas.

St. Thomas Aquinas most prominent work, the *Summa Theologica*, was written between 1266 and 1273. The purpose of the writing served as an instructional guide for novices and teachers of the faith. In addition, it served as a compendium of the approved teachings of the Catholic Church[1]. St. Thomas Aquinas continues to hold a position of honor in Western philosophy and religion both within and outside the Church. He composed the *Summa Theologica* as a series of questions, thoughts, and objections to matters related to the faith, virtue, and in offering ways to be a better Christian.

In Volume Two, Question 114[2] of the *Summa Theologica*, St. Thomas Aquinas discusses the virtue of friendliness of affability. He asks the question, "Is friendliness of special virtue?" He also asks the question in Article Two related to this topic, "Is friendship a part of offering justice to others?" These are excellent questions to ponder considering this discussion on whether affability plays any significant role in evangelization. In addition, if friendliness does play a

---

[1] The first use of the term "Catholic Church" (meaning universal) came from St. Ignatius of Antioch (50-140) in his letter to Smyrnaeans (110 AD). https://www.orderofstignatius.org/files/Letters/Ignatius_to_Smyrnaeans.pdf

[2] St. Thomas Aquinas, *Summa Theologica*. Volume II. Christian Classics. Westminster, MD, 1948, Question 114, Article One.

role, how imperative is it in the overall picture of living out the virtues of faith?

Friendliness as a Special Virtue

The question at hand in Question 114 related is whether friendliness is "special" in terms of its measure in living the virtues of faith. The first Objection in Article One argues that affability is only a consequence of every virtue. In the article, it states that "any virtue can cause friendship"[3]. Although St. Thomas Aquinas does not elaborate in this specific question, he proceeds to answer the objections in the proceeding paragraphs. In Objection Two[4] he discusses the concept of showing love to those we do not love in a natural or organic way. He says this kind of friendliness is not virtue. Lastly, he states that the kind of love that only shares the pleasures of life but not the pain is also not virtue. Regarding responses to all of these questions, St. Thomas Aquinas quotes scripture, "Make thyself affable to the congregation of the poor" (Sirach 4:7[5]). He states that these precepts are laws of the faith. He states further that "deeds and words" must go together in terms of human relations and the "becomingness of this order" points to the virtue of friendliness.

After his initial response to the objections at hand, he continues forward to address each one: Objections One, Two, and Three. In his reply to Objection One, St. Thomas Aquinas mentions that it is not just "words and deeds" that suggest the virtue of friendship; it is the

---

[3] Ibid., Question 114, Article One.
[4] Ibid., Question 114, Article One.
[5] Sirach 4:7, NOAB.

behavior of friendship[6] which makes it a virtue and something to strive for. It is the manner of action and behavior which make it affable in nature. In his reply to Objection Two, he speaks of love[7] which signifies the signs of friendship. His statement describes the difference between strangers and friends:

> Hence there is not dissimulation in this, because we do not show them signs of perfect friendship, for we do not treat strangers with the same intimacy as those who are united to us by special friendship.[8]

In this statement, he speaks of "perfect friendship"[9] as one that recognizes those considered close in relationship through the bonds of charity and dialogue. This is what it means to be a devoted friend, and St. Thomas Aquinas brings to the forefront the virtue of having friends and of being a friend to others. In Objection Three of the question at hand, St. Thomas Aquinas utilizes scriptural references to prove his point that affability is indeed a virtue in and of itself since it is rooted in the love of God. He speaks of mourning with those who mourn and in sharing pleasures, but not lustful pleasures. He adds to his thought a verse from Psalm 132:1: "Behold how good and

---

[6] The "behavior of friendship" is related to the morality of a friendship and whether is it virtuous or not.

[7] St. Thomas Aquinas, *Summa Theologica*. Volume II. Christian Classics. Westminster, MD, 1948, Question 114, Article One.

[8] Ibid., Question 114, Article One.

[9] "Perfect friendship" is one that is infused with the love of God, and one that is morally virtuous in all aspects.

how pleasant it is for brethren to dwell together in unity."[10][11] Based on his responses to the objections, St. Thomas Aquinas reveals that friendly attitude toward others must be based on real charity, care, and genuine concern for the other. He proves his point that affability is not only relevant but *needed* in relationships and in Christian awareness of others.

Friendship as a Part of Justice

The next question at hand has to do with friendship as a part of justice. In Objection One of the questions, it is stated that friendship is indeed *not* a part of justice. The simple definition of "justice" in the Objection is "giving a man his due"[12]. Objection Two makes it a point to state that friendliness is not a part of justice, but it is included with the virtue of temperance. The simple definition of temperance in the paragraph is, "to moderate the greatest pleasures"[13]. Objection Three simply states that friendliness is opposed to justice because it, "treats in like manner known and unknown companions and strangers"[14]. In the proceeding paragraphs of Question 114, Article Two, St. Thomas Aquinas answers that, yes, friendliness *is indeed* under the

---

[10] Psalm 132:1, NOAB.

[11] St. Thomas Aquinas, *Summa Theologica*. Volume II. Christian Classics. Westminster, MD, 1948, Question 114, Article One.

[12] St. Thomas Aquinas, *Summa Theologica*. Volume II. Christian Classics. Westminster, MD, 1948, Question 114, Article Two.

[13] Ibid., Question 114, Article Two.

[14] Ibid., Question 114, Article Two.

Chapter Six: St. Thomas Aquinas on Friendliness

title or the umbrella of justice[15]. It is also a moral virtue. In his reply to Objection One he mentions the fruit of the spirit is joy. He states: "Now, as man could not live in society without truth, so likewise, not without joy, because as the Philosopher says, no one could abide a day with the sad not with the joyless"[16]. In his reply to Objection Two, he states:

> It belongs to temperance to curb pleasures to the senses. But this virtue regards the pleasures of fellowship, which have their origin in the reason, in so far as one man behaves becomingly toward another. Such pleasures need not to be curbed as though they were noisome.[17]

The above response from St. Thomas Aquinas indicates that he believes that it is *improper* to place friendliness under the category of temperance. Lastly in his reply of Objection Three, he speaks of the fact that we, the faithful, should treat everyone with due respect and kindness. He states:

---

[15] Friendliness as "under the umbrella of justice" refers to the fact that friendliness and affability are one of the moral virtues of justice; therefore, it is justice due to another out of love and respect for them as humans and children of God.

[16] St. Thomas Aquinas, *Summa Theologica*. Volume II. Christian Classics. Westminster, MD, 1948, Question 114, Article Two.

[17] Ibid., Question 114, Article Two.

It is not fitting to please and displease intimate friends and strangers in the same way. This likeness consists in this, that we ought to behave towards all in a fitting manner.[18]

The idea of treating everyone in a "fitting manner" suggests that joyful and kind interactions are integral in following the commands of God to love others. There is much to ponder in examination of all of these questions, and perhaps there may be a bit of confusion in full understanding of all of St. Thomas' points related to the questions and topics. It can be concluded that in the final analysis, friendship is a virtue, and a justice offered to others especially when friendship is exercised in a virtuous manner.

Passions

Along the same lines as this discussion on friendship is an examination of passions[19] and Aquinas' thoughts on how the passions relate to moral virtues. In *Summa Theologica*, a question is presented as to whether passions increase or decrease related to the goodness of an act also relating to friendship.

Objection One. It would seem that every passion decreases goodness of a moral action for anything that hinders the

---

[18] Ibid., Question 114, Article Two.
[19] "The term 'passions' belongs to the Christian patrimony. Feelings or passions are emotions or movements of the sensitive appetite that incline us to act or not to act in regard to something felt or imagined to be good or evil." CCC, 1763.

judgment of reason, on which depends the goodness of moral acts, consequently, decreases the goodness of the moral act. But every passion hinders the judgment of reason, for Sallust say (Caitlin): 'All those that take counsel about matters of doubt, should be free from hatred, anger, friendship, and pity': therefore passion decreases the goodness of a moral act.[20]

Aquinas addresses the question in part:

Accordingly, just as it is better that man should both will doing good and do in his external act; so also does it belong to the perfection of moral good, that man should be moved unto good, not only in respect of his will, but also in respect of his sensitive appetite; according to Ps. 83:3: 'My heart and my flesh have rejoiced in the loving God': whereby (heart) we are to understand the intellectual appetite and by 'flesh' the sensitive appetite.[21]

One thing is clear, which is the fact that vice decreases the goodness of a moral act. Passions which are not directed toward good will minimize efforts to act in the ways of the Lord and to live in charity with others. This same concept applies to friendship since it is in friendship that charity and justice will *prevail*. Additionally, since

---

[20] D.J. Kennedy, *Summa Theologica* Parts I and II. Pars Prima Secunda. Kindle Edition. Jazzybee Verlag. July 21, 2012, Third Article, Q. I and II, Article Three, p. 378.

[21] Ibid., p. 380.

friendship is a justice and also a moral virtue, we, Christ's followers, should strive to be virtuous in all matters related to relationships which blossom into friendship. There is much more to read and understand pertaining to the work, writings, and charism of Aquinas; however, these sections presented from the *Summa Theologica* display a basic understanding of his work related to affability. The nature of his writing style is the question-and-answer method which aims to reveal specific truths of the faith related to virtuous living. It can easily be summed up based on the evidence presented that Aquinas believed and taught that affability is not only relevant but necessary especially in holy friendship with others.

Understanding the Language of St. Thomas Aquinas

The *Summa Theologica*, written in the thirteenth century, had specific language of the day and presentation of words on paper. St. Thomas Aquinas uses logical thinking and precise language in each question and objection to demonstrate a point. In the above writings related to Question 114 on friendliness and affability, it seems that St. Thomas Aquinas wishes *to dispel any myths* on friendliness and its importance in living the virtues of our faith. He aspires to assure his audience that friendliness is not temperance; it is a justice owed to others by virtue of their dignity as humans and as beloved children of God.

In addition, his responses also indicate that we, as followers of Christ, are indebted to others in giving them due justice as human beings and God's beloved. Although his language is not "casual" in a modern sense, St. Thomas Aquinas communicates clearly that

Chapter Six: St. Thomas Aquinas on Friendliness

affability is valuable, and we are obligated to show friendliness as a justice offered. He also mentions the poor in this section of the *Summa Theologica*. He states that we, God's people, are to remember the poor in our interactions which alludes to the fact that friendliness is a major part of the equation of affability. One should not be confused by St. Thomas' "back and forth" commentary in the *Summa Theologica*. Instead, those who wish to comprehend more fully can read his final answers for clarity related to affability as a worthwhile and virtue to be exercised in light of seeking a virtuous life.

II. Comparison: Aristotle and St. Thomas Aquinas

Aristotle[22] is known as one of the greatest philosophers to have ever lived, and he has impacted Catholic philosophy and thought in the area of politics, metaphysics[23], and ethics. His body of work has greatly impacted in particular the field of Catholic education. This ancient Greek philosopher was born in the year 384 B.C.E. and died in 322 B.C.E. He has also made impacts in the fields of rhetoric[24], physics, and in psychology. He was the son of a physician, Nicomachus[25], and his father also served as king of Macedonia.

---

[22] Oliver Shields, *Biography of Aristotle by Ptolemy*. Kindle Edition. December 14, 2021, p. 1-7.

[23] Metaphysics is a branch of philosophy dealing with identity, time, space, being, knowing, and substance.

[24] Rhetoric is the use of effective or persuasive speaking or writing and other techniques.

[25] Nicomachus was an ancient Greek philosopher and the father of Aristotle. Nicomachus is also the name of the son of Aristotle, and he was

Nicomachus came from a prominent family including supposed lineage to Asclepius, who was also known at the time as the Greek god of healing. His parents played a major role in his love to education and innovations in philosophy, as he was exposed to a variety of ethnicities and cultures and a wide range of perspectives.

His formal education began when he moved to Athens to study under Plato[26]. After Plato died in 347 B.C.E. he traveled to several Greek cities, and he began to fine tune his own ideas on topics related to philosophy and science. It was at this time he began to publish his own works. In addition to all of his studies in these fields, he developed genuine interest in nature including plants, animals, and the human body. One of the major aspects to be admired on his philosophies is his appreciation for critical thinking. His teachings continue to have an impact on Western civilization in the shaping of our understanding of the world.

One of Aristotle's most prominent pieces of work is the Nicomachean Ethics[27]. In this writing, he presents ideas on ethics, the nature of a good life, and morality. He made the argument that the goal of human life is to achieve happiness, which in his definition is to flourish and to be in a positive state of well-being. Two other

---

born in 60 and died in the year 120. His son was a philosopher and a mathematician.

[26] Plato is a prominent ancient philosopher born in 428/427 B.CE. and died in 348 B.C.E. His most prevalent contribution is his theory of idea or forms.

[27] The *Nicomachean Ethics* is one of Aristotle's best-known writings on ethics. The book is about the science of the good centered on human life. The book is essential in understanding the ethics of Aristotle and of his teachings.

major contributions in his lifetime are his writings on politics and the education system. He argued that the best political system is a constitutional government balancing both those who govern and all people. He taught that the goal of education is in providing adequate education and in the state being responsible for all of its citizens. His work in the field of logic includes his piece, *Organon*[28], which was groundbreaking at the time. In his works related to logic, he discusses systems and reasoning which are still used in modern times. He argued that logic is essential for a better understanding of the world at large.

Additionally, his contribution to physics and the concept of motion lead to a belief that the universe is in constant motion. He also developed ideas on natural movement in which he stated that motion was inherent in all objects. In all of the areas of biology, metaphysics, physics, and logic, he brought forth groundbreaking ideas and concepts[29] which were very new to the understanding of the world. His centering on the importance of analysis and careful observation and his contribution to the pursuit of education inspired and informed great thinkers around the globe. The *Peripatetics*[30] school of philosophy founded by Aristotle in the fourth century made a major impact on the fields of logic and reasoning. This is where Aristotle developed his work the *Organon* which helped to

---

[28] The *Organon* by Aristotle is a collection of Aristotle's six works on logical analysis and dialectics.

[29] Most of Aristotle's concept center around three areas: classification, function, and hierarchy. He emphasized the search for proper and accurate definitions in terms of their properties.

[30] *Peripatetics* is a school founded by Aristotle in the year 355 B.C.E. It was an informal institution based around philosophy and science.

bring understanding to the world of logic, giving tools for developing sound arguments and making the best-informed decisions. The school of logic proceeded to thrive after his death, and Aristotle continued to influence the world of philosophy and of science for centuries to this day. Great theologians, such as St. Thomas Aquinas, were influenced by him, and by his Peripatetic school. Aristotle died in 322 B.C.E.

Aristotle's Contribution to Catholicism

Aristotle[31] has and continues to have influence in the world of Catholicism and in Catholic education. His teachings and ideas have affected many aspects of Catholic thought, ethics, science, metaphysics, and theology. He has made major contribution to natural law[32]. He believed there is an objective and a universal moral law that is inherent in the order of things. He debated with others that this law is discernable and made through observation and through reason, and this law governs the behavior of all things living. Theologians over centuries have incorporated his understanding of ethics and morals into their own writings. The Church has maintained there are specific morals and principles which are objective and universal, and these truths are brought about through observation and reason as Aristotle taught. His teachings on philosophy have influenced

---

[31] Brother Azarius, "Aristotle and the Christian Church. An Essay." The Brothers of Christian Schools. Published by William H. Sadlier. New York, NY. 1888, Article XII. https://www3.nd.edu/~maritain/jmc/etext/aatcc.htm

[32] Natural law is a body of unchanging moral principles as a basis for all of human conduct.

Chapter Six: St. Thomas Aquinas on Friendliness

Catholic social teaching as it promotes that commitment to social justice is rooted in the belief that God's people all have inherent dignity[33] which is also rooted in natural law.

He has been embraced by Catholic theologians and scholars throughout the history of the Church especially these contributions to natural law and to justice. Since the Catholic Church has long held that faith and reason go together, the study of the natural world helps to bring greater awareness of all of God's creation and in promoting a just society. His contributions to philosophy have long inspired theologians in the area of the moral teachings of the Church. His body of knowledge has made an impact from fields ranging from science to theology. St. Thomas Aquinas, in particular, drew heavily on Aristotle's knowledge and ideas, and he incorporated them into his works bringing them into Catholic intellectual reasoning and tradition and solidifying Aristotle as a major contributor to areas of theology and of natural law.

A Comparison of the Two: Aristotle and St Thomas Aquinas

St. Thomas Aquinas read extensively the works of Aristotle, and Aquinas is known as one of the most influential interpreters of Aristotle's writings in the medieval period. St. Thomas regarded Aristotle as one of the greatest philosophers of all time. The Catholic perspective in terms of the differences between Aristotle and Aquinas are in the realm of virtue. This has to do with how virtue comes about in our lives. Aristotle points to *reason* as to why virtue occurs and how

---

[33] Inherent dignity refers to the fact that every person has dignity as we are made in the image of God.

right decisions come about, and St. Thomas Aquinas expresses that through love virtue is attained. The difference between the two is in *how virtue comes about*. The similarity between the two is that like Aristotle, Aquinas believed that ethical understanding comes through virtue and that virtue is a skill that is developed.

Aristotle's body of knowledge and his expertise is rooted primarily in biology and politics while Aquinas is known as one of the greatest theologians in medieval times. In terms of virtue, Aristotle pointed to *habituation*, while St. Thomas Aquinas states that *God's grace* working within us helps us to obtain the virtues. This same theory indirectly pertains to God's existence and work in one's soul in doing good and avoiding evil.

> A difference exists between Aristotle and St. Thomas, in both we encounter the same hierarchy of second causes both subordinated to a first cause, but of the lack of passing beyond the plane of efficiency to the plane of being, Greek philosophy fails to emerge from earlier becoming. However at a glance, St. Thomas has enough to show that his proof moves on quite other lines, for him the proof of the existence of God by efficient causality is typical proof of creation. Thus, it can be readily seen that the basic difference between the two philosopher is the idea of revelation and religion in the case of St. Thomas. Christianity has done very much for philosophy as evidenced in the works of St. Thomas, who undoubtedly

presents to man the clearest philosophy ever written. We thank him for giving to us pure theology.[34]

The idea of revelation and religion in the case of St. Thomas in the existence of God carries the same theme related to virtues versus habits. St. Thomas Aquinas' theology has given the framework and includes the "whys" of God's presence and existence but also in allowing the grace of God to work in obtaining virtue. Aristotle has given the framework for determining what it means to be a "good person" and a person of virtue. This difference is a primary piece in understanding how the two are alike but also varied in their ways of thinking. Aquinas deepened the teachings of Aristotle and infused God and his grace as a way to live out virtue in daily life.

The moral doctrine of St. Thomas Aquinas as compared to Aristotle points to the *infusion of God* and in keeping in mind our eternal end and beatitude. One thing is clear, St. Thomas learned from Aristotle his approach to living a good, moral life, and he geared it toward the service of the Church.

This sketch of the moral doctrine of Thomas Aquinas will have to suffice for present purposes. It is of course tempting to add to the sketch from the vast number of pages Thomas devoted to the presuppositions, concomitants, corollaries, and consequences of the few matters we have mentioned. The

---

[34] Edward M. Danaher, "A Comparison of the Theories of Aristotle and St. Thomas Aquinas Regard to the Existence of God." Marquette e-publications. Marquette University. 1938. https://epublications.marquette.edu/bachelor_essays/124/

hope is that, however skeletal the presentation, it may nonetheless serve to suggest the basic structure of Thomas's moral philosophy. One who knows Aristotle well will find much that is familiar in the account we have given, and this is no accident. And yet, as our discussion of ultimate end makes clear, Thomas put the Aristotelian approach to the service of elucidating moral theology as well as moral philosophy. When man's end is recognized to be a supernatural one, the means to achieving it can scarcely be thought of as virtues a man can acquire through his natural capacities alone. Thus Thomas will speak of infused as well as of acquired virtues. Indeed, his moral theology, as is only to be expected, gathers round the preeminent Christian virtue of charity. Man's ultimate purpose is to love God with his whole heart and soul and his neighbor as himself. Reflection on what this ennobling task consists of reflection at the level of generality as to how this aim can be realized, could never be confused, as will be obvious, with the acts of charity that are the ultimate concern of such reflection.[35]

As McInerny states above, "Man's ultimate purpose is to love God with his whole heart and soul and his neighbor as himself." This ultimate goal was understood well by Aquinas, and all that he learned from Aristotle related to moral theology led him to deepening and

---

[35] Ralph McInerny, "A First Glance of St. Thomas Aquinas." Chapter Two: St. Thomas and Aristotle. Jacques Maritain Center. University of Notre Dame Press. 1990, No. 71. https://www3.nd.edu/~maritain/jmc/etext/peeping.htm

expanding the meaning of Christian virtue and widening these theories throughout the Church and the world. In relation to the moral virtue of justice and most particularly affability, Aquinas not only recognized this virtue as of immense value, but he also made it a point to include this virtue in his greatest body of work, the *Summa Theologica*.

III. St. Thomas Aquinas and the Virtues

In addition to his great writing, the *Summa Theologica*, St. Thomas Aquinas also wrote the *Treatise on the Virtues*[36] which offers additional insights on Church teachings on virtue. In this piece, St. Thomas Aquinas wrote about: the habits, the essence of virtue, morality, the cardinal virtues, and more. It is relevant to bring this piece of writing into the discussion as St. Thomas Aquinas touches upon the meaning and relevance of living out good habits which in turn becomes virtue in our lives.

Living out the Good

St. Thomas Aquinas suggests that good actions translate into virtues which then lead us to living better lives for God and others:

---

[36] John A. Oesterle, *St. Thomas Aquinas Treatise on the Virtues*. University of Notre Dame Press. Notre Dame. 1966.

> In order that man's actions be good, not only must his reason be well disposed by a habit of intellectual virtue but also his appetitive power by a habit of moral virtue.[37]

Intellect has much to do with following good moral conduct. An act of will is when there is a firm decision to do good and to avoid evil. It is beneficial to the soul in making the decision to develop and follow good habits which lead in the direction of God and of helping others. In terms of the topic of affability, a firm decision may also be made in one's heart in becoming more compassionate and friendlier. This is one way to live out the good in relation to affability and justice in offering friendliness toward everyone.

St. Thomas Aquinas suggests throughout his writings that virtue does indeed lead to happiness. As Catholics, we are taught that happiness is not something to seek after, but it is the result of living a virtuous life. Joy can be obtained through the love of God despite circumstances,[38] whereas it has been said that happiness is dependent on circumstance.

St. Thomas Aquinas suggests that happiness occurs in this willingness to do right and to follow a virtuous path. Therefore, happiness is dependent on this circumstance: that in doing good, we are more susceptible in finding true happiness which can only come from God.

---

[37] Ibid., p. xiv.
[38] I Peter:8-9, NOAB.

Happiness in this Life

St. Thomas Aquinas points to virtue as the key to both joy and happiness. Joy is not dependent on situations in life, but in love of God and others through the pains presented in daily encounters. Since happiness is dependent, to obtain it, one must seek after the good.

> The whole purpose of virtue is to achieve happiness, but happiness is twofold. The happiness which is proportioned to man's nature, and obtainable by means of man's natural capacities, is the happiness to which the moral and intellectual virtues are immediately ordered.[39]

The moral and intellectual virtues are "immediately ordered" meaning that all true happiness stems from this idea of seeking after virtue through the will of God and out of love for him and others. This is a brilliant summary on the teaching of St. Thomas Aquinas in all his writings that living virtue brings peace, heals the soul, and helps one to do the will of God. On the same note, in exercising the virtue of affability, we, as disciples of Jesus, can make a difference in fulfilling our God give mission to love and serve. We can also experience the happiness we so desire in reaching outside of ourselves to show openness and friendliness.

---

[39] John A. Oesterle, *St. Thomas Aquinas Treatise on the Virtues*. University of Notre Dame Press. Notre Dame. 1966, p. xv.

IV. Living Out the Virtue of Friendliness

Following a virtuous mission leads to an ordered and Godly life according to St. Thomas Aquinas. Friendliness is the quality of being affable and open to others. It is the unexpected smile received, the invitation to converse with someone new, and the cheerful attitude of spirit to those we encounter. St. Thomas Aquinas alludes to the fact that it is not just a behavior, it is a virtue. He goes as far as to categorize affability under the title of justice, which is one of the most integral of the cardinal virtues of the Church. With this said, living out friendliness should be in the forefront of evangelization practices. As discussed in Chapter Four, Section One, of this book on Human Development, friendliness is monumental in healing those who have been traumatized and marginalized. In examining both the psychological and spiritual ramifications in not practicing the virtue of affability, friendliness is a needed element in bringing God's love to the world in the greatest of ways.

Friendliness is a concrete virtue of faith making a colossal difference in the lives of the lost and forsaken. St. Thomas Aquinas recognized it to the level of educating others on the meaning of affability by including it in the *Summa Theologica,* as mentioned. There are specific ways those who practice the faith can live the valuable virtue of friendliness. Aquinas and other saints of the Church knew and understood well the meaning of virtuous friendship and outreach to those in need.

Josef Pieper

Josef Pieper, (1904-1997), a German Catholic Philosopher of the twentieth century keenly studied Aquinas and included in his writings thoughts and teaching on the value of holy friendship. Pieper is greatly responsible for a resurgence in Thomistic teachings and in promoting the Aquinas body of work to the world. He writes:

> There is no way of grasping the concreteness of man's ethical decisions from outside. But no, there is a certain way: that is through the love of friendship. A friend, and a *prudent* friend can help to shape a friend's decision. He does so by virtue of that love which makes the friend's problem his own, the friend's ego his own (so that after all it is not entirely 'from outside.') For by virtue of that oneness which love can establish he is able to visualize the concrete situation for decision, visualize it from, as it were, the actual center of responsibility. Therefore it is possible for a friend and only a *prudent* friend – to help with counsel and direction, to shape a friend's decision or, somewhat in a manner of judge, help to reshape it.[40]

Pieper emphasized prudence in friendship which transforms it into something virtuous and worth striving after. It is in the attaining of virtue in relationship to others that we, the faithful, are able to model Christ and to do good. In this striving for prudence, the Holy Spirit enables Christ's followers to be a true friend to others and to

---

[40] Josef Pieper, *The Four Cardinal Virtues*. Harcourt, Brace, & World, Inc. 1965, p. 37.

guide those struggling toward good and away from evil. In this way, members of the Church can help to lead people in the right direction in following Christ. Theologians, saints, and scholars of the Church open doors of understanding on the proper meaning of real friendship.

Aelred of Rievaulx

St. Aelred of Rievaulx (1109-1167) is a saint to look on the wisdom of spiritual friendship. As an abbot, he had a charism for friendship, and during his lifetime, he had developed deep bonds of friendship with other monks prior to his death in 1167. His love of others was rooted in the love outpoured from the Holy Trinity.

> Now the spiritual, which we call friendship, is desired not with an eye to any worldly profit or for any extraneous reason, but for its own natural worth and the emotion of the human heart, so that its fruit and reward is nothing but itself. Hence our Lord says in the Gospel, "I appointed you to go and to bear fruit that is to 'love one another.' For one goes by making progress in the fruit of friendship, and one bears fruit by savoring the sweetness of its perfection. So spiritual friendship is begotten by likeness of life, habits, interests, that is, *by agreement in things human and divine with good will and charity*.[41]

---

[41] Marsha L. Dutton, *Aelred of Rievaulx Spiritual Friendship*. Cistercian Publications. 2010, p. 77-78.

St. Aelred recognized the connection between love of God and neighbor through intimate, spiritual friendship with others. He states in the above quote that through "life, habits, and interests" we are able to develop the type of bonds worthy of virtuous friendship which is a true demonstration of charity. He stresses that friendship is mutual and in agreement with one another, which points to affability.

Cicero on Friendship

Marcus Tullius Cicero (106-43 B.C.E) offers wisdom on friendship along on the same vein of thinking as Aquinas and Aelred in certain instances. Cicero was a Roman poet, philosopher, and humorist. Educated in Rome and Greece, he was considered one of Rome's greatest orators. He wrote and spoke about friendship and its meaning in detail for reflection and practice.

> Well between men like these the advantages of friendship are almost more than I can say. To begin with, how can life be worth living, to use the words of Ennius, which lacks that repose which is found in the mutual good will of a friend? What can be more delightful than to have someone to whom you can say everything with the same absolute confidence as to yourself? If it not prosperity robbed of half its value if you have no one to show your joy?[42]

---

[42] Marcus Tullius Cicero, *Treatises on Friendship and Old Age*. Good Press. 2022, p. 7-8.

Obviously, Cicero understood well the value of friendship including the confidence placed in a true and trusted friend. He states that having the ability to speak one's mind to a friend is something to not only treasure, but to be joyful about. He knew and understood the absolute value of having a trusted confidant, which is a mutual good when shared in unison with one another. Along the same lines, there is great significance in recognizing the values of friendship taught by Cicero, Aelred, and Pieper.

Recognizing Others

In addition to saints and scholars of the past, the teachings of Aquinas, and the wisdom of the Church, the first step in living out the virtue of affability is recognition of the value of the human person. This entails being keenly aware of those who lack support, friends, and confidence. There are people in daily life who are experiencing challenges and trauma, and who need the care of others to make it through life. The faithful can find those people in all the familiar surroundings of living, such as: at home, in neighborhoods, churches, workplaces, schools, and public places. Our ability, as followers of Christ, to recognize others enables us to live the mission God has given us to reach the rejected.

Active Listening

A second way to live the virtue of friendliness is to be a good active listener. Active listening involves carefully paying attention to the words of another person in conversation. It also involves not interrupting and allowing that person to explain themselves and to "have" their feelings. It is in giving and showing love and concern for the things that matter to someone else in their life that have exceptional meaning. A significant number of people undergo trials and adversities which impact their lives of faith and make them feel powerless over what is happening. In allowing them space to be listened to and cared about, fosters authentic healing, and helps them to understand how much God loves them.

Staying Connected

Another key element in living out affability is in staying in touch and keeping the lines of communication open. When people go through trials, part of the trauma is not having support and in losing family, friends, and others during times of crisis. Having people to care about their needs and foster fellowship is key for ongoing healing. Relationships come and go in life, but those who have faced alienation and loneliness need to be aware that there is always someone they can call. This could be someone to talk to, pray with, or just be there for. This is how we, as Catholics who love the faith, can make a monumental difference by offering ongoing care and friendship to those who suffer.

Not everyone has the natural gift of a friendly demeanor, but it can be learned just like any good habit. In taking the time to smile, listen, and to not give up on another, members of the Church can create a kinder world. St. Thomas Aquinas knew that the virtue of affability is an integral one in living out Catholic identity. As Christ's followers take seriously the lessons presented by St. Thomas

Aquinas, we, as people of faith, can make an impact for those who will benefit from our gifts. Doing so makes a difference for the domestic and universal churches.

The Church's Definition of Friendship

In addition to discussing friendship in light of Aquinas and other influential thinkers of the Church, we can turn directly to the Catechism of the Catholic Church for a precise, modern definition of how best to manifest friendship with others. Human friendship is best lived out in human solidarity within families and in society.

> The principle of solidarity, also articulated in terms of 'friendship' or 'social charity,' is a direct demand of human Christian brotherhood. An error, 'today abundantly widespread, is disregard for the law of human solidarity and charity, dictated and imposed by both our common origin and by the equality in rational nature of all men, whatever nation they belong to. This law is sealed by the sacrifice of redemption offered by Jesus Christ on the altar of the Cross to his heavenly Father, on behalf of sinful humanity.[43]

Friendship to be efficacious and rooted in Christ must always keep in mind solidarity with our brothers in sisters who need God's love and of our love. The Catechism offers a definition of "friendship" which includes social charity. Real and authentic friendship and affability is inclusive and in union with Christ and the Paschal Mystery.

---

[43] CCC, 1939.

As we go forth in search of friendship, the faithful must never forget the role of solidarity in making outreach to the marginalized as instructed by Christ.

Chapter Seven

Teachings of Pope Francis Related to Exercising Mercy and Sensitivity

I. What is Love?

Although this chapter will explore the question, "what is love" according to the teachings of Pope Francis, I will also discuss the proper theological definitions of love according to Church teachings, additional modern pope's definitions of love, and some of the saints . The most basic definition of love according to the Catechism of the Catholic Church is below:

> "To love is to will the good of another." All other affections have their source in this first movement of the human heart toward the good. Only the good can be loved. Passions 'are evil' if love is evil and good if it is good.[1]

The Church recognizes and teaches that the primary definition of love is, indeed, to "will the good of the other." Throughout this book it is clear that teachings on affability as a moral virtue of faith is rooted in this same kind of love. The catechism states, "In Christ, human feelings are able to reach their consummation in charity and divine beatitude"[2]. To clarify, as humans we experience a variety of

---

[1] CCC, 1766.
[2] Ibid., 1769.

feelings including those of "love," but in order to obtain the perfection of love and its consummation, this is only attained through God in meeting him face to face in eternal beatitude. As followers of Christ, we can look forward to heaven as we strive throughout life to live and love according to the commands of the Lord in following the two Great Commandments. In a *basic* way, this is love, however there is much more to discover when it comes to knowing and understanding deeper questions related to the definition of love.

Pope Francis on Love

Much of this book is focused on Pope Francis writing *Amoris Laetitia* which centers to a great extent on love as it pertains to family. From the family, comes life and the essence of God's love which then goes on mission in imitation of Christ to love and serve. Pope Francis writes:

> The triune God is love, and the family is its living reflection. Saint John Paul II sheds light on this when he said, "Our God in his deepest mystery is not solitude, but a family, for he has within himself, sonship, and the essence of family, which is love. That divine love, the divine family, is the Holy Spirit."[3]

Pope Francis recognizes that God *is*, indeed, love, and this love is part of the deepest mysteries of the faith. According to the teachings of Francis, it is not overly simplistic or theologically incorrect to make a statement that *God is love* and also that *love is God*. He states

---

[3] *Amoris Laetitia*, p. 15.

that love is found in family, and the mystery itself is not solitude but communion. This communion is what draws the human person to act in imitation of Christ by offering oneself to others in charity. Beginning in the family and then taking this message of hope and charity to the world there is much to do for the modern disciple of Christ.

As this book speaks of frequently, *love is not rude*, and this teaching is related to Pope Francis' instructions on showing and demonstrating love. This pertains to the *action of love*. He speaks of love as a giving of one's heart, time, and sacrifice for the good of the other.

> Its actions, words, and gestures are pleasing and not abrasive or rigid. Love abhors making others suffer. Courtesy 'is a school of sensitivity and disinterestedness' which requires a person to develop his or her mind and feelings, learning how to listen, to speak and at certain time, to keep quiet.[4]

Related to the topic of affability, love becomes materialized through the action of kindness and of demonstrated care, concern, and in genuinely acting in love. Although love, according to the teachings of the Church is "willing the good of the other," Pope Francis offers an expansion of this definition by stating that "love abhors making others suffer." With this in mind, the manner in which we, the faithful, not only open ourselves to others but how we treat them in terms of friendliness and kindness is how we take love to an even *higher level* than just desiring what is best for them. In consciously acting on becoming more compassionate toward those who suffer

---

[4] Ibid., p. 79.

while continuing to "will" the best for their lives, we become missionary disciples for Christ through commitment and action. Additionally, we imitate the saints of our faith when in taking steps to comfort those who suffer and by loving them *not just through our wills* but through active service. If there is a barrier to being able to help marginalized people in bringing them the love of God, prayer is an eternal and timeless gift.

Pope John Paul II on Love

In Pope John Paul II's first encyclical, *Redemptor Hominis*, which he authored in March of 1979, he writes of what is needed in order to gain a deeper understanding of the human person and of the life of faith. This encyclical was, at the time, and excellent precursor to what was to come with his many writings including the *Theology of the Body*. In *Redemptor Hominis*, he speaks of the mystery of redemption.

> The redemption of the world – this tremendous mystery of love in which creation is renewed is, at its deepest root, the fullness of justice in a human heart – the heart of the firstborn Son – in order that it may become justice in the hearts of many human beings, predestined from eternity in the Firstborn Son to the children of God.[5]

---

[5] Pope John Paul II, *Redemptor Hominis. Encyclical Letter.* Kindle Edition. Liberia Editrice Vaticana. March 4, 1979, Location 300-323.

He speaks of "justice" as a means to be renewed, and this is all part of the mystery of God which is of love. St. John Paul II says that at its "deepest root" fullness if found. The deepness he is speaking of is the mystery of love itself, which is God. This is also the heart of Jesus which is that self-giving and self-sacrificing love he offered on the cross for our redemption. Redemption is at the heart of love. He states that justice is what will reign in the hearts of human beings as they are "predestined from eternity" within the Son as children of God. These thoughts expressed by St. John Paul II have everything to do with love and justice.

Theology of the Body

Perhaps one of the most influential writings from St. John Paul II are the series of talks he gave from September 1979 to November 1984 related to the *Theology of the Body*. Books have been written over the last thirty years or more pertaining to this school of thought by Pope John Paul II on the meaning of our bodies and the theology behind how we are made in the image and likeness of God. In these talks and in the books written on the topic, there is one commonality, and it is that humans are *made to love*. We, as God's children, are made not only to love him but also to love others through the gift of our bodies. He articulates in detail by discussing the male and female persons and their complementarity as a communion of persons. At the heart of his writings, he speaks of the wonder of every person with those basic questions of existence.

So many people wonder: Who am ? Why am I here on this earth? The answer is found in self-giving love. We were created by love, and we're called to love in return. A man can only find his true self in giving himself away.[6]

The statement by St. John Paull II that "a man can only find his true self in giving himself away"[7] refers to the love generated between man and woman, but it also alludes to the fact that giving oneself away extends to the outer world. Giving time and love to the needs of others does not just pertain to the communion of love experienced in marriage but also in the gift of love between them that gives outwardly. The domestic church, the family, is an offering to the world that both gives and receives love, which imitates the love between the Father and the Son producing the fruits of the Holy Spirit in the world. This is love.

Additionally, this gift of love is the justice given to others; this is affability which is the friendliness of spirit demonstrated and shown to sow peace. In the many writings of St. John Paul II, he understood the tremendous gift of man and woman and their relationship in marriage and how the family unit can strive to bring God's love by offering justice to the needy. St. John Paul II understood the importance of every facet of justice including affability.

---

[6] Pope John Paul II, *Theology of the Body in Simple Language*. Kindle Edition. Philokalia Books. April 30, 2014, Location 443.

[7] Ibid.

Pope Emeritus Benedict XVI

Perhaps Pope Emeritus Benedict XVI's most profound statement on the meaning of love is his choice of the title of first encyclical written in 2005 called *Deus Caritas Est* translated as God is love. For anyone in the academic world or elsewhere who may doubt the relevance of this straightforward but far-reaching definition of love; it is perfectly *theologically correct*. Benedict makes it clear as presented in the introduction of *Deus Caritas Est* that this definition is precise.

> God is love, and we he who abides in love abides in God, and God abides in him' (1Jn 4:16). These words from the First Letter of John express with remarkable clarity the heart of the Christian faith; the Christian image of God and resulting image of mankind and its destiny. In the same verse, Saint John also offers a kind of summary of the kind of the kind of Christian life: 'We have come to know and to believe in the love God has for us'.[8]

When we recognize God is love in the most basic understanding of love, it opens up doors in loving God more each day and in carrying out his will. Pope Bendict spoke often of the love experienced in family, and the role each member of the domestic church in bringing the gospel of Christ to the world.

---

[8] Pope Benedict XVI, *Deus Caritas Est. God is Love.* Liberia Editrice Vaticana. Kindle Version. December 25, 2005, Location 40.

Love in Truth

In his 2009 encyclical *Caritas in Veritate* translated as *Love in Truth*, Pope Benedict expands on the meaning of love and truth. Pope Benedict Emeritus XVI broadens the same pattern of thought on love which he discussed in *Deus Caritas Est*.

> Charity is at the heart of the Church's social doctrine. Every responsibility and every commitment spelt out by that doctrine is derived from charity which, according to Jesus is the synthesis of the entire Law (cf. Mt. 22:36-40). It gives real substance to the person relationships with God and with neighbour; it is the principle not only of micro-relationships (with friends, with family members or within small groups) but also of macro-relationships (social, economic and political ones.) For the Church, instructed by the Gospel, charity is everything because, as Saint John teaches (cf. 1 John 4:8, 16) and as I recalled in my first Encyclical Letter "God is Love" *(Deus Caritas Est): everything has its origin in God's love, everything is directed towards it.* Love is God's greatest gift to humanity, it is his promise and our hope.

Benedict states that all relationships whether micro or macro have their basis in God, and the faithful should never forget this fact. Not only does he stress these thoughts in the paragraph above, but also throughout his writings, especially in *Deus Caritas Est* and *Caritas in Veritate*. He states that "Charity is at the heart of the Church's social doctrine"[9]. It is also at the heart of this book and the teachings on affability. As Pope Emeritus Benedict XVI was attuned to charity, truth, and justice, he certainly understood and practiced the virtue of affability in his own life.

Eros and Agape

A chapter on love would not be fully complete without a mention of eros and agape love. Bendict speaks of the two forms of love in his encyclical *Deus Caritas Est*.

> In philosophical and theological debate, the distinctions have often been radicalized to the point of establishing a clear antithesis between them: descending, ablative love - agape – would be typically Christian, while on the other hand ascending, positive or covetous love – eros- would be typical of non-Christian, and particularly Greek culture. Were this antithesis to be taken to extremes, the essence of Christianity would be detached from the vital relations fundamental to human existence and would become a world apart, admirable perhaps, but decisively cut off from the complex fabric of human life. Yet eros and agape – ascending and descending love – can never be completely separated.[10]

Bendict continues on this thought:

---

[9] Ibid.
[10] Pope Benedict XVI, *Deus Caritas Est. God is Love*. Liberia Editrice Vaticana. Kindle Version. December 25, 2005, Location 143-153.

The element of agape thus enters into the love, for otherwise eros is impoverished and even loses its own nature. On the other hand, man cannot love alone. He cannot always give he must also receive. Any who wishes to give love must also receive love as a gift.[11]

What Pope Emeritus Benedict XVI is communicating about eros as well as agape is that they enter into one another as ascending and descending love. He states that "man cannot love alone;" therefore the gift of the other comes into play in terms of human love and the giving and receiving involved in it. He admits that there have been debates on the definitions and understanding of eros and agape, but he clarifies that love is the fabric of human life, therefore there is a place for the different forms of love. When God is infused into all of love and charity, this is the gift man not only receives but gives back through giving of himself. As Catholics and people of faith, we understand this giving to be self-sacrificing. In imitation of Christ, and in incorporating the Corporal and Spiritual Works of Mercy into our lives it is essential in the offering of love. When we, as members of the Church, do acts of charity, seek justice, and learn to offer a friendly and affable spirit toward others, we are living in God's love.

The Saints on Love

The saints have had much to say on the topic of love and its meaning. For the purpose of this book, I will focus on four saints in a discussion on love and a small sampling of each one. Doctor of the

---

[11] Ibid.

Church, St. Therese of Lisieux in the piece *Story of a Soul,* she spoke extensively on her relationship with God and the depths of his love.

> All our sacrifices seemed quite petty compared with this regard, and I wanted so much to love Jesus with my whole heart and prove it in a thousand ways while it still had the chance.[12]

This is a small example of Therese's thoughts on her love of Jesus and her constants recognition of his presence in her life. As many are aware, the love she had for Jesus led her to be able to give herself in the Carmelite monastery as she was surrounded by those whom she felt challenged to love. Her outpouring of love toward the heart of Jesus and in pleasing him is a good example of affability and openness to God's plan on a day-to-day basis. She is an excellent example of holy friendliness for the sake of the Lord.

Blessed Pier Giorgio Frassati a young man who devoted himself to the poor and who died at the young age of twenty-four, is another holy example of care and self-giving. Frassati was known as a friendly and positive young man who also celebrated a profound faith in Jesus and in the sacraments of Church. He died after contracting an illness attempting to bring medicine to an infirmed elderly woman. He made it a daily practice to live the virtues and to care for the sick and suffering.

> Blessed Pier Giorgio Frassati's life remains a shining example of virtue, faith, and compassion. His unwavering commit-

---

[12] Saint Theresa of Lisieux, *The Story of a Soul.* Tan Classics. 2010, pg. 76.

ment to serving others, his deep love for God, and his indominable spirit continues to inspire generations.[13]

His commitment to being an active listener, sacrificial, and loving is not only an example for younger people but to *all* people. In terms of love, Pier Giorgio Frassati demonstrates that he knew and understood what it means not only to receive love but to give it away, especially to the marginalized.

St. Francis of Assisi is another saint who lived a life of devoted to the love of God through poverty, chastity, and obedience to Christ. This Italian mystic saint was led to live a life devoted to Christ in every sense including making a conscious decision to give up all worldly possessions and to offer his whole self as a living sacrifice to God.

> Blessed are the peacemakers for they shall be called the children of God. They are truly peacemakers who amidst all they suffer in this world maintain peace in soul and body for the love of our Lord Jesus Christ.[14]

Being a peacemaker oftentimes involves suffering in modeling after Christ and bringing the love of God to the world. St. Francis of Assisi is an ideal saint in imitation of Christ and in demonstrating

---

[13] Vincent Neumann, *Blessed Pier Giorgio Frassati. Chronicle of a Man of Beatitude.* Kindle Edition. Sacred Lives Collections. February 6, 2024, Location 168.

[14] *The Writings of St. Francis of Assisi.* Kindle Edition. E-Bookarama. February 12, 2023, pg. 29.

the meaning of love and self-gift. Affability, for him, was lived out through his recognition and offering of peace to all he encountered, and this became the over-arching theme of his life.

Lastly, on the topic of "what is love," St. Teresa of Calcutta has various quotes over the years, but mostly what is striking is the demonstration of her life which was centered on the poorest of the poor. She understood well that love at various times is much more than "willing the best" for another, but it is also in *doing what we can*, if we are able to help and care for those who need it most. She lived and preached that love is what the world needs more than anything else.

> Being unwanted, unloved, uncared for, forgotten by everybody, I think that this is a much greater hunger than a person who has nothing to eat.[15]

St. Teresa of Calcutta said a great deal more than this simple quote, but this statement says much about her commitment to those who are hungry for love and in need of pastoral accompaniment. She comprehended that love is an immense gift from God meant to be given away. She knew the power of giving a kind smile to someone, and she exercised charity to those who feel rejected by offering an affable and friendly spirit.

The lives of the saints show us, the faithful, that love is oftentimes more than wishing the best for others. When opportunities arise, as people of faith, we can offer our lives in simple and practical ways to

---

[15] Sr. Jennifer Juliet, *The Prayers, Quotes and Sayings of Saint Teresa of Calcutta (Mother Teresa)*. Kindle Edition. September 13, 2016, pg. 8.

give love to those who need it most. We can materialize love through prayer, compassion, and self-gift. Modeling after Christ, Christians can demonstrate affability and charity in order to bring needed peace to the world. Not only will offering love bring peace, but it will usher in needed order to the chaos and confusion brought on through sin and discord which has become prevalent in the modern age. It is for this reason that this book has been written.

II. *Amoris Laetitia* and Exercising Mercy

In Pope Francis' piece *Amoris Laetitia*, he emphasizes the journey that families make together on the path of faith throughout life. He speaks of how families must never lose sight of their mission and not lose heart because of human limitations. This message of hope is dispersed in every chapter of his writing in *Amoris Laetitia*. Mercy[16] is the most common theme in all his writings and especially in this one. Chapters vary in topic starting with "In Light of the Word,"[17] and progressing to the "Experiences and Challenges of the Family."[18] He continues with "Love in Marriage,"[19] "Love Made Fruitful,"[20] and "Some Pastoral Perspectives."[21] He ends with topic titles of "Towards a Better Education,"[22] "Accompanying, Discerning and Integrating

---

[16] Mercy is the most common theme in *Amoris Laetitia* since the encyclical is geared for families who may be experiencing crisis.

[17] *Amoris Laetitia*, p. 13

[18] Ibid., p.27.

[19] Ibid., p. 73.

[20] Ibid., p. 127.

[21] Ibid., p. 153.

[22] Ibid., p. 197.

Chapter Seven: Teachings of Pope Francis

Weakness"[23], and lastly, "The Spirituality of Marriage and the Family"[24]. These sub-chapter summaries offer a synopsis of *Amoris Laetitia* and are included within this book because of their prime importance in the overall presentation of this topic.

In each of the chapters of *Amoris Laetitia*, Pope Francis integrates mercy and how it is made real for families in day-to-day life. He speaks in a conversational tone[25] and with compassion. His goal in each chapter is to integrate mercy into the daily lives of families. He states, "The joy of love experienced by families is also the joy of the Church."[26]

In the Light of the Word

Chapter One, Pope Franics lays the groundwork by citing Psalm 128:1-6 which speaks of the fruitfulness of marriage and of the gift of children to the family:

> Blessed is everyone who fears the Lord, who walks in His ways!
> You shall eat of the fruit of your labor of your hands;
> You shall be happy, and it shall go well with you.
> Your wife will be like a fruitful vine within your house; your children will be like the olive shoots round your table;

---

[23] Ibid., p. 221.

[24] Ibid., p. 245.

[25] The "conversational tone" of *Amoris Laetitia* is common in Pope Francis' writings as his goal is to present in a manner which most people can relate to.

[26] *Amoris Laetitia*, p. 9.

> Thus shall the man be blessed who fear the Lord.
> The Lord bless you from Zion!
> May you see the prosperity of Jerusalem all the days of your life!
> May you see your children's children! Peace be upon Israel!"
> (Psalm 128:1-6)[27]

Pope Franics states that both Christian and Jewish communities use the above passage in wedding ceremonies. It gives a high quality visual of the biblical perspective of the gift of marriage and family. He then chooses to speak first of the gift of "You and Your Wife" which is a section dedicated to integrating sound biblical theology regarding the marriage of husband and wife. He speaks of the solitude of man before Eve was given as a gift to Adam in the Book of Genesis and how the encounter of husband and wife gives life to the meaning of "family":

> This encounter, which relieves man's solitude, gives rise to new birth of the family. Significantly, Adam, who is also the man of every time and place, together with his wife, starts a new family.[28]

By using the verses of Psalm 128, Pope Francis integrates what he feels is most important to communicate to his audience regarding the *Joy of the Gospel*. He reminds his readers that the gift of marriage

---

[27] Ibid., p. 13-14.
[28] Ibid., p. 17.

is not just sexual union; it is a self-giving and sacrificial love[29]. It is a love which when rooted in God, is bound in the Lord's mercy for one another. It is a positive attribute of the encyclical that Pope Francis chose to use Holy Scripture as the basis for *Amoris Laetitia* especially at the beginning of his writing.

Children are the primary gift of marriage, and Pope Francis goes directly to speaking of this fact in the initial chapter. In terms of the "olive shoots" around the table, this is a reference to children as a gift of God to parents. The image of the olive shoot speaks of "the presence of children as a sign of the community of the family"[30]. This community consists of the parents and any children given to them because of their intimate union. This extends not only to living out the life of the domestic church, but also to the life of faith. Pope Francis continues to explain the biblical significance of family life and in raising children to know, love, and serve God[31]. The responsibility of parents is given to them directly from God. Pope Francis writes, "The Gospel goes on to remind his readers that children are not the property of family but have their own lives to lead." The circle of life is not just that of "life." It is also a circle of faith for all the future generations of a family to continue to be the domestic church.

He speaks of "A Path of Suffering and of Blood," "The Work of Your Hands," and "The Tenderness of An Embrace." In all three sections, he refers to both Old and New Testament passages which

---

[29] Ibid., p. 17.

[30] Ibid., p. 18.

[31] Pope Francis repeats the theme of "teaching children to know, love, and serve the Lord" throughout his writing to solidify the importance of passing on the faith.

allude to God's love and mercy, and of the gift of family. He reminds his audience that the "word of God is not a series of abstract ideas, but rather a source of comfort and companionship for every family who experiences difficulties or suffering"[32]. In these visualizations he does an excellent job of laying the framework to delve into how to create joy in daily living, especially for those who are immersed in family life and in raising children in the faith.

The Experiences and Challenges of Family

Families experience a variety of challenges in daily living. There are also many external factors, such as tensions, traumas that occur, and the reality of sin which affects everyone. In this section, Pope Francis speaks of the "Current Reality of the Family"[33]. He is honest in explaining that factors from the outside such as culture expectations and other realities make it more difficult for families to experience the joy and fulfillment of living out the Gospel day-to-day. He speaks of freedom and way to obtain it. He explains that freedom must never be self-centered:

> Freedom of choices makes it possible to plan our lives and to make the most of ourselves. Yet if this freedom lacks noble or personal discipline, it degenerates into an inability to give oneself generously to others.[34]

---

[32] Ibid., p.22.
[33] Ibid., p. 28.
[34] Ibid., p. 29.

Chapter Seven: Teachings of Pope Francis

He discusses the *correct* definition of freedom. Freedom must include truths[35] and values which help to guide the faithful in the proper direction of living a good life. Living in freedom enables God's people to live in the Lord's grace[36] and to exercise free will[37] properly ordered toward the good. The relation of free will ordered to the good is in the submission to do the will of God in living at each moment. If we, the faithful, are not rooted in Christ and are in a state of mortal sin, it is possible to choose an action that is "not good" causing further separation from the Lord's grace.

Those who follow the voice of God in their lives and make a conscious effort to avoid sin can still fall. Confusion occurs when those who are not catechized, do not understand, or reject the good that is before them choose incorrect paths. This lack of certainty can occur with both a good and a perceived good when there are wrong steps or actions taken toward a poor direction of life. This is the nature of sin, and it is what separates us from God. The freedom we seek is found in choosing to do what is right and avoiding evil. Pope Francis speaks of additional elements which contribute to the breakdown of

---

[35] "Truth as an uprightness in human action and speech is called truthfulness, sincerity, and candor. Truth or truthfulness is the virtue which consists in showing oneself true in deeds and truthful in words, and in guarding against duplicity, dissimulation, and hypocrisy." CCC, 2468.

[36] "The grace of Christ is the gratuitous gift that God makes to us of his own life, infused by the Holy Spirit into our soul to heal it of sin and to sanctify it." CCC, 1999.

[37] "Freedom is the power, rooted in reason and will, to act or not to act, to do this, or that, and so to perform deliberate action on one's own responsibilities. By free will one shapes one's life. Human freedom is a force for growth and maturity in truth and goodness, it attains its perfection toward God, our beatitude." CCC, 1731.

society and the family. One of those factors is when unmarried people decide to live together before marriage, and it has become prevalent in the modern world.

Cohabitation is a factor which has affected all of society and the faithful since it disregards the sanctity of marriage and the relevance of the domestic church in our culture. Pope Francis describes "independence" as a goal of many in modern society. The thought process of those who deem independence as a goal of life is a "me-first" attitude, and it does not take into consideration the effects this kind of mentality has on the family unit. When younger people enter first into cohabitation, without realizing they are placing themselves and their own personal goals above their significant other; they are planning, without realizing it, on choosing selfishness as a guiding force.

In addition to cohabitation and its societal affects, external factors such as the lack of affordable housing[38], and money related issues have played a part in the challenges of family life on a global scale. In caring about the needs of families and of their well-being, Pope Francis states that this is the mission of the Church. We all have a responsibility in not only caring about the welfare of families, but also in supporting them through prayer, care, and outreach.

Families, which include those who have special needs, must also be part of this mission of consideration and support. Pope Francis says, "People with disabilities are a gift for the family as an opportunity to grow in love, mutual aid and unity."[39] He makes it a point to remind members of the Church that people with special needs have a need for a great deal of care and affection. They need to know

---

[38] Ibid., p. 37
[39] Ibid., p. 31.

and feel accepted not only on the familial level but within the community and the world at large. The Church, especially, can minister and care for those who have disabilities. In addition to those with physical, psychological, and mental challenges, Pope Francis mentions the needs of the elderly. Most families have older adults represented in their family units as grandparents, aunts, uncles, neighbors, and others. It is all of our responsibility, as members of the Church, to love and make outreach to them. The response we have to the care of those with special needs and of the elderly are excellent opportunities to work for the Church as missionary disciples. We, Christ's followers, do this through loving protection, outreach, and simply by "being there" for others.

One of the greatest challenges for families is when family breakups occur. This is a result of separations and divorces. Families break apart for several reasons including addictions such as alcoholism and/or drug addiction, immaturity, spousal infidelities, financial hardships, communication problems, and more. The Church must continually pray for and support families through outreach, care, prayer, and support. Domestic abuse is also a major issue and a reason for separations and divorce. Pope Francis mentions the precedence of reaching out and helping those affected by this type of abuse within family life:

> I think particularly of the shameful ill-treatment to which women are sometimes subjected, domestic violence, and various forms of enslavement which, rather than show a masculine power, are craven acts of cowardice.[40]

---

[40] Ibid., p. 47.

The statement above from Pope Francis is a stark reminder that the Church has a responsibility to be concerned about these situations, but to do something about it by prayer, action, and outreach. Over centuries, women in particular, have suffered tremendously in marriages where there has been disrespect and abuse. Abuse comes in a variety of forms and, of course, affects both females and males. Pope Francis is attempting to bring greater awareness to these problems so the Church can act through the lives of the faithful in helping families who go through times of trauma and adversity.

Although there are a variety of obstacles facing families in the modern age, Pope Francis reminds the Church that there is much hope because of the presence of Christ in our lives. The reality of healing will occur on a larger scale when the faithful take ownership of the issues at hand and attempt to make a difference by offering both healing and the mercy of God. Through reaching out in tangible ways, mercy can and will be materialized both now and in the future in moving forward together. Affability combined with mercy brings healing to families who face the difficult circumstances of life.

Looking to Jesus: The Vocation of the Family

Pope Francis spells out that the answer to all the problems within marriage and family come from Christ himself through the teaching of the Church and of the sacraments. Most of all, families are given a mission of love and of tenderness. Pope Francis discusses the fact that tenderness is necessary in the daily lives of all of us, but in a particular way in the vocation of marriage and family life. As he discussed in previous sections of *Amoris Laetitia*, there will always be challenges in family life, and love and tenderness are gifts of the spirit enabling members of the family to get through crises and hardships together as a family unit.

Jesus is the one who can restore the family to the fullness which is deemed by God himself. Pope Francis reminds his readers in *Amoris Laetitia* that the Lord can transform each of us by way of the cross[41]. Not only does he do this for the individual person, but the transformative power of the cross is for families. When couples and families turn to their faith in full trust of God, the Lord can work miracles in the hearts of those who have been wounded by sin. He states:

> God's indulgent love always accompanies our human journey, through grace, it heals, and transforms hardened hearts, leading them back to the beginning through the way of the cross. The Gospels clearly presents the example of Jesus who…proclaimed the meaning of marriage as the fullness of revelation that restores God's original plan.[42]

God's original plan can restore the hurt and brokenness of life and help to bring full restoration in his time to families who go through trials. Pope Francis also presents the Holy Family, which consists of Jesus, Mary, and Joseph as an example to follow in terms

---

[41] Pope Francis refers to the "way of the cross" as the method and way in which individuals and families will find healing. This also refers to the Paschal Mystery, which is the life, death, resurrection, and ascension of Christ.

[42] Ibid., p. 53.

of family life. The covenant of love shared within the family unit of the Holy Family demonstrates to the world the power of love and fidelity, and that of covenantal and sacrificial love, as well. This kind of love is what perseveres during times of trauma and difficulty.

Pope Francis speaks of the covenantal love of marriage, and the beauty of the sacrament. He clarifies the fact that marriage is much more than a contract between two people or a social convention. It is sacramental sign of Christ and the Church:

> The sacrament of marriage is not a social convention, an empty ritual or merely an outward sign of a commitment. The sacrament is a gift given for the sanctification and salvation of spouses, since their mutual belonging is a real representation, through the sacramental sign, of the same relationship between Christ and the Church.[43]

The sacrament is a mutual self-giving lived out daily by the spouses. He states that married couples are the "heart of the entire family"[44] of faith, and an example to their children and to the world. Christian marriage is a covenantal relationship which offers strength to the couple to continue the journey in trust of God and of his plan. Their physical relationship, when rooted in the mystery of the cross and of the sacraments, is filled with grace affecting all aspects of their lives including the spiritual, emotional, and mental. God is at work in every part of the lives of couples who are rooted in Jesus and in following him daily.

---

[43] Ibid., p. 59.
[44] Ibid., p. 60.

There are also irregular situations in marriage and challenges associated with raising families that Pope Francis alludes to. Blended families, divorced/annulled and remarried couples, single-parent families are just a few of the irregular situations. Pope Francis reminds the faithful that as a Church we should prayerfully support[45] families with irregular situations and have compassion. There is an array of factors which cause challenges and difficulties in raising children. He mentions not only the role of the church but that of the educational system and the community. He states the significance of the awareness of all facets of community life and how the Church can work together with those who work closely with families in helping to bring restoration and healing when problems arise. He reminds all of us that forgiveness plays a major role in healing within families, and in the recognition of the beauty of each member of the family. When couples and children respect and care for each other within the family unit, the Lord is present through the sacramental graces of marriage.

Love in Marriage

Pope Francis takes a considerable amount of time in *Amoris Laetitia* explaining the nature of love. He bases his discussion on verses from I Corinthians 13. The verses below are often read at weddings as a reflection on what love is and what it is not:

---

[45] Pope Francis alludes to the relevance of prayerfully supporting families throughout *Amoris Laetitia*.

Love is patient; love is kind; love is not envious our boastful or arrogant or rude. It does not insist on its own way; it is not irritable or resentful; it does not rejoice in wrongdoing, but rejoices in the truth. It bears all things, hopes all things, endures all things. Love never ends. But as for prophesies, they will come to an end; as for tongues, they will come to an end. But we know only in part, and we prophesy only in part, but when the completion comes, the partial will come to an end. When I was a child, I spoke like a child, I thought like a child, I reasoned like a child; when I became an adult, I put an end to childish ways. For now, we see in a mirror, dimly, but when we see face to face. Now I know only in part; then I will know fully, even as I have been fully known. And now faith, hope, and love abide; these three; and the greatest of these is love.[46]

Pope Francis speaks of the patience of love. He says, "We encounter problems whenever we think that relationships or people should be perfect, or when we put ourselves at the center and expect things to turn out our way." [47] This is sound advice for families since problems arise when the expectations of others are not met. Even within "devout" families, there will be this sense of impatience that happens in daily living. He continues in the chapter to speak of love being at the service of others and not jealous. In terms of being at the service of other people, he emphasizes that patience is not a passive virtue, it must be alive and active, and this is where service comes into play. Love is also not jealous, and Pope Francis reminds us, Christ's

---

[46] I Corinthians 13:4-13, NOAB.
[47] *Amoris Laetitia*, p. 75.

followers, that love "values the other person's achievements"[48]. When a spouse or family member succeeds, the Christian response is in not seeing the other person as a threat. Love is not boastful speaks of not being "puffed up" or proud. Pope Francis explains that sadly even those who claim to be religious or devoted to their Catholic faith may become boastful. He states, "Such people think that, because they are more 'spiritual' or 'wise,' they are more important than they really are." He explains that power destroys love within family life, and the answers comes to us through following the humble example of Jesus.

The section in the book on love is quite interesting because it has a direct correlation with the topic of this book. This is the section called "Love is not rude." He states:

> To be open to a genuine encounter with others, 'a kind look' is essential. This is incompatible with a negative attitude that readily points out other people's shortcomings while overlooking one's own. A kind look helps us to see beyond our own limitations, to be patient and to cooperate with others, despite our differences. Loving kindness builds bonds, cultivates relationships, creates new networks of integration and knits a firm social fabric.[49]

The above passage is a beautiful way of describing affability or openness. Friendliness is, therefore, an integral part of love. Openness shown through body language, through the ability to actively listen, and in giving a simple smile to others offers kindness and love.

---

[48] Ibid., p. 77.
[49] Ibid., p. 80-81.

Pope Francis also states that, "Antisocial persons think that others exist only for the satisfaction of their own needs."[50] He speaks of the words of Jesus:

> These were the words that Jesus spoke: 'Take heart my son!' (Mt 9:2); 'Great is your faith!" (Mt 15:28); 'Arise!' (Mk 5:41); "Go in peace" (Lk 7:50); 'Be not afraid" (Mt: 14:27). These are not words that demean, sadden, anger, or show scorn. In our families, we must learn to imitate Jesus' own gentleness in our way of speaking to one another.[51]

There is a far-reaching connection in the section on love in *Amoris Laetitia* to the deep relationship of affability both within family life and in living out the Christian vocations. Pope Francis emphasis on love not being rude and his description of it clearly demonstrates a tie to affability.

Pope Francis continues that love is generous, love is not irritable, or resentful, and love forgives. He states, "Saint Thomas Aquinas explains that it is more proper to charity to desire to love than to desire to be loved"[52]. He discusses the ties between loving and that of justice since love transcends and overflows the demands of justice. In other words, loving another person deeply[53] and sacrificially is a way to exhibit justice and care. In terms of irritability and resentfulness,

---

[50] Ibid., p. 81.
[51] Ibid., p. 81.
[52] Ibid., p. 82.
[53] Loving another person deeply refers to offering sacrificial love and active listening.

Chapter Seven: Teachings of Pope Francis

Pope Francis states, "Our first reaction when we are annoyed should be one of heartfelt blessing, asking God to bless, free and heal the other person"[54]. This is sound advice for both family matters and issues that occur outside of home life. Forgiveness is a major piece of offering love in family life. Forgiveness is the engine that enables couples and families to continue the journey when challenges occur in terms of relationship issues. Pope Francis states:

> Today we recognize that being able to forgive others implies the liberating experience of understanding and forgiving ourselves. Often our mistakes, or criticism we have received from loved ones, can lead to a loss of self-esteem. We become distant from others, avoiding affection and fearful in our interpersonal relationships.[55]

This idea of the liberation in forgiveness is integral in marriage and family life. It is important to note that Pope Francis also states that without forgiveness that "family life will no longer be a place of understanding"[56] and that families need to place forgiveness at the center of interactions to be able to move on in full trust of God and of the future.

Pope Francis expands on love rejoicing with others, love in bearing all things, love in believing all things, love in hoping all things, and lastly love in enduring all things. All these subtitles are

---

[54] Ibid., p. 83-84.
[55] Ibid., p. 85.
[56] Ibid., p. 86.

references of the verses from I Corinthians 13[57] notes earlier in this chapter. Pope Franics makes an invitation to his readers to rise to the occasion of real love and service to one another. He uses Holy Scripture and practical guidance to demonstrate the duty of love is difficult but worth all the sacrifice. Love is transformation in every sense. He describes how true love is accomplished through understanding and authentic charity. He explains that various aspects of love including marriage, and those who are called to the celibate life or virginity are how love is manifested to the world.

Love Made Fruitful

When Pope Francis speaks of a love made fruitful. He discusses the lifespan, and he begins the discussion by talking about new life, which begins with the love of a mother and father toward their child. He states:

> Children, once born, begin to receive, along with nourishment and care, the spiritual gift of knowing with certainty that they are loved. This love is shown to them through the gift of their personal name, the sharing of language, looks of love and the brightness of a smile.[58]

Again, this suggests how friendliness and openness play a part even in the preliminary stages of life. It makes an overwhelming difference when love is expressed. Pope Francis expands his thoughts

---

[57] I Corinthians 13, NOAB.
[58] *Amoris Laetitia*, p. 132.

when he mentions adoption and foster care along with other ways families serve together. He also discusses extended families and their roles in the domestic church. The wider family includes not only the extended family, but our communities and our world:

> The individualism so prevalent today can lead to creating small nests of security, where others are perceived as bothersome or a threat. Such isolation, however, cannot offer greater peace or happiness; rather, it straitens the heart of a family and makes its life all the more narrow.[59]

Individualism is the opposite of what Pope Francis speaks as he focuses on sibling relationships and of the elderly. He concludes this segment on the topic of having a "big heart" for others. The tie to affability is the openness of spirit to all members of the family. The community of love in a family which includes the extended family remembers all members including those with disabilities, the elderly, and the infirmed. He refers to the larger family unit as the wider family:

> The wider family can help make up for the shortcomings of parents, detent and report possible situations in which children suffer violence and even abuse and provide wholeness love and family stability in cases when parents prove incapable of this.[60]

---

[59] Ibid., p. 145.
[60] Ibid., p. 151-152.

Pope Francis continues to express that every member of the family has value. As Catholics, we understand this includes the entire domestic church. Love is at the core of the Church, and the domestic church is the family unit.

Some Pastoral Perspectives

In pastoral perspectives, Pope Francis discusses proclaiming the Gospel and preparing engaged couples for marriage. He continues with thoughts on marriage preparation and accompanying couples during the first years of married life. It is key to note that he brings up casting light on crisis, worries and difficulties in marriage and family. He mentions the fact that crises happen in most family units. He states:

> Crises need to be faced together. This is hard, since persons sometimes withdraw in order to avoid saying what they feel; they retreat into a craven silence. At these times, it becomes all the more important to create opportunities for speaking heart to heart. Unless a couple learns to do this, they will find it harder and harder as time passes.[61]

It is inevitable that challenges will occur in family life in some form over the years. The response is critical in the survival of the marriage and of the family unit. When Pope Francis speaks of creating opportunities for dialogue, this is necessary for the family to be able to move forward together in faith. Withdrawing and avoiding

---

[61] Ibid., p. 179.

discussions creates extra unneeded space when dialogue[62] and love is the answer. There are also old wounds, and situations related to divorce which may come up in conversations that need attention and care. Pope Francis discusses the complexities which occur related to divorce, separation, and annulments. He dialogues on the sting of death in relationships. Death is something we will all face, and Pope Francis offers words of wisdom on this acceptance. He says that when we accept death, we are also preparing ourselves for it. All the above situations need prayer and deep care to accompany those who are affected.

Towards a Better Education for Children

Pope Francis asks questions such as: where are children? He is referring to the fact that parents and the community have the responsibility of caring for our children and doing our part to protect and guide them. There is the ethical formation of children and a value in correction as an incentive. He instructs that children need our guidance, care, and most of all our love. As Catholics, the moral education of children is imperative. He also speaks of ethical formation:

> Ethical formation is at times frowned upon, due to experiences of neglect, disappointment, lack of affection or poor models of parenting. Ethical values are associated with

---

[62] Throughout his writing, Pope Francis discusses the fact that for every situation of life, dialogue opens the doors to hope and healing.

negative images of parental figures or the shortcomings of adults.[63]

He mentions the aspects of ethical formation since this area has a monumental influence on the development of children. With a variety of crises and aspects that affect family life including behavior issues and poor decisions, ethical formation has immense value in family life. Additionally, Pope Francis discusses the educational settings of children, sex education, and passing on the faith. All these areas are not only relevant but have a major impact on the lives of children. Parents and families have the responsibility of guiding children in the proper direction to lead good moral and ethical lives in the future.

Accompanying, Discerning, and Integrating Weakness

Pope Francis discusses gradualness in pastoral care and irregular situations. It is important to mention both areas since gentleness and accompaniment are necessary for both. Openness of spirit or affability are integral virtues to exhibit since these circumstances are delicate, and adequate pastoral care is needed. In terms complicated situations related to divorce or separation or to blended families Pope Francis states:

A sincere reflection can strengthen trust in the mercy of God which is not denied anyone. What we are speaking of is a

---

[63] Ibid., p. 205.

Chapter Seven: Teachings of Pope Francis

process of accompaniment and discernment which guides the faithful to an awareness of their situation before God.[64]

In dealing with delicate situations of marriage and family, the mercy of God is the best antidote. There is a certain discernment and reflection needed to be guided by the Holy Spirit in full trust of God in all circumstances including ones which are difficult to deal with. Those situations include single parent families, step-parenting, and all conditions related to divorce and separation. Pope Francis goes into detail on the pastoral logic of mercy which is an approach that places charity at the forefront of all interactions with those in need of pastoral care.

The Spirituality of Marriage and Family

Pope Francis highlights the momentousness of spirituality in marriage and family. He says relationship with God and prayer is an invitation to all to develop a deep spirituality. This development is a supernatural communion of persons both within the family and ultimately with Jesus and with the entire universal church. We gather in prayer in the light of Easter, since we are people of resurrection. We center on Christ and on his love for us. This is expressed through family prayer[65] and by the love we show every member of our family. This love is shown not only within the confines of a home. It extends out to the community and to the world. Prayer is at the center of it

---

[64] Ibid., p. 231.
[65] Pope Francis emphasizes the primacy and importance of family prayer in daily life.

all. Pope Francis states, "All family life is a 'shepherding' in mercy. Each of us by our love and care, leaves a mark on the life of others"[66]. We are led by the spirit and gathered in a circle of love. This circle of love leads us in the footsteps of Christ to fulfill our mission both personally and as a family. This same concept can be imitated globally as a Church as we strive to care for all members of the human family. In relation to the topic on the relevance of affability in our culture, one vehicle to demonstrate this love is through friendliness and openness to all. The virtue of affability aids in enhancing the evangelization of the current culture of the Church.

Pope Francis reminds each of Christ's followers to intercede to the Holy Family: Jesus, Mary, and Joseph. They are the perfect role models for family life in terms of virtue and charity. He ends *Amoris Laetitia* with a prayer to the Holy Family:

> Jesus, Mary, and Joseph, in you we contemplate the splendor of true love; to you we turn with trust Holy Family of Nazareth, grant that our families too may be places of communion and prayer; authentic schools of the Gospel and small domestic churches. Holy Family of Nazareth may families never again experience violence, rejection, and division; may all who have been hurt and scandalized find ready comfort and healing. Holy Family of Nazareth, make us once more mindful of the sacredness and inviolability of the family, and its beauty in God's plan. Jesus, Mary, and Joseph, graciously hear our prayer. Amen.[67]

---

[66] Ibid., p. 252.
[67] Ibid., p. 255-256.

This prayer is a call on God for his blessing of families and of people. It is done in a gracious manner. The prayer calls for healing of all who have been hurt and scandalized and asks for God's comfort for them. By exercising the virtue of friendliness and affability, we, as a Church, can spread God's love in a far-reaching manner. The prayer to the Holy Family of Nazareth is a perfect model and guide for holiness and openness to God's plans for the domestic church, the family.

III. Mercy and Sensitivity

In whole, *Amoris Laetitia* speaks greatly on mercy, sensitivity, and affability. The responsiveness Pope Francis speaks of starts within the family and branches out to extended family, and to community. As a Church, we must begin to care more and show deep concern for the welfare of others. This is done through active listening, attentiveness, and through prayer to the Lord for guidance and direction in ways to make an impact for those who suffer and those who lack support.

The mercy exhibited does not come from us, it comes to us from the Lord. Prayer is at the heart of this request of God to help us to show greater compassion for those within the domestic church. It is not an easy task, but it can be done through and with Jesus. Pope Francis states:

> May we humble ourselves in such a way that it becomes easy for our God and our brothers and sisters to communicate with one another through us. May our Heavenly Father feel,

as he feels about the beloved Son, that through us, he can reach the least of his children with his blessing and his word. May people feel, as they feel about Jesus and the Virgin, that through us they can offer to the Lord their daily sacrifices, those that weave together their work and family life, and tell God that they love him, that they need him, and that they worship and praise him from the heart. I ask that we take care of our priesthood by this offering.[68]

The message above was directed to priests and religious, but this communication from Pope Francis is relevant for all people. Each person has a part in exhibiting the mercy of God within families and to the world. Pope Francis speaks of how through love given and shared aids in directing those who need to know God's love in a tangible way. This is how the mercy of God is transmitted to others.

In the same way, affability is an avenue in showing mercy in something as simple as a smile or in the way we, as Christ's followers, forgive others for their mistakes and sins. In *Amoris Laetitia*, Pope Francis makes it a point to discuss the varied areas of sensitivity in family life such as those who have been traumatized or marginalized in some form. These difficult situations are opportunities for the faithful to exhibit extra charity in letting family members and close community know they are supported. Lending a listening ear and concern is the way this is accomplished.

---

[68] Pope Francis, *I Ask You, Be Shepherds. Reflections on Pastoral Ministry*. Crossroads Publishing. 2015, p. 90-91.

IV. The Practicality of Mercy

Pope Francis has spoken often and in plain language over the years about mercy and how to live it out. In some of his main writings of *Amoris Laetitia, Fratelli Tutti,* and *Laudato Si,* he weaves mercy throughout his communications. He seems to indicate repeatedly that it begins with the relationships we, the faithful, have within our homes and with those closest that we can exercise the mercy of God. This mercy is given as a gift from the Lord through the Paschal Mystery[69] and through the continual gift of the Holy Spirit. Christ's life, death, resurrection, and ascension is this mystery. Jesus' sacrifice is an everlasting gift which has eternal benefits. Mercy is always at the core of Jesus love for humanity. The practicality of mercy are those daily opportunities and grace-filled moments where we call upon the Lord for guidance in dealing with the complexities of life.

The practicality of mercy is inclusive and not exclusive. This refers to the fact that the love and mercy extended includes those who feel left out, judged, not cared for, or made to feel different and set aside from the rest of a group. As Catholics, we must remember to be people of inclusion and of love of *all people.* Pope Francis writes:

> Differences between persons and communities can sometimes prove uncomfortable, but the Holy Spirit, who is the source of that diversity can bring forth something good from all things and turn it into an attractive means of evangelization. Diversity must always be reconciled by the help of the Holy Spirit; he alone can raise up diversity, plurality, and

---

[69] *CCC,* 1085.

multiplicity while at the same time being about unity. When we, for our part, aspire to diversity, we become self-enclosed, exclusive, and divisive; similarly, whenever we attempt to create unity on the basis of our calculations, we end up imposing monolithic uniformity. This is not helpful for the Church's mission.[70]

Diversity is a gift from God to the world. Pope Francis reminds members of the Church that when we call on the Holy Spirit for guidance to be able to seek unity, the Lord will assist. We must put aside any pre-judgements of other cultures aside. Inclusivity means that we recognize the beauty of diversity, and we seek to be unified with *all* of our brothers and sisters. This is an integral piece of the practicality of mercy both within family life and beyond.

There is also a "logic to pastoral mercy" which Pope Francis discusses in *Amoris Laetitia*. This logic refers to the simple ways we, as individuals, can make a difference in others' lives for the better. Younger people need to know they are cared for, loved, and watched over. In this chapter, he discusses all aspects of family including children and younger people. He weaves into the discussion the Gospel, the heart of God, and God's will for his people. He states:

> We cannot forget that 'mercy is not only for working of the Father; it becomes a criterion for knowing who his children are. In a word, we are called to show mercy because mercy was first shown to us.' This is not sheer romanticism or a

---

[70] *Evangelii Gaudium*, p. 66.

lukewarm response to God's love, which always seeks what is best for us, for 'mercy is the very foundation of the Church's life. All of her pastoral activity should be caught up in the tenderness which she shows to believers; nothing in her preaching and her witness to the world can be lacking in mercy.[71]

This is excellent advice for the faithful as it demonstrates the love of the Father. We can be vessels of his mercy in opening our hearts to his will. Pope Francis invites all the faithful to partake in the mission of mercy and of tenderness. Tenderness[72] is an extremely integral aspect of the logic of mercy as it is the vehicle to better communication and interactions with those who feel rejected. Exercising this virtue is key in bearing witness to Christ's love for all of humanity.

The practicality of mercy is a foundation of love. Pope Francis reminds the faithful to be flexible with others in hearing their stories and in order to help them to process the hurts of life. We must help them to find the right kind of help such as counseling or other avenues of healing which are available. People who refer to themselves as "devout" or "believers" must especially put their faith into action to work in mission. He states, "At times we find it hard to make room for God's unconditional love in our pastoral activity. We put so many conditions on mercy that we empty it of its meaning and real

---

[71] *Amoris Laetitia*, p. 241.

[72] "Tenderness" is another word for gentleness combined with kindness.

significance"[73]. This is a call to all people including serious-minded Catholics to put faith into tangible action. Saying daily prayers, Mass attendance, and avoiding sin are only the basics. Getting one's "hands dirty"[74] and making a substantial difference for those who have been traumatized and who suffer are ways to partake in the practicality of mercy, as suggested by Pope Francis.

This "practicality" reminds the faithful that there will always be sensitive situations both in family life and as presented to the Church. The answer to all the challenging issues related to the handling of delicate family intricacies and discernments falls to the guidance and teachings of the Church. This must be done with great care and through accompaniment and good pastoral leadership. Each situation is different and unique. Mercy and love point to listening, and then to respond carefully with love. Pope Francis calls on pastors:

> I also encourage pastors to listen to them with sensitivity and serenity, with a sincere desire to understand their plight and their point of view, in order to help them live better lives and to recognize their proper place in the Church.[75]

Pastors and clergy are to be the face of Christ to those who need to know that the Church cares and is there to help. The role of clergy is in administering the sacraments with love, and to act as a "father" to those people and families who need pastoral guidance. Pope

---

[73] Ibid., p. 242.

[74] Getting ones "hands dirty" refers to taking seriously the mission of mercy and practicing the Corporal and Spiritual Works of Mercy.

[75] Ibid., p. 243.

Francis reminds them to listen with sensitivity and serenity. Mercy can be exercised with practicality, according to his writings. Charity is at the center of all dialogue and communications with families and those who need pastoral assistance. The central values of the Gospel must be prevalent in all interactions. Conditions must not be present in this dialogue so that the Holy Spirit may work through the faithful and by clergy. A culture of encounter[76] and of love is at the center. This love is not shared and given out of obligation. It is given in all sincerity. It is exercised through the gift of affability and openness.

---

[76] A "culture of encounter" is one that calls the domestic church to the mission of mercy in every aspect of life.

Chapter Eight

On-going Conversion

I. Prayer: The Key to Conversion

The Catechism of the Catholic Church has a great deal to say on prayer, its roots, and why we are to pray. Prayer is also the key to our conversion since it is where relationship with God becomes real, tangible, and alive within our spirits.

> Christian prayer is a covenant relationship between God and man in Christ. It is the action of God and of man, springing forth from both the Holy Spirit and ourselves, wholly directed to the Father, in union with the human will and the Son of God made man.[1]

Christian prayer, when it is infused with the Holy Spirit enables those who are devoted to Christ and his Church to live out the Gospel and to make love known and experiential to all the world. Again, it is a "covenant relationship" which depends on opening ourselves to the work of the spirit in daily living. On the topics of justice and affability, it is only through a deep prayer life that one may be able to offer the gift of friendliness especially toward those who need it most.

---

[1] CCC, 2565.

Types of Prayer to Grow in Virtue

In the Christian life, there are various ways to pray, and there is no "right way"[2] to pray in terms of growing in virtue. The most important aspect of prayer is that *we do it*. The Catechism also discusses the fact that prayer is communion. It is not only communion with the Lord but with all we encounter on the journey of life.

> In the New Covenant, prayer is the living relationship of the children of God with their Father who is good beyond measure, with his Son Jesus Christ and with the Holy Spirit. The grace of the Kingdom is "the union of the entire holy and royal Trinity . . . with the whole human spirit. Thus, the life of prayer is the habit of being in the presence of the thrice-holy God and is communion with him. This communion of life is always possible because, through Baptism, we have already been united with Christ. Prayer is Christian insofar as it is communion with Christ and extends throughout the Church, which is his Body. Its dimensions are those of Christ's love.[3]

In going to the Catechism for clarification and understanding, it is because in the modern time period, it is the *primary sources* Catholics refer to. In order for the faithful to bring greater depth and

---

[2] The term no "right way" to pray refers to the fact that there are various methods of prayer. What is most important is that prayer is developed and nurtured through relationship with God and with the Church.

[3] Ibid., 2565.

Chapter Eight: On-going Conversion

understanding to those who are not involved in the theological or academic world, it is vital to look to sources which most people will seek guidance for meaning and understanding. The Catechism states that prayer is found in the presence of the Holy Trinity[4], which is where this communion will take place. Since communion takes place in prayer, this is where all virtue is derived and where Christ's love can be found. The Father is "good beyond measure"[5], and in prayer those who seek to know God will find him. There are various ways to pray in order to live in communion with Christ and in living out God's will.

Whether one chooses to pray traditional prayers of the Church such as the Our Father[6], Hail Mary[7], or other various prayers, prayer leads to relationship with God. Some may choose to pray the Holy Rosary,[8] visit a Eucharistic Adoration Chapel,[9] or pray litanies[10] and

---

[4] The Holy Trinity is the Father, Son, and Holy Spirit. It is the central Christian doctrine concerning the nature of God.

[5] CCC, 2565.

[6] The Our Father prayer is also known as the Lord's Prayer. It is the central Christian way to pray as Jesus Has taught us.

[7] The Hail Mary prayer incorporates the greeting of Mary in the Gospel of Luke (Luke 1: 26-28). It is the main prayer of the Holy Rosary.

[8] The word "Rosary" means a chain of roses. The prayer consists primarily of the Our Father prayer and the Hail Mary prayed in succession along with the Glory Be and additional prayers. There are a total of Sorrowful, the Glorious, and the Luminous. It is widely believed that St. Dominic was given the Rosary by the Blessed Mother in the year 1214.

[9] A Eucharist Adoration Chapel is a space or small building usually located on the premise of a parish, dedicated to adoring Jesus Christ in the Holy Eucharist.

[10] Litanies are a form of prayer containing a series of petitions and fixed responses. Some examples of Litanies are the Litany of the Sacred Heart,

novenas. Others may prefer contemplative[11] or meditative prayer,[12] of charismatic prayer.[13] All of these ways of seeking to "be with the Lord" are beautiful and appropriate in growing in faith, hope, and love. Since the goal of prayer is communion with God, any method of prayer is beneficial to the soul. *Time in prayer* is what helps one to love God more, to serve him, and to be better stewards. The greatest prayer of all is the Holy Sacrifice of the Mass,[14] and our union with Christ in Mass is the most perfect form of prayer. Attending Sunday Mass is an obligation and one of the Precepts of the Church,[15] and it is a celebration of the most excellent way of prayer and the opportunity to receive the body, blood, soul, and divinity of the Eucharist.[16]

---

the Litany of the Precious Blood, and Litany of the Blessed Virgin Mary, and more.

[11] Contemplative prayer is a form of Catholic prayer where the use of the imagination is prevalent. It is a time of "being one with the Lord" in prayer.

[12] Meditative prayer uses silence and stillness while meditating on a scripture passage, a spiritual reading, or another aspect within Catholic spirituality.

[13] Catholic Charismatic prayer is a method of prayer to the Holy Spirit sometimes done outwardly within a prayer meeting with other like-minded individuals. Some elements of a charismatic prayer meeting are praise and worship, testimonials, and discernment of spiritual gifts.

[14] The Holy Sacrifice of the Mass is one single sacrifice of the Paschal Mystery of Jesus Christ. It is the sacrifice of the Eucharist and the sacrifice of Christ where the priest offers the sacrifice once and for all.

[15] The Precepts of the Church are attending Mass on Sundays and days of obligation; to confess your sins at least once a year; to receive the Eucharist at least once a year; to observe days of fasting and abstinence; and to provide for the needs of the Church.

[16] The Eucharist is the Blessed Sacrament also known as Holy Communion. It is the true body and blood of Jesus Christ.

Attending daily Mass[17], although not obligatory, is another avenue to grow closer to the Lord in prayer each day. As we, the faithful, pray, we can ask the Lord to help us to grow in virtue. On the subject of this book, we can ask him to enable us to develop affability in our lives of faith as a justice given to others.

Prayer and Affability

Prayer, which helps one grow in deeper union with the Lord, also impels the faithful to make outreach to those in need. Affability is not necessarily a "personality trait," but through prayer and in exercising virtue, one can attain the ability to become more open to the needs of others. Through prayer, members of the Church can learn more fully the relevance of community and of living together not only in God's presence but also in union with the domestic church.

> In the Gospel, Jesus is clear, 'Ask, and it will be given you; search and you will find, knock, and the door will be opened to you.' And so we understand that example of the man knocking on his neighbor's door at midnight for three loaves of bread, unconcerned that he may be perceived as rude; his only interest is to get food for his guests. And although her timing is bad, we see the Canaanite woman (Matthew 15:21-28), who risks being sent away by the disciples (v. 23) and

---

[17] Daily Mass a daily opportunity to receive the Eucharist and to celebrate the Paschal Mystery of Jesus Christ in communion with the Church. Daily Mass is oftentimes shorter than Sunday Mass and, in many circumstances, does not have music.

being called a "dog" (v. 27), what is required to get what she wants; the healing of her daughter. That woman really knows how to fight courageously in prayer.[18]

In the above reflection, Pope Francis speaks of prayer as something "courageous" when the Canaanite woman refuses to give up praying for her daughter. This is the type of prayer which trusts God and perseveres despite all circumstances. He describes Jesus words in the Gospel as being "clear" that what we ask of the Lord, the door will be opened. This kind of trust in God's providence is what is necessary to be able to grow in deeper commitment to the spreading of the Gospel. The same is true with praying for justice for a world that is in dire need of it. Additionally, Francis writes:

> The Lord's promise of trust and perseverance goes far beyond what we can imagine: in addition to what we ask for, he will give us the Holy Spirit. When Jesus exhorts us to pray insistently, he throws us into the very bosom of the Trinity, and through his sacred humanity, he brings us to the Father, and he promises the Holy Spirit.[19]

Through the Holy Spirit, we, Christ's followers, are immersed together with the Holy Trinity. We are able to begin to know the heart of God. We can be led to deeper conversion in the daily walk with Jesus. In order to live the virtues to the fullest extent, deeper

---

[18] Pope Francis, *I Ask You, Be Shepherds. Reflections on Pastoral Ministry.* Crossroads Publishing. 2015, p. 20-21.

[19] Ibid., pg. 21.

conversion of faith is *necessary*. It will help one to do the will of God in all matters of life. The Lord works in the hearts of those who trust him.

Conversion to Become More Affable

Becoming more affable is something that not only takes awareness, but it takes prayer and perseverance. A certain conversion of heart is necessary in order to be able to live the virtues and to recognize that affability is something to strive after. The Catechism states:

> The human heart is heavy and hardened, God must give man a new heart. Conversion is first of all a work of the grace of God who makes our hearts return to him, 'Restore us to thyself, O LORD, that we may be restored!' God gives us the strength to begin anew. It is in discovering the greatness of God's love that our heart is shaken by the horror and weight of sin and begins to fear offending God by sin and being separated from him. The human heart is converted by looking upon him whom our sins have pierced.[20]

In prayer, penance, and in offering oneself daily to God and to the needs of others, conversion begins to take place. It is in prayer and discernment that moment by moment, followers of Christ can become more virtuous and live in the love of the Lord. In doing so, the faithful begin to experience deeper conversion through prayer in

---

[20] CCC,1432.

using the gifts bestowed by God to be more open and friendly in all the encounters of life.

II. Our Baptismal Call to Holiness

The first sacrament, Baptism, brings us into the Church, the family of God, where we, his followers, are cleansed of original sin, and made new by the power of the Holy Spirit. It is the gateway to the Christian life of the Church as everything stems from Baptism:

> Holy Baptism is the basis of the whole Christian life, the gateway of life in the Spirit, and the door which gives access to the other sacraments. Through Baptism, we are freed from sin and reborn as sons of God; we become members of Christ, are incorporated into the Church and made sharers in her mission: Baptism is the sacrament of regeneration through water and the word.[21]

This regeneration of life propels us, as Christians, to conversion and to mission. Baptism is just the beginning of this journey, with holiness as the goal in the life of grace. In the sacraments of Confession, the Holy Eucharist, and Confirmation, the journey of love and mission continues.

The baptized become body of believers or "living stones" of the Church in its outreach; for Baptism enables one to live fully in Christ, freed from sin, in order to partake in the mystery of salvation given by Christ:

---

[21] CCC, 1213.

Chapter Eight: On-going Conversion

The baptized have become 'living stones' to be 'built into a spiritual house, to be a holy priesthood.' By Baptism they share in the priesthood of Christ, in his prophetic and royal mission. They are a 'chosen race, a royal priesthood, a holy nation, God's own people, that (they) may declare the wonderful deeds of him who called (them) out of into his marvelous light.' Baptism gives a share in the common priesthood of all believers.[22]

Living out this mission of a "holy priesthood" does not mean that only clergy or consecrated religious are called. On the contrary, it refers to the fact that as baptized members of the Church we are all part of this "priesthood" and as priest, prophet, and king, we share in ministry of the universal Church. Each member is part of a family, which is a "little church" (domestic church) and is integral to the worldwide Church.

Pope Francis has called the entire Church, namely the baptized body of believers, to become active in the mission of bringing God's love to every people. This is no easy task as no one is excluded from partaking. Joy is found is following Christ and in taking the baptismal call seriously. Saying "yes" to God is both a gift and a momentous calling of life. It is an integral step in the process of ongoing conversion. This is a joy because service to God and others brings true and eternal happiness to the soul. Sin is "an utterance, a deed, or a desire contrary to the eternal law"[23]. Sin affects each person in differing ways. The Catholic Church offers the antidote to sin which are the

---

[22] CCC, 1268.
[23] Ibid., 1871.

sacraments. Being baptized in Christ, Pope Francis states we are then called to become disciples through evangelization:

> Evangelization takes place in obedience to the missionary mandate of Jesus: 'Go therefore and make disciples of all nations, baptizing them in the name of the Father and of the Son and of the Holy Spirit, teaching them to observe all that I have commanded you' (Mt. 28:19-20). In these verses we see how the risen Christ sent his followers to preach the Gospel in every time and place, so that faith in him might spread to every corner of the earth.[24]

This is the core of missionary discipleship which calls the faithful to partake in this effort to bring God's love to the world in an intense way. In receiving these sacramental graces of the Church through Baptism and the other sacraments, the road to conversion is marked ahead in the embarkment of living the Gospel through the Corporal and Spiritual Works of Mercy. This calling is a gift to God and to the world. Incorporating merciful acts in daily living marks the path of healing and the awakening of the spirit of God within us.

Corporal and Spiritual Works of Mercy: A Path of Conversion

The Corporal and Spiritual works of mercy offer a path of transformation in becoming more closely identified with Christ in the daily walk. The Corporal Works of Mercy are those tangible actions, such as: feeding the hungry, giving drink to the thirsty, sheltering the

---

[24] *Evangelii Gaudium*, p 11.

homeless, and more[25]. These actions of love help to bring tactile goods to help sustain the poor and those in need. In doing so, the mercy of God is given in an authentic way to someone who is lacking basic needs. The path of conversion becomes more visible and tangible in seeing the faces and hearing the stories of people who have suffered and are alleviated in some fashion through the generosity of a giver. Friendships are developed because this kindness can establish bonds of trust which are priceless and lasting. An example is a baptized Catholic who has made a conscious decision to leave the Catholic Church, but after contemplation and the guidance of the Holy Spirit, decides to return. We, as followers of Christ, can patiently lead others "home" to the Church. Bridges are built to enable a person who may have had trust issues in the past. Charity and trust help to demonstrate God's love in a heartfelt way making an impact on both the giver and the receiver. This is an on-going conversion at work since spiritual transformation is not usually a one-time decision or simplified prayer to the Lord in a time of need. It is in having a daily and close relationship with Jesus in all moments of life.

The Call to Holiness

In the call to ongoing conversion, the sacraments give one the grace to follow Christ more closely and to live out the baptismal call to holiness. The *Dogmatic Constitution of the Church: Lumen Gentium* written in 1964 at a time of profound change and awakening in the Church, cites that in Baptism, we are challenged and sent out to live this declaration of faith:

---

[25] CCC, 2447.

In that Body, the life of Christ is poured into the believers who, through the sacraments, area united in the hidden and real way to Christ who suffered and was glorified Through Baptism, we are formed in the likeness of Christ: 'For in one Spirit we were all baptized into one body.' In this sacred rite of oneness with Christ's death and resurrection is both symbolized and brought about: 'For we were buried with Him by means of Baptism into death' and if we have united with Him in the likeness of His death, we shall be so taken up into communion with Him and with one another. 'Because the bread is one, we though many, are one body, all of us who partake of the one bread.' In this way all of us are made members of His Body, 'but severally members one of another'.[26]

We, the faithful, are formed in the likeness of Christ, and this is a major component of the groundwork of the entire Christian life. We are called forth to live and proclaim the Gospel through the manner of our lives keeping in mind our eternal end. Christ joins the members of his body to live together in harmony and in love. This is done through the gifts of the sacramental life of the Church, through prayer, and adherence to God's will. The call to holiness enables its members to work in mission but also to rejoice. "Christ loves the Church as his bride"[27] and the Church as given its members the priceless gifts of the sacraments of the faith. The Church commissions God's people to love and serve especially those members who

---

[26] Pope Paul VI, *Lumen Gentium. The Dogmatic Constitution of the Church*. 1964, Chapter 1, pg. 2. *This book will refer to this source as *LG*.

[27] *LG*, Chapter 1, pg. 3.

Chapter Eight: On-going Conversion

are downtrodden, forsaken, and marginalized. Affability is an avenue for believers to reach those people who may feel abandoned by the world and the Church, as well. This is an integral part of this calling to "be Christ" to others.

Affability and the Call to Conversion

Affability calls members of the Church to respect the dignity of others by remembering that love is not rude. Pope Francis speaks of "genuine encounters"[28] we have with those around us giving us the ability to overlook the shortcomings of others. It is not an easy task to do this, and we must call on the Holy Spirit to accomplish this effort. The kind behavior we, as followers of Christ, exhibit toward a difficult person is a practical way we become more deeply converted to the Christian life. He states, "Loving kindness builds bonds, cultivates relationships, creates new network of integration and knits a firm social fabric"[29]. Cultivating relationships is a prime area of importance in evangelization and in building a culture of life and of love. Friendliness and openness are clearly a major piece in our *own conversion* of living each day.

The larger picture of our baptismal call invites the faithful to become more compassionate in all interactions of life. The Ten Commandments, the Beatitudes, and the catechetical teachings of the Catholic Church are not a spiritual checklist for getting to heaven or of being a "good person" in earthly life. Rather, they are the treasured teachings of the faith meant to guide one in the proper direction

---

[28] *Amoris Laetitia*, p. 80.
[29] Ibid., p. 81.

toward eternal salvation. Christ has won salvation for us. It is through *identification* with Christ in living out the sacramental life of the Church, adherence to the will of God, and by exercising the Corporal and Spiritual Works of Mercy that directs the faithful toward ongoing conversion. Affability is a call to conversion through holiness of life exercised by way of a charitable demeanor toward all. Pope Francis speaks on the topic of "Love is not rude" in *Amoris Laetitia*. This teaching is crucial in terms of understanding the relevance of friendliness in the work evangelization of Church:

> To love is also to be gentle and thoughtful, and this is conveyed by the next word, *aschemonei*. It indicates that love is not rude or impolite; it is not harsh. Its actions, words, and gestures are pleasing and not abrasive or rigid.[30]

Being gentle and thoughtful calls us to speak with kindness in *all* interactions. There were times in which Jesus[31] displayed anger such as when he turned the tables in the temple[32]. Serious-minded Catholics and Christians sometimes use this example to make a point that

---

[30] *Amoris Laetitia*, p. 80.

[31] "Jesus Christ is the true God, and true man, in the unity of his divine person, for this reason he is the one and only mediator between God and men." CCC, 480. (His actions in reprimanding sin especially of those who sinned against God and others is the action of the Holy Spirit to correct a wrongdoing which was being done before his eyes. His reaction to the moneychangers is a reaction of fraternal correction.)

[32] Matthew: 21:12-17, NOAB.

Chapter Eight: On-going Conversion

Jesus lost his temper[33]; and therefore, justified anger is acceptable. The Gospels clearly demonstrate that Jesus' interactions and teachings call for care of the poor, with kindness, justice, and charity[34]. When anger is expressed in life or within ministry, it must be utilized with care in order to teach an important lesson just as Jesus demonstrated the acceptable use of anger in the temple to show those who were making the house of God a marketplace[35]. Pope Francis indicates that loves "actions and gestures are pleasing and not abrasive." We are not to use examples of Jesus' anger in Holy Scripture to justify being rude or harsh. It is not the will of God[36] that we exercise this mentality in our actions with those we wish to "teach a lesson." Sensitivity toward others and their situations of life will enable to us to love sinners but to teach and educate them on the dangers of sin in the world.

Conversion as an Invitation

Christ is at the center of the conversion of the Church since he is our founder, our teacher, and our savior. We are part of the whole body of the Church, and we, his followers, are called to mission and

---

[33] Jesus' anger in temple when he overturned the tables of the money changers is not an example of any "sin" on Jesus' part. This example is justified anger toward those who were making God's house a marketplace. Jesus displayed anger because they were using religion to threaten the dignity of other people in God's holy place. Matthew 21:12-17; Mark 11:15-19; Luke 19:45-48; John 2:13-16, *NOAB*.

[34] Matthew: 5:3-12; Luke: 6:20-23, NOAB.

[35] Matthew: 21:12-17, *NOAB*.

[36] CCC, 1822.

conversion starting with Baptism. Just as an individual person grows in body, mind, and spirit, the Church also grows in a similar fashion. Conversion is Jesus' call to all who claim to love and follow him. This is the commission of both Christ and of his Church. It is by Christ's power that the Church continues in all its ministries and missions. Each person has a vocation or mission from God. Part of this ministry is conversion of heart and faith. We have gifts to share as missionary disciples which includes the evangelization of the world. This is accomplished in small but heartfelt ways by exercising mercy and care for those who feel rejected and cast aside. Affability's piece of this larger picture is momentous as it has to do with demeanor, care, and social interactions with people in all levels of society.

Pope Francis invites all Christians everywhere to partake or to at least consider being a part of mission in the future. He made this proclamation in his writing *Evangelii Gaudium* where he asks the faithful to take this invitation: "I invite all Christians everywhere, at this very moment, to a renewed personal encounter with Jesus Christ, or least an openness to letting him encounter them; I ask all of you to do this unfailingly each day." It is interesting to note that Pope Francis does not *demand* this of us, for he uses the words "at least an openness." This again points to affability, which of course, is another word for openness. Evangelization, which has a certain broad-mindedness and respect for others, is worthy of imitation in efforts toward conversion.

III. Catechizing the Young and Newly Initiated Catholics on Conversion of Life

Catechizing both the young and newer Catholics to conversion is a major component in evangelization and the overall mission of the Catholic Church. Every age, stage, demographic, religion, and creed are invited to become Catholic and to accept the godship of Jesus into their lives. Younger and newly initiated Catholics are especially important to this calling since they are learning the various aspects of what it means to be a disciple of Christ and the momentousness of making a conscious decision to live a sacrificial life of service to God and to others. We are all part of this one body of Christ.

Catholic unity is at the core of this mission and this oneness is an invitation to the world. As we profess our faith in the Creed[37], we make a promise to the Lord to give ourselves in taking part in discipleship of the Gospel of Christ. Catechesis begins in the pilot stages of this journey, and as Catholics this pathway of faith does not cease until our life on earth has ended. At the conclusion of our lives, we go home to the Father with hopes of heaven and of everlasting life with Jesus and the communion of saints. The promises we make publicly at Mass when we profess the Creed is a call to evangelization in daily living. Saying "I believe" is the first step in evangelizing others and more importantly our very selves:

> Celebrated in the liturgy and lived in observance of God's commandments and in prayer, we must first know what 'to

---

[37] CCC, 26.

believe' means. Faith is man's response to God, who reveals himself and gives himself to man, at the same time bringing man a superabundant light as he searches for the ultimate meaning of his life. Thus, we shall consider first that search, then the divine Revelation by which God comes to meet man, and finally the response of faith. We begin our profession of faith by saying: 'I believe' or "We believe' before expounding the Church's faith, as confessed in the Creed.[38]

Believing in this mission calls one to become active in both evangelization and in catechizing others including those closest, namely our families. Proper parenting is the most effective way to teach children the beauty and responsibilities of living and loving the faith. Pope Francis speaks of the challenges of parenting and of catechizing younger people and those new to the Catholic faith. He understands that the mission to evangelize individuals of all ages is a task for every member of the Church, and we must stay relevant in terms of grasping the complexities of modern life. The answer he offers is related to the simplicity of our faith:

> Only if we devote time to our children, speaking important things with simplicity and concern, and finding healthy ways for them to spend their time, will we be able to keep them from harm. Vigilance is always necessary and neglect is never beneficial. Parents have to help prepare children and

---

[38] Ibid.

adolescence to confront the risk, for example, of aggression, abuse, or drug addiction.[39]

The first step in catechizing faith, whether to our own children or someone else, is devoting time. Caring about the well-being of an individual is of utmost importance, and this includes every aspect of their life, their health, mental and emotional lives, and their spiritual lives. This is never a "once and done" approach, but a process of accompaniment. This holistic method of concern highlights the nucleus of what is at the heart of it all, and this is the faith-life of the individual and their relationship with Jesus Christ and the Church.

Newly Initiated Catholics

People who decide to convert to Catholicism are sometimes those who have not practiced any religion in the past. These individuals are called to conversion of life by entering the salvific works of the Church, firstly the sacraments of the faith. Of the most relevant teachings of the faith is to believe fully in *grace* which is given to us by the Lord, and this is taught in the *Catechism of the Catholic Church*[40]. Various elements of our faith point to this grace. Faith[41] is a free, human act enabling us to love God more fully. In understanding faith as a gift from God and our own decision, we, the faithful, can find freedom through the practice of faith. Faith as a *grace* is a primary teaching:

---

[39] *Amoris Laetitia*, p. 198.
[40] CCC, 1997.
[41] Ibid., 166.

Grace is the participation in the life of God. It introduces us into the intimacy of Trinitarian life: by Baptism, the Christian participates in the grace of Christ, the Head of His Body. As an 'adopted son' he can henceforth call God 'Father,' in union with the only Son. He receives the life of the Spirit who breathes charity into him and who forms the Church.[42]

Faith as a grace refers to the fact that we would not have the ability to do anything on our own without the Lord. God the Father is at the helm, and his son Jesus Christ's gift of self for the salvation of the world in the Paschal Mystery of our faith is the nucleus. The Trinitarian life[43] is our life in communion as "adopted sons" of God. For newly initiated Catholics, this understanding is the beginning of wisdom. It is at the heart of work of catechesis in order to educate them on where our faith comes from.

In communicating with those who are new to the faith, we must not only teach them of God's grace, but of all the elements of a living faith, including proper formation about each of the sacraments and living out the mission given to us directly from God, as followers of Christ. We may be able to speak to them about the fulfillment found in walking alongside Jesus and in giving one's life to the Lord through daily conversion of heart. Christianity as expressed through Catholicism is a place for constant growth. There is a temptation for many, including those new to the faith, to consumerism and complacency which are to be avoided. Followers must accept the encounter with

---

[42] Ibid., 1997.
[43] CCC, 234.

Chapter Eight: On-going Conversion

the living Christ to live God's grace and to be converted at each moment. Discipleship is a gift from God, and for newer Catholics, this understanding is beneficial for the evangelization of the Church and the world.

The Conversion of Youth and Young Adults

Those who have a heart for evangelization often care deeply about the conversion of both youth and young adults in the Church. This is understandable since younger people are not only the future of the Church, but in an authentic way, *they are the present.* This means that in observing this thinking, that youth and young adults are part of the present moment, we can take full advantage of present-day evangelization efforts making a difference for the Church and the world in the here and now. The same thought processes and ideas for catechesis come into play as with newly initiated Catholics. Catechizing in an effective way, including instructing on the beauty of each of the sacraments of the faith and in living out the call to holiness is at the center. In addition, by recognizing the gifts of younger people, we must do our best to communicate with them in a language that they understand considering modern culture. Younger people are unique, and we, as a Church, would do better in recognizing their gifts.

> Young adults give to the Church their own unique way of looking at faith and life, their idealism that is tempered by real-life experiences, and their passions and dreams for themselves and for the world. Young adults are a vital part of

the intergenerational faith community. They provide energy and hope to older adult, asking their elders the 'why' of the Catholic faith in holy and healthy ways. They serve as role models and mentors for adolescents and children who look up to them.[44]

The role of younger adults is of prime importance as they continue the legacy of faith to those families who have passed on the torch of our Catholic beliefs and practices to the next generation. Profound respect for younger people is in order since as children of God they deserve recognition for their gifts and talents. Some of those talents include energy, desire to do good, and innovative thinking on ways of bridging the gap between the old and the new. These abilities, when used properly, help to expand the mission of the Church in impactful ways helping to bring Christ to the entire world.

The conversion of younger people also involves not only teaching them the basics of the faith, but also going deeper to instruct them on the relevance of practicing the Corporal and Spiritual Works of Mercy[45] and of living virtuous lives. These teachings on mercy are relevant in today's world since oftentimes younger people are drawn to compassion and making a difference for the marginalized. Included in this type of catechesis is instructing younger people on the virtue of affability which has an impact on reaching those who feel abandoned and left out. With modern emphasis toward the young

---

[44] United States Conference of Catholic Bishops. *Connecting Young Adults to Catholic Parishes. Best Practices for Catholic Young Adult Ministry.* USCCB Publishing. Washinton, D.C. 2010, p. *ix*.

[45] CCC, 2447.

Chapter Eight: On-going Conversion

on anti-bullying and care for the rejected, affability is an avenue to reach people we may never have been able to offer Christ's love to in decades past.

The contribution of younger adults in the Church has much to do with the mission of justice which includes affability and openness. Young adults who have a passion for helping others and in making their faith materialize into action will be intrigued to give their lives to God in service of those who are forsaken. It is imperative that members of the Church keep eyes and hearts open to the gift of service and of love offered by younger adults.

> Young adults contribute to the richness of parish life, but they may not automatically connect with or stay connected with, the Church in the way generations before them did. It takes a conscious effort on the part of each community of faith to welcome the gifts and meet the needs of the young adults who live within their boundaries.[46]

The conscious effort is an invitation for the domestic Church and for the universal Church. All of the faithful have a part in this effort to invite youth and young adults to partake in the missionary efforts of the faith. This is done through genuine catechesis which offers the rich teachings of the ancient Church including the history and the lives of the saints. When younger people learn about saints and the fact that they were real people who lived lives of heroic virtue; this

---

[46] United States Conference of Catholic Bishops. *Connecting Young Adults to Catholic Parishes. Best Practices for Catholic Young Adult Ministry.* USCCB Publishing. Washington, D.C. 2010, p. *ix.*

can make a lasting impression on them. When they investigate the lives of younger saints such as Blessed Pier Giorgio Frassati[47] or Blessed Carlo Acutis[48], oftentimes they can relate better to how saints lived lives devoted to Christ and to the Church. They can also see and experience the impact of kind interactions at the heart of effective evangelization.

One way to evangelize and catechize younger people is in building a responsive church. This is related to not only the entire worldwide Church but also the smaller church, the domestic church. When we see, understand, and honor the gifts of youth and young adults, we are also able to respond to them in ways that make a difference in their lives. Jesus is at the heart of this mission.

> A young adult-responsive parish has Jesus at its core everything the community does, from Sunday liturgy, to parish potlucks, serves as a way to connect parishioners with Jesus. This connection in itself is appealing to young adults, who seek a personal relationship with Jesus that is supported by the Word of God and the church community.[49]

The appeal to young people is authenticity. Younger people are attracted to what is real and not what is false or hypocritical. For that

---

[47] Luciana Frassati, *A Man of the Beatitudes. Pier Giorgio Frassati*. Ignatius Press. 2001.

[48] Francesca Pollio Fenton, "*10 things you should know about Blessed Carlo Acutis*". National Catholic Register. October 12, 2023.

[49] United States Conference of Catholic Bishops. *Connecting Young Adults to Catholic Parishes. Best Practices for Catholic Young Adult Ministry.* USCCB Publishing. Washington, D.C. 2010, p.1.

Chapter Eight: On-going Conversion 257

matter, all of us are attracted to the good, true, and beautiful of our world which all come from God, himself. There is a real connection in meeting youth and young adults where they are and in leading them to God through virtue and humility. They are also often drawn to wanting to develop an authentic and personal relationship with the Lord in fully giving of themselves. Again, the lives of the saints are a wonderful guide for their pathway of faith both in younger life and in the years ahead. Affability and openness give them tools to evangelize others and in practicing authentic care toward those who are in need. Friendly attitudes and actions creates harmony and offers hope and healing to those who suffer. Younger people can offer their gifts to materialize love and charity in our world.

IV. Creating a Gentler World through Mercy

The Church calls members of the Church to exercise mercy[50] in response to God's love. This, in turn, creates a kinder and gentler world. In terms of conversion of heart, when the love of God is felt in a more intimate and personal way, the ultimate response to his love is to give back to others. This an integral part of not only the conversion of hearts but also in helping to create a kinder world which is the kingdom of God. It is the Lord's desire that members of the Church partake in this mission of mercy. Mercy drives one to have compassion for the misery of others, and to act on the desire to pray and do good for other people. The faithful can help to carry the crosses of others and lighten their burdens.

---

[50] CCC, 2447.

Following the Gospel of Christ means accepting the cross, which comes in numerous ways in the lives of the young, the old, and those in between. The cross is the way we, as followers, identify with Christ which ultimately is the road to heaven. Holy Scripture states, "Whoever wants to be my disciple must deny themselves and take up their cross and follow me"[51]. It is in this decision to take up the cross daily that there is a recognition of the gifts of God. Without the acceptance of crosses, there is no salvation as all are called to follow and imitate Christ. These "crosses" are offerings from the Lord because they lay the groundwork to make crucial decisions on whether we, the faithful, will say "yes" to becoming his disciples on a daily basis. Life presents many trials, traumas, and adversities which can be temptations to give up on the life of faith. In addition, there are beauties of life such as good friends and family, God's providence, and blessings which fosters feelings of love of our Creator. The combination of both the challenging elements and the joyful times has an influence on one's decision to move forward in faith or to give up. Pope Francis speaks about the importance of taking up the cross:

> However, the temptation for the Church was and will be the same: evading the cross (Matthew 16:22), negotiating the truth, mitigating the redemptive power of the cross of Christ to avoid persecution. Impoverished is the lukewarm Church that shuns and avoids the cross! It will not be fruitful; it will be politely socializing in sterility on the edges of acceptable culture. This is the price people of God pay for being

---

[51] Luke 9:23, NOAB.

Chapter Eight: On-going Conversion

ashamed of the Gospel, for giving in to the fear of witnessing.[52]

The cross is the salvation of the Church. Pope Francis reminds and warns the faithful that to be truly fruitful, we must never forget the cross. We cannot and should not be ashamed of it. He says politely standing on the edges is not the right thing to do in making faith real to the world. For this reason, the faithful must understand exactly what the Gospel is requiring in order to proceed. We turn to the teachings of the Church to better know and understand what it means to be an authentic follower of Christ and how to best live out the ministry of the Church. As lay people, members of the Church have a specific mission in the domestic Church. This mission encompasses knowing, loving, and serving God. We are to be the salt of the earth, as Jesus states in Holy Scripture, "You are the salt of the earth"[53]. We are to model Christ in all interactions and in missionary work.

We are called to make the Church present. This means being fully present in our will. This is a missionary task that takes prayer, perseverance, and charity in our hearts to present Christ in the proper way to the unchurched and those who are abandoned and marginalized. When we show the living Christ alive in our hearts and actions, we become true missionary disciples in the effort to evangelize the world. *This is mercy in action.* Mercy in action is a daily task, and we must not lack in it. Pope Francis states, "All of her pastoral activity

---

[52] Pope Francis, *I Ask You, Be Shepherds. Reflections on Pastoral Ministry.* Crossroads Publishing. 2015, p. 96-97.
[53] Matthew 5:13, NOAB.

should be caught up in the tenderness which she shows to believers; nothing in her preaching and her witness to the world can be lacking in mercy."[54] Tenderness is a key component in exercising mercy, as well.

Our Christian spirituality needs to model after the life of Christ, which was about humility, service to others, and in ultimately giving his life for the salvation of the world. In our personal mission to live mercifully, we, his followers, are to do the same. In addition, we are also called to live moderately, and not to be people of consumption. Pope Francis writes:

> Christian spirituality proposed a growth marked by moderation and the capacity to be happy with little. It is a return to that simplicity which allows us to stop and appreciate the small things, to be grateful for the opportunities which life affords us, to be spiritually detached from what we possess, and not to succumb to sadness for what we lack. This implies avoiding the dynamic of dominion and the mere accumulation of pleasures.[55]

These are excellent reminders that living the Christian life impels us not to be people of excess. Merciful living requires members of the Church to be more concerned in giving than to possess. We are encouraged to exercise a deep care for the poor to a point where we wish to do something about the poverty we witness. The poor are often those people who have a lack of the necessities of life. They are

---

[54] *Amoris Laetitia*, p. 241.
[55] *Laudato Si*, p. 144, 145.

also people who we know and see every day, such as those in our families, friends, co-workers, parishioners, and strangers, as mentioned. Marginalized people are always in our company, and Jesus calls us to recognize them and make outreach. Our life with Christ calls us to let them know we care as we put love into action for their sake.

Attentiveness to and Ongoing Conversion

A major part of exercising mercy is through attentiveness and ongoing conversion. Secular culture teaches a "me-first" attitude and way of living. Starting with early life, a certain competitiveness in society with others fosters an unhealthy attitude of life. Children as early as toddlerhood and preschool are compared to others in school there is a certain "branding" in terms of intelligence and adeptness, and this mentality often continues through life. Consumerism gives way, and as we age, we may become more self-focused as a culture instead of offering love and attention to those in need. Children are taught to compete in terms of grades, status, relationships, and other areas causing those on the fringes to be ignored. Unfortunately, this attitude has crept into the Church, hence the term "clericalism"[56] has come forth which describes those priests and religious who view their vocations as "careers." The Catholic faith teaches that these attitudes are *incorrect*. For us to move forward on a missionary journey with Christ, we must accept our crosses and help others to carry their

---

[56] "Clericalism" refers to priests, bishop, and religious having entitlements and should be treated as nobility.

crosses, as well. Taking up the cross is major part of conversion of heart. Pope Francis states:

> We are speaking of an attitude of the heart, one which approaches life with serene attentiveness, which is capable of being fully present to someone without thinking of what comes next, which accepts each moment as a gift from God to be lived to the full.[57]

This serene attentiveness is how we, the faithful, avoid selfishness, competitiveness, and unkindness. The wisdom of these words helps us to understand that we live one moment at a time with God's grace. This grace gives members of the Church the ability to use the extraordinary gifts God has given in order to make an impact. Attentiveness is done simply through active listening and in giving of oneself especially when there is someone who needs time and care.

Making Mercy Tangible

Creating a kinder world for God's sake, it is not done in a sterile or highly academic way. The teaching of Jesus and of the Church must be real and tangible to others. Making mercy real for those who suffer encompasses our own conversions and growing closer to Jesus. Christ used parables in his teachings which he understood to be easy to understand to the listener. His followers are to do the same. In the work of evangelization, we will be in the presence of people with varying degrees of intelligence, understanding, and cultural back-

---

[57] Ibid., p. 146-147.

Chapter Eight: On-going Conversion

grounds. The faithful are encouraged to deeply understand the evangelizing work of the Church and do our best to offer faith in action. This is how it is possible to make God's love real, tangible, and tactile in their lives. This experience is part of one's own *personal conversion*, as well. God instructs us to be spirit-filled in communicating his love to those we encounter. The truths of faith are factual and intellectual but also alive, vibrant, and full of joy.

> Spirit-filled evangelizers are evangelizers to pray and work. Mystical notions without a solid social missionary outreach are of no help to evangelization, nor are books or social or pastoral practices which lack spirituality which can change hearts.[58]

It is interesting that Pope Francis mentions books since these research papers are what produces doctoral degrees in academia. Pope Franics is stating that "mystical notions" which don't have any kind of missionary reach will become *ineffective*. Spirituality is encouraged to include mercy and the mission of the Church in practicing Works of Mercy. Catechesis should additionally be comprised of outreach to the disenfranchised, the lonely, and rejected. Changing the hearts of others requires the faithful not to fall into hypocrisy. Our faith implores us to go beyond a clique of like-minded friends to reach past boundaries which are safest in the work of evangelization. Additionally, those who work in the theological world are asked not to fall into presenting faith as a list of facts and theories and to be

---

[58] *Evangelii Gaudium*, p. 126.

mindful that the audience is the world and not just the highly educated. It is not the will of God that the teachings of the Church be directed only to those of a certain IQ or EQ level, intellect, educational background, socio-economic status, or living situation. Jesus taught everyone, and *no one* was excluded from his teachings. He preached and spoke to those of the upper classes, to the lowly, and to those who were considered in between in terms of status. It is our job to imitate these virtues of living. We should seek out the marginalized at every opportunity.

In the mission to create a gentler overall world, we are asked not to forget the poor. Jesus honored them as the focus of his outreach when he lived on the earth. The impoverished are those who do not have the love and support they deserve in some fashion of life. They may be materially poor and also those who are left without hope, care, or compassion. Members of the Church are to seek them out and to selflessly serve them. The antidote to fill the gap is in listening and developing strong bonds of love with those who are cast aside. Pope Francis states, "The ability to sit down and listen to others, typical of interpersonal encounters, is paradigmatic of the welcoming attitude shown by those who transcend narcissism and accept others, caring for them and welcoming them into their lives."[59] The Holy Spirit creates the needed space between one individual and another for the divinity of Christ to be made present.

His divine life is our reason for being and the cause of our joy. He gives hope to carry on despite the crosses encountered in our own lives. He helps each person through his Holy Spirit to have the grace

---

[59] *Fratelli Tutti*, p. 34.

to carry out personal missions of faith and the works of the Church as a whole. This is conversion in action when we encompass God's will for the salvation of the world. In doing this work of evangelization, the virtue of friendliness and openness is integral. It enables one to know and understand that love is not rude. Love is gentle, kind, and affable. Prayer and relationship with God lay the groundwork for this to happen, especially within family life:

> It is within the family that we are trained for a relationship with the Lord and the conversation with Him: "Ever since we were children, our parents taught us to start and end the day with a prayer, to teach us to feel that the friendship and the love of God accompanies us.[60]

Prayer and charity combined will enable the faithful to enter an even deeper level of love for the Lord. Christ's divinity shines forth in service to those who lack materially and/or spiritually. As Christ's followers live in the love of God and in his spirit, charity can be expressed to a greater degree. This can only be done through God's grace and through acceptance of his will in every aspect of life and through conversion of heart. This mission is taught to the young, new Catholics, the old and infirm, to the middle-aged, and to every person. Gentleness and mercy act conjointly with the virtue of justice and affability in the process of ongoing conversion. This is the mission of the Church, and friendliness is a valuable attribute to encompass and practice each moment of existence.

---

[60] United States Conference of Catholic Bishops. *Pope Francis and the Family*. Libreria Editrice Vaticana. 2014, p. 49-50.

Chapter Nine

Loving and Serving as Catholics

I. Church Teachings on Loving and Serving Others

There are thousands of teachings related to loving and serving others, but it is necessary to point to some of the key teachings in relation to the virtue of affability and its relevance in modern evangelization. Perhaps one of the most prevalent teachings are the Corporal and Spiritual Works of Mercy of the Church as discussed throughout this book. Through these acts of loving and serving faithful members of the Church are in imitation of Christ and of the Gospel message. These acts enable one to model the life of Christ and to continue his work on earth. In terms of affability, the Works of Mercy are powerful ways to evangelize in doing the work of the Lord.

Some of the lives of the saints will be discussed in the next subchapter at length. In addition to their lives, the Christ's followers can take a moral inventory in terms of service to others. Part of this service is the treatment of people, which is the openness of spirit in all of the instances of life. A major piece of this is in respecting others. The Catechism states:

> Respect for the human person proceeds by way of respect for the principle that 'everyone should look upon his neighbor (without any exception) as 'another self,' above all bearing in mind his life and the means necessary for living it with dignity. No legislation could by itself do away with the fears,

prejudices, and attitudes of pride and selfishness which obstruct the establishment of truly fraternal societies. Such behavior will cease only through charity that finds in every man a 'neighbor,' a brother.[1]

In addition to having an openness of spirit, the respect given to others assists us to live out the virtue of affability to a greater degree. It is in treating others exactly as we would desire to be treated that we are giving them the justice they deserve. We, Christ's followers, cannot love and serve properly without doing so. Additionally, the Catechism states:

> The duty of making oneself a neighbor to others and actively serving them becomes even more urgent when it involves the disadvantaged, in whatever area this may be. 'As you did it to one of the least of these brethren, you did it to me.'[2]

The activity of making oneself like a neighbor to another person is at the heart of the Gospel and of teachings on affability and evangelization. Members of the Church must remember at all times the urgency in acting as missionary disciples for Christ and in carrying out the mission of mercy. When the call to love and serve is taken seriously, the Gospel comes alive. This is part of work Christ has laid out for all Christians.

---

[1] CCC, 1931.
[2] Ibid., 1932.

Chapter Nine: Loving and Serving as Catholics

How to Carry Out Loving and Serving

Church teachings found in the Catechism of the Catholic Church communicate that justice is served when the faithful fulfill the ministry of being missionary disciples toward each person as Christ would. It is our duty to remember that in God's eyes, all are of equal dignity and deserve to be treated as such. In following the Lord's command to love and care, we, his followers, begin to carry out this missional journey. How is this done? It is done through the acts of mercy which are the Church's teachings on love and service. Pope Francis speaks of the work in God's kingdom as seeds which are growing:

> Because we do not always see these seeds growing, we need an interior certainty, a conviction that God is able to act in every situation, even amid apparent setbacks 'we have this treasure in earthen vessels' (2 Cor 4:7). This certainly is often called "a sense of mystery," it involves knowing with certitude that all those who entrust themselves to God in love will bear good fruit (cf. Jn 15:5). The fruitfulness is often invisible, elusive, and unquantifiable. We can know quite well that our lives will be fruitful, without claiming to know how, or where, or when. We may be sure that none of our acts of love will be lost, not any of our acts of sincere concern for others. No single act of love will for God will be lost, no generous effort is meaningless, no painful endurance is wasted.[3]

---

[3] *Evangelii Gaudium*, p. 135.

Nothing that is done for God and for the good of others will be lost, and this includes all the acts of mercy and of love that are done for the disparaged of the world. Pope Francis articulates well that all that is done for the Lord in service to our brothers and sisters is somehow eternal. We should keep this in mind as we endure various trials for the good of others. Members of the Church can offer prayers knowing that in following the Lord through sincere care and concern, we imitate Jesus.

The spiritual instruments of loving and serving others consist of prayer, sacrifice, and knowledge of the teachings of the Church. When the faithful understand how these teachings are to be materialized, they can evangelize to the poor. This service of the Church works within the realms of family life, communities, and the world. In doing so, Christ's followers begin to fully understand the teachings of the Church as they tangibly live it out.

II. Lessons from the Lives of the Saints

All of us as Christians are called to sainthood. The lives of the saints teach the world about what is most valuable in living out the mission of the Church and destiny toward heaven. Faith in living action is how sainthood occurs when a conscious decision to do God's call is lived out no matter the cost. Saints live lives of heroic virtue[4] demonstrating their profound love of God and of his people. Their lives illustrate a variety of personalities, demeanors, likes, dislikes, and ways in which they lived God's will in becoming the most excellent version of themselves through the work of the Holy Spirit.

---

[4] CCC, 828.

Chapter Nine: Loving and Serving as Catholics

Although some saints' personalities are demonstrated as being more inward and less outgoing, nonetheless, affability and openness is prevalent in some fashion in their lives. Their impartiality is revealed through a mission of mercy toward every individual encountered in willing the good for others in a heartfelt and authentic manner.

St. Thomas Aquinas, St. Faustina, Blessed Pier Giorgio Frassati, and St. Francis de Sales are saints which exhibited the virtue of affability in their lives of virtue. These four saints are a sampling of those who have lived heroic virtue and who have illustrated openness of spirit both in action and in their relationship with God the Father. Each has his/her own charism and way of expressing themselves in demonstrating the valuable virtue of affability.

St. Thomas Aquinas

As mentioned earlier in this book, St. Thomas Aquinas, doctor of the Church, is one of the most prevalent teachers of the medieval Catholic Church. An Italian Dominican friar, and preacher who lived from 1225-1274, his systematic works are the *Summa Theologica*[5], *Summa Contra Gentiles*, and the *Scriptum Super Sententiis*. These writings are his greatest contribution to the Church. His work, *Summa Theologica*, was unfortunately never completed; and the piece details the whole of Catholic theology. His dedication to writing, which he did with fervor and care, has had a massive influence on the passing on of the faith for centuries and will continue to do so for generations to come.

---

[5] St. Thomas Aquinas, *Summa Theologica*. Volume II. Christian Classics. Westminster, MD. 1948.

Aquinas' primary objective in his writing endeavors, especially in the *Summa Theologica*, were in developing questions and thought-out replies toward every aspect of the Catholic faith to present it in a logical and calculated manner for understanding. One of those areas of study includes detailed writings on virtue and vice and what each entail. He was concerned in differentiating them in a concise way so the reader would gain full knowledge of Catholic doctrine and tradition.

In the *Summa Theologica* Part II, Questions 114[6], Aquinas speaks of the friendliness called affability as discussed earlier in this book. His diligence in this matter related to affability and its relevance suggests his placement of it under the cardinal virtue of justice as integral in daily living. In his piece on affability, he mentions that to live in peace, the virtue of affability brings joy, and this is of immense value. In the *Summa Theologica*, his attention to areas such as virtue, vice, the causes of sin, and the law gives clarity to his method of preaching and teaching the truths of the faith. St. Thomas Aquinas' lessons on affability remind the faithful that this virtue implores us to give due justice to our neighbor through a kind and affable spirit which is open to the needs of others.

The application of this virtue is one that must be thought-out and applied in the way St. Thomas Aquinas suggests which is through awareness, practice, and guidance of the Holy Spirit. His writings speak of a practical approach to affability which begins by comprehending the opposite vice which is being closed off and unwilling to listen to the voice of God within interactions and in relationships.

---

[6] Ibid.

Chapter Nine: Loving and Serving as Catholics

According to the thoughts and ideas of Aquinas, seeking virtue and avoiding vice is key to living a life of saintliness which is dedicated to doing God's will alone and in completely avoiding sin as much as possible. Without a doubt, St. Thomas Aquinas is biblical, theological, and sensible in terms of executing the practice of this valuable virtue. St. Thomas speaks about the order of faith, charity, and justice:

> Faith and charity supply a special directing of the human mind to God by the intellect and will; whereas justice implies a general rectitude of order. Hence this transmutation is named after justice rather than after charity or faith.[7]

The writing above is on the effects of grace in our lives from the *Summa Theologica*. This is the same section where Aquinas speaks about the virtue of affability. Affability is a justice due to others *lived out by the grace of God*. Throughout all his writings, he demonstrates a logical order of thought in his presentation related to these invaluable virtues of faith. It is interesting to note that St. Thomas Aquinas has ordered affability as a noteworthy attribute as a way to offer God's justice to one another in life.

St. Faustina

St. Maria Faustina Kowalska lived from 1905 to 1938 in west-central Poland. She was an uneducated Catholic nun who joined the Congregation of the Sisters of Our Lady of Mercy in 1925. She had a

---

[7] Ibid., p. 1145.

deep interior life and had received revelations[8] from the Lord. These revelations, which were given to her by Jesus, were recorded in a diary, and included directives to have an image produced with a picture of Jesus wearing white with both red and white rays coming from his body outward. The image is a depiction of God's living mercy for humanity since the rays represent both his blood and water, his gift of self and of the cleansing sacraments of the faith which bring new life. The message of mercy is related to God's unconditional love and mercy for humanity throughout life but especially the hour of death. When the Chaplet of Divine Mercy[9] is recited at the bedside of a dying person, the prayer is for a happy death and the remissions of the corporal punishment of any sins of the past so that the person may enter heaven. It is a powerful prayer which encompasses Jesus total gift of self and his undying mercy for his children.

St. Faustina had a naturally inward personality, and she shared an intimate relationship with both Jesus and the Holy Spirit. Jesus spoke to her in plain language about the mission of mercy in her own life and offered ways that she could spread the devotion of mercy to the world. This type of openness to the Holy Spirit required her to also be affable since there is a direct connection with our relationship with God and with others. Although her natural personality was

---

[8] The "revelations" St. Faustina received from the Lord are accepted as private revelations of the Church. These revelations have been approved by the Vatican.

[9] The "Chaplet of Divine Mercy" is a prayer given to St. Faustina Kowalska (1905-1938) referred to as "Divine Mercy." Rosary beads are used to pray the prayer. For information on how to pray the Chaplet: https://www.thedivinemercy.org/message/devotions/pray-the-chaplet

Chapter Nine: Loving and Serving as Catholics

more introverted, affability was evident in her life not as an occurrence but through an awareness of God and others in her life in exercising virtue. Her affable demeanor and spirit created a broad-minded acceptance to the will of God and the way she interacted with those around her. There are a variety of writings in her diary on mercy and how one can do the will of God by performing acts of charity and kindness toward others. She wrote:

> Everyone in the word can belong to this group. A member of this group ought to perform at least one act of mercy per day, at least one, but there can be many more, for such deeds can easily be carried out by anyone, even the very poorest. For there are three ways of performing an act of mercy: the merciful word, by forgiving, and by comforting; secondly, if you can offer no word, then pray – that too is mercy; and thirdly, deeds of mercy. And when the Last Day comes, we shall be judged from this, and on this basis, we shall receive the eternal verdict.[10]

Jesus gave her the devotion to Divine Mercy, in 1931. Mercy is present when as followers of Christ, we find the ways and means to offer God's love to another in some acceptable form. St. Faustina refers to doing acts of mercy, offering prayer, and deeds of mercy. All these tasks when done with love are ways that charity is expressed. This demonstrates affability, as well, since in leaving oneself open to offer the Corporal and Spiritual Works of Mercy, great good can be

---

[10] Saint Maria Faustina Kowalska, *Divine Mercy in My Soul. Diary.* Marian Press Stockbridge, MA. 2004, 1157-1158.

done in building up the kingdom of God. This is also the will of God that the faithful offer openness of spirit to the Lord and others. This receptivity fosters kindness, goodness, and brings joy to the receiver. The life of St. Faustina, which encompassed great interior suffering and prayer along with carrying out God's will for her own life, is another example of the affable spirit willing to take the necessary steps to bring healing and redemption to countless lives. She is a saint to be modeled after in her demonstration of affability of heart and spirit.

St. Francis de Sales

St. Francis de Sales was a priest, a missionary, and a pastor. Born in 1567 and died in 1622 in the Chateau de Sales, he was a gifted and brilliant man who lived a life of purpose. His demeanor was said to be affable, charming, and virtuous which was directed to his intense love of God and the Church. At the age of thirty-five, he became of the Bishop of Geneva where he continued his mission of preaching, hearing Confessions and of catechizing. Two of his most famous books are the *Introduction to the Devout Life* and *A Treatise on the Love of God*. He had a deep, spiritual friendship with another saint, St. Jane Frances de Chantal. St. Jane de Chantel was a widowed mother of four adult children who had later founded a religious order, the Visitation of Holy Mary. St. Francis de Sales and she developed a close spiritual friendship over many years starting with spiritual direction. The two of them prayed in unison and acted together in virtue for the good of the Church and others.

In his writing *Introduction to the Devout Life*, he speaks of humility, gentleness of spirit, and of the value of Christian friendship. He alludes to the treasure of real, mature friendship which when rooted in virtue has its value within the heart of God as a gift. This offering is much like the affable person who is open to befriending, helping, and guiding those in need. The open-spirited man or woman keeps the Holy Spirit close at heart when in conversation and in exercising mercy toward others. This is God's compassion in action, and St. Francis de Sales spent his life living out these virtues, and he taught others to do the same. This was done through preaching and teaching. One way that he accomplished this was through writing and distributing pamphlets to explain Catholic doctrine. In addition, his writings on the differences between good and evil friendships and of virtue versus vice, pave the way to gaining knowledge on what it means to develop God-filled relationships which are based on prudence and charity.

St. Francis de Sales is another example of an affable saint who taught and preached on God's mercy and in living a truly virtuous life of faith.

Blessed Pier Giorgio Frassati

Blessed Pier Giorgio Frassati[11] [12]was born in 1901 and died in 1925 at the age of twenty-five. He was born to a wealthy Italian

---

[11] Luciana Frassati, *A Man of the Beatitudes. Pier Giorgio Frassati.* Ignatius Press. 2001.

[12] Maria DiLorenzo, *Blessed Pier Giorgio Frassati. An Ordinary Christian.* Pauline Books and Media. 1973.

family, and he became a favored model of an exemplary life not long after he died. While his parents were agnostic, and he modeled his faith after his grandmother who had a major influence on his life at an early age. In his youth, he joined the Marian Sodality and the Apostleship of Prayer. He also asked permission to be a daily communicant at an early age, which was rare at the time. Pier Giorgio is known for devoting his life to the needs of the poor and forsaken. He would give money and alms to those who needed it, and he brought medicine and material goods to the sick and elderly. Pier Giorgio did these deeds oftentimes in secret as even his family and close friends were not fully aware of the sacrifices he made for the marginalized. At the age of twenty-four, he contracted polio which eventually took his life. His family believed that he contracted the disease while visiting the sick which he continued to do up until his own premature death.

Blessed Pier Frassati's openness of spirt is demonstrated in his determination to do God's will and in exercising the Corporal and Spiritual Works of Mercy in his daily life. Even in the face of his own death, he continued to do good carrying out charitable acts which made a difference to the suffering. In addition to his affable spirit, he also had a charming and friendly demeanor toward everyone he came into contact with. He was a natural extrovert, and his life of virtue came forth in his utilizing friendliness and affability in every encounter he experienced. This was evident in his personal relationships with his peers and in his outreach to the forsaken of the world. His example of virtue is the perfect instance of both an affable spirit toward others and of genuine cheer and kindness. Blessed Pier Giorgio Frassati is a model to both younger people and to those of all ages as his life is a clear picture of what affability lived out looks like from the inside. This is a reference to his interior life which demonstrated his deep connection with God and care for others.

Additional Saints and those Previously Mentioned

There are a host of saints, perhaps too numerous to list, who have lived the virtue of affability and have taught others to do the same. These saints lived humble lives dedicated to others, and they did it with an affable demeanor and in full charity. It seems that one commonality of all the saints who exercised this virtue is their determination to do God's will. Despite sickness, pain, suffering, or any other aspect which separates, saints who lived with openness of spirit care deeply in doing the will of God and of loving others as commanded by Christ. Saints teach us, Christ's followers, how to be kind and affable in all relationships of life.

III. Exercising Kindness, Goodness, and Charity

Exercising charity and kindness toward everyone is part of what it means to be Christian. In loving and following the faith, it is not just a set of rules. The Paschal Mystery[13] encompasses the life, death, resurrection, and ascension of our savior, Jesus Christ. Since the Paschal Mystery is the cornerstone of all that Christians believe, there is a connection with the practicing of virtues. Living virtue entails understanding the Corporal and Spiritual Works of Mercy and living them out. This kind of love is a major part of the virtue of affability

---

[13] CCC, 571.

which is the openness of spirit needed to make outreach to the marginalized and in finding them in the first place. The beginning of understanding the significance of the mission of mercy is in having respect for the dignity of each human person encountered.

> Respect for the human person entails respect for the rights that flow from his dignity as a creature. These rights are prior to society and must be recognized by it. They are the basis of the moral legitimacy of every authority: by flouting them or refusing them in its positive legislation, a society undermines its own moral legitimacy. It is does not respect them, authority can rely only on force or violence to obtain obedience from its subjects. It is the Church's role to remind men of good will of these rights and to distinguish them from unwanted or false claims.[14]

Respect is first in all efforts to evangelize and in exercising greater charity. Members of the Church must first see and revere all that is good in the people. Without this ability, we fall short in attempting to spread the Gospel. The Church has a key role in reminding followers of Christ to be people of justice and of love. Spreading and living God's word requires us to remove the barriers we place between ourselves and other people. All prejudices and judgements must be cast aside.

Modern society is more aware of the prejudices of the past, but there is still much work to be done in the Church and in the world. The faithful must put forth best efforts and avoid at all costs judging

---

[14] Ibid., 1930.

others based on race, religion, sex, socio-economic status, education, age, or any other factors. Without doing so, we may fall into sin, and we will not be able to execute God's will in this regard. Recognizing our own sin and going to the foot of the cross for repentance and receiving the Sacrament of Reconciliation, we can be restored from the sin of prejudice, judgment, and neglect of others. Our sin is before us, and the remedy is in following our faith and repenting for sins of the past.

> The Church that is holy does not reject sinners. She does not reject us all; she does not reject because she calls everyone, welcomes them, is open to even those furthest from her, she calls everyone to allow themselves to be enfolded by the mercy, the tenderness, and the forgiveness, of the Father who offers everyone the possibility of meeting him of journeying toward sanctity.[15]

We have a loving God who calls us to him no matter the circumstance. His tenderness and mercy can restore us to all that is good and to begin to see more clearly the dignity of every person in the world despite our many differences. This is our journey toward sanctification.

Kindness and Affability

The virtues of kindness and affability go together since kindness encompasses those kind, daily interactions we have in exercising acts

---

[15] Pope Francis, General Audience. www.vatican.va. October 2, 2013.

of mercy which make a difference in people's lives. Affability is the openness of spirit in dialogue, conversations, and behaviors toward others, especially those who are different from us in some way. Snobbery, ignoring people, and pre-judging are sinful behaviors, and sadly in society they are commonplace. In addition, competitiveness, and a throw-away attitude about friendships and relationships fosters a closed-off mentality which is the opposite of friendliness and kindness. Some people are naturally more outgoing and perhaps empathetic, but with prayer, patience, and an attitude of care, even the most introverted and overly self-aware person can learn to become kinder and gentler, especially to those who are rejected and cast aside. A key component in all of this is sincerity. Natural personality traits related to extroverted versus introverted are less important in comparison to acting in true compassion with a sincere heart.

Goodness and Affability

Goodness is holiness which is practiced in daily living. It is a result of sanctification and of a deep relationship with God. As God's children, he has made each of us good, but we need to stay on course with him through lives of prayer, virtue, and in doing good. The Corporal and Spiritual Works of Mercy offers a myriad of opportunities in practicing virtue including friendliness. When affability is combined with goodness in the practice of virtue, the results are positive. Instead of doing charitable deeds for the sole purpose of doing God's will, when combined with friendliness and joy, those on the receiving end can see and feel the difference when acts of charity are done in a spirit of joy and of gladness. Those who have been rejected by others can see and understand when an act is being done only out of obligation, and the results are negative. Incorporating affability in all acts of goodness makes a major difference for both the giver and the recipient.

Charity and Affability

Charity is love; and love is the greatest of all virtues, and without love, nothing is of value. Society equates love with emotion and not much more. The Catholic faith teaches that love is in willing the good of the other. Christ died for us to obtain salvation for eternity. It is love in action, and in imitation of Jesus, we do the same. We offer ourselves for the good of other people, and namely, for their eternal salvation. Sacrificial love is not offered in systematic way to gain heaven for us or others alone. It is freely given out of love for Christ, and out of this love, we pray to be more willing to give of ourselves for the salvation of others. Freely offering oneself for the good of another is the definition of love, and members of the Church are called to love everyone despite anything that separates.

Affability and charity are virtues which complement each other the most since every act of friendliness and kindness is done with love. Without love, any "niceness" and openness displayed does not amount to much. With Christ at the center of loving interactions, especially with those who are on the fringes of society, the Gospel of Christ is carried out. Everyone has passions, thoughts, and feelings, but through virtue, the faithful can discern what is of God and what is not.

Strong feelings are not decisive for the morality or holiness of persons, they are simply the inexhaustible reservoir of images and affections in which the moral life is expressed. Passions are morally good when they contribute to a good action, evil in the opposite case. The upright will order the movements of the senses it appropriates to the good and to beatitude, an evil will succumb to disordered passions and exacerbates them. Emotions and feelings can be taken up into the virtues or perverted by the vices.[16]

It is important to understand that humans have "feelings" and sometimes those emotions may or may not coincide with the will of God in terms of how we as act on those emotions. In developing greater awareness on the role of passions in life, we, Christ's followers, grasp how to act in situations and how to do God's will at all costs. When true charity is at the heart of all moral decisions and actions, a positive result will come out of most every interaction and decision. When love is not present, then the opposite will occur; evil will prevail. The way to conquer evil passions is through prayer, perseverance, and by staying close to Christ through life and living out the sacramental life of the Church. There will be struggles along the way, and this is expected. Once we gain a greater understanding of what love *is*, we can exercise the virtue of affability and make friendliness a part of who we are even if we, the faithful, are not naturally open to others. We can pray to become more compassionate so that

---

[16] CCC, 1768.

in encountering people who need love and support, we can support them in a greater capacity.

As we continue the journey to become more open with others, we will be able to grow in relationship with Christ. Kindness, goodness, and charity are rooted in the love of Jesus, and the affable spirit will make an even greater difference in evangelizing those who are away from the Church and who need to know and understand God's love. Our role as disciples is to carry out the wishes of Christ to "go and make disciples of all nations"[17]. This is accomplished one person at a time and through charity and compassion. As we, the faithful, go forth as a church in becoming kinder and gentler, our friendly spirit will pave the way to opening doors which may have never been opened in the past. This relates not only to the domestic church but also to the universal Church, as well. Affability refines and perfects kindness, goodness, and charity which is exercised in a spirit of sacrificial love for humankind.

IV. A Living and Breathing Faith

A faith that is alive in the spirit of God can transform the world by the power of the Gospel. This is done through an active relationship with Christ in giving ourselves to him for the sake of others and for the world. The Catholic Church offers the antidote to finding and living out a faith that is truly living and active and which make a difference in the lives of others, especially the poor and forgotten. The domestic church consists of the smaller units made up of families who strive together to live in harmony with Christ and others. Each

---

[17] Matthew 28:19-20, NOAB.

family makes a tremendous difference to the world as they are "little churches" where lessons of life and of love are shared and expressed. Pope Franics recognizes this fact as he has expressed in in his many writings and homilies in the past.

In the work of evangelization, the focus on families is imperative to the growth of the Church and in fulfilling the work of Christ on earth. From the youngest to the oldest as members of the Church, we are called to love, serve, and be charitable in using our gifts for the good of world. It is a union of love that begins with parents and is expressed outward to children, and further to society. Pope Francis has stated:

> Through their union, the couple experiences the beauty of fatherhood and motherhood, and shares plans, trials, expectations, concerns; they learn care for one another and mutual forgiveness. In this love, they celebrate their happy moments and support each other in the difficult passages of their life together. The beauty of this mutual gratuitous gift, the joy which comes from the life that is born and the loving care of all family members-from toddlers to seniors-are just a few of the fruits which make the response to the vocation of the family unique and irreplaceable both for the Church and society as a whole.[18]

The picture given by Pope Francis reminds the faithful that every life has value and purpose no matter how young or how old. Each

---

[18] *Amoris Laetitia*, p. 72.

life is irreplaceable and holds a unique place in the human family and the universal Church. This is what it means to be pro-life, when we recognize the Lord in people and in all of creation. This openness of heart and of spirit is invaluable in efforts to evangelize those who have walked away from the faith and those who have been cast aside by society at large. The Catholic mission is a calling which is rooted in the family but also that recognizes each individual person in a distinct way regardless of anything that separates. This is how the Church expresses a living and breathing faith both inside and outside the walls of the Church.

Ways to Accomplish this Goal

Accomplishing the goal of creating a Church which is alive and active in terms of evangelizing efforts is the work of God and in obedience in doing his will. Efforts which are rooted in any type of force, or which are not guided by the Holy Spirit will fail. Therefore, prayer is the primary way in which the Church can and will be guided to open itself up to the world in a more distinct way. This begins with an awareness of God in all circumstances of life. There are numerous ways to offer prayer within family life, and one of the simplest ways to begin is by offering prayer at mealtime and by thanking the Lord for his offerings which give life. Pope Francis states:

> One expression of this attitude is when we stop and give thanks to God before and after meals. I ask all believers to return to this beautiful and meaningful custom. That moment of blessing however brief, reminds us of our depend-

ence on God for life; it strengthens our feeling of gratitude for the gifts of creation; it acknowledges those who by their labors provide us with these goods; and it reaffirms our solidarity with those in greatest need.[19]

The prayer which is referred to as "grace before meals" has a meaningful impact as it draws attention to prayer as a family unit. "Grace after meals" is a prayer that is often forgotten but that remembers to give thanks to God after the meal is consumed. Families who make this a practice can pray together that day even if other prayers are neglected as a family unit. Once the regularity of the prayer of "grace" is fully established, it can lead to more opportunities for family prayer such as prayers in the morning, evening, and at night. The more a family takes the time to pray together, God's graces are instilled, and families begin to look forward to praying and will notice the days and times that a prayer is neglected. These opportunities for prayer create an open spirit which is affability.

As family prayer life is more deeply established, additional prayers such as the recitation of Holy Rosary, spending time in an Adoration Chapel, and attending Daily Mass, together may come into play. The value of taking time to pray in a deeper way fosters spiritual growth and enables families to have a desire to not only practice the faith, but to *love the faith*. Evangelization efforts in this regard are not manufactured, they grow and are sustained through a living faith which makes a difference for both the family itself and for the whole of society and the Church.

---

[19] *Laudato Si*, p. 147.

Chapter Nine: Loving and Serving as Catholics

We Need One Another

Pope Francis speaks of the fact that in addition to prayer and relationship with Christ, it is essential to recognize more deeply that we need each other both within the domestic church, the Church at large, and the entire world which includes everyone. In his writing *Laudato Si*, he speaks about not only the gift of human relationships but also the gift of the earth and our responsibility in caring for all of creation which includes the whole planet and all creatures of God. He says that "we need each other," and in working together with the Lord's guidance and care, we can make a difference for the Church and the world.

> We must regain the conviction that we need one another, that we have shared responsibility for one another and for the world, and that being good and decent are worth it. We have had enough of immorality, and the mockery of ethics, goodness, faith and honesty. It is time to acknowledge that light-hearted superficiality has done no good. When the foundations of social life are corroded, what ensues are battles over conflicting interests, new forms of violence and brutality, and the obstacles of a genuine culture of care for the environment.[20]

Pope Francis reveals wisdom in the above writings as he communicates to his audience that it is time for a change in terms of our responsibilities to God and to others. The Catholic faith summons

---

[20] Ibid., p. 148.

us, Christ's followers, to do good not just within the confines of our homes but in making a difference through life choices and care for humankind and all of God's creation. In doing so, this is doing God's will since it is clear that selfish attitudes and behaviors create war and discord even if done indirectly. As Catholics, it is imperative to act in a responsible manner. It is proper to care for our world, and this includes understanding and implementing better environmental practices which will produce a cleaner, kinder, and safer world. In being an effective steward of God's creation, we have the responsibility of caring for everyone and for the earth. The combination of care for human life and God's earth is indeed "pro-life." Adopting an attitude of awareness and of active stewardship also fosters affability of heart and mind. Affability is not just about openness to people but in doing God's will and in caring for the earth which can be done both individually, as a domestic church, and together in unison with the entire Church and the world.

As families pray together, care for one another, and foster kindness and love in the smaller unit of the family itself, the mission is established. When this occurs, families can put prayer into action which is a major part of becoming disciples of Christ and in fulfilling the Church's goal of true evangelization to those who have been cast aside and forgotten. Every person makes a difference through prayer, compassion, and mercy. This is not a one-time effort for anyone. It is something that is accomplished in daily living and in being ministers of reconciliation and love. Pope Francis states:

> Saint Therese of Lisieux invites us to practice the little way of love, not to miss out on a kind word, a smile, a gesture which

sows peace and friendship. An integral ecology is also made up of simple daily gestures which break with the logic of violence, exploitation, and selfishness. In the end, a world of exacerbated consumption is at the same time a world which mistreats life in all forms.[21]

It is interesting to note that the openness of spirit, which includes both kind actions toward people is important to combating our world of consumption which Pope Francis mentions in the above quote related to St. Therese of Lisieux. The "little way of love" is an avenue of self-giving and of deep awareness of our surroundings. Selfishness is at the heart of why there is a disconnect both in the hearts of people within human relationships and the reason there is discord throughout the world starting with a spirit of over-consumption. Care for all of God's creation and an attitude of graciousness and of openness is a step in the proper direction in making the world a truly better place. In understanding holistically Pope Francis' thinking on this topic of self-gift and care for everyone and everything, we can begin to go forward in living our faith in deeper ways which are not superficial. His call to all of us to begin with prayer, to foster good relationships with others, and in caring for the environment and the world is how individuals and families can live and spread the Gospel of Christ.

---

[21] Ibid., p. 148.

Openness of Spirit and Friendliness

The life of St. Therese of Lisieux is a prime example in creating a living and breathing faith which is alive and well. Pope Francis states, "Love overflowing with small gestures of mutual care, is also civic and political, and it makes itself felt in every action that seeks to build a better world."[22] It is critical that we take these words of advice seriously when it comes to implementing the virtue of affability which is that positive openness of spirit that every child of God deserves. As we put aside sinful tendencies, we open ourselves up to the goodness of God. In doing so, we begin to live our personal mission of virtue in creating a more compassionate world based on the teachings of Christ and in living the overall mission of the Catholic Church. This is affability in action in striving for holiness of life as a family and as an individual.

---

[22] Ibid., p. 148.

Chapter Ten

Faith Interweaved
through Daily Action and Sincere Charity

I. Outreach to the Marginalized

In the Church's mission to reach the abandoned and marginalized of the world, it is imperative we do something active in accordance with this call to become missionary disciples. It takes a daily commitment to Christ and his teachings to exercise sincere charity in this work. Outreach to the marginalized is optimal when members of the Church understand the significance of a friendly spirit and an attitude of graciousness toward those who feel lost and without hope. Pope Francis states, "The joy of the Gospel fills the hearts and lives of all who encounter Jesus"[1]. When people on the fringes meet Christ's followers, those who have a desire to live the Gospel message have an opportunity to be evangelized through love commonly shared. In this process, Jesus is present. This is love in action as the faithful make outreach to the marginalized. Steps can be taken to seek out the lost, accompany and guide them on their journey back to Jesus.

---

[1] *Evangelii Gaudium*, p. 1.

Finding the Marginalized

Discovering lost and forgotten people in our own lives is something which takes time and skill. This book has discussed the fact that those who feel alienated from others and the Church are often those people who go unnoticed within families, workplaces, neighborhoods, parish communities, and other places. The one commonality they often share is the feeling of having lost hope in God and in the love of those around them. When this occurs, despair can set in, resulting in some people losing all sense of community. Some may even fall into poverty and become completely isolated from society. It is our mission as Catholics to recognize the disenfranchised in our midst and to help them to feel supported and guided by the love of God.

The experience of feeling a sense of isolation and sadness by the rejected is something that continues to happen within the domestic church and the world. One solution according to Pope Francis is for the faithful to become missionary disciples for Christ. Pope Francis writes:

> There are those whose lives seem like Lent without Easter. I realize of course that joy is not expressed the same way at all times in life, especially at moments of great difficulty. Joy adapts and changes, but it always endures, even as a flicker of light born of our personal certainty, that when everything is said and done, we are infinitely loved. I understand the grief of people who have to endure great suffering, yet slowly but

surely, we all have to let the joy of faith slowly revive as a quiet yet firm trust, even amid great distress.[2]

Although each of us may undergo tribulations of life and we ourselves may become rejected by others, it is important to recognize the abiding joy of the Lord. In returning to Jesus, just as the prodigal son[3] went back to his Father, we, as faithful Catholics, can find true happiness, which is joy itself. In our efforts toward looking for and ministering to those who are on the fringes, we are encouraged to stay immersed in prayer and the love of God. In doing so, we, as members of the Church, are given the grace and the strength to do the missionary work of ministering to those who feel unloved and unsupported.

Finding those who feel abandoned also requires us to go outside of comfort zones in terms of evangelization. For those who are extroverted, this may result in finding ways to talk less and listen more. Those who are more inward or less engaging, may learn to become more affable toward others and to make new friends. There are various people who fall in the middle of the spectrum of personalities and are neither outgoing nor shy. For people who are even-tempered or varied in response to others, a good inventory of self through prayer and discernment will enable them to find a good balance in finding avenues to make outreach to the marginalized. The Holy Spirit can guide the faithful to find ways to be more aware of surroundings and to befriend the friendless within communities.

---

[2] Ibid., p. 3-4.
[3] Luke 15:11-32, NOAB.

Accompanying Those Who are Abandoned by Others

Accompaniment is spiritually supporting others, especially those who have gone through trials and challenges; and it encompasses deep care, compassion, and the desire to help someone in need. In essence, in accompanying another, members of the Church walk alongside those who are on the fringes, especially during challenging times. Other words for "accompany" are in standing by someone and in walking alongside them through tough circumstances. Those who have suffered a loss such as a divorce or separation, the death of a loved one, unexpected unemployment, relationship issues or additional factors may experience insecurity and despair. Accompaniment allows those who struggle to feel the compassion of the Christ during times of crisis. Even after an adversity has passed, as disciples, the faithful can continue with loving actions toward those who need support. Instead of walking away after a trial, we can assure people of our ongoing friendship and love. This is what it means to offer real, Christian friendship to others in the commitment made to stay the course through life's challenges.

In the process of accompaniment, there may be times when healthy boundaries must be put into place in this evangelizing work for the Church. Placing proper parameters in these relationships aids in determining the time needed to help others. The reason for this is to distinguish the amount of time and help available. Those who do not have an adequate amount of support from family or others may tend to become "needy," and this may affect our own personal relationships in the future. By deciphering what types of boundaries need to be placed, Christ's followers can learn healthy methods of communication which are much better overall. Those on the outskirts of society often need to be shown what healthy relationships look like, and with the Holy Spirit, the faithful can model this for their betterment in the future.

In God's time, we learn best how to communicate and how to love others in a language they understand. It takes practice, and it takes a great deal of love and compassion. Pope Francis states, "We must know how to meet each other. We must build, create, construct a culture of encounter."[4] This culture of encounter includes accompaniment and guidance. As we call on the spirit of the Lord to guide us, we learn how to direct others in the path of God's love and encounter for the future. Additionally, at the heart of it all is acting in God's grace in order to accomplish the work of exercising affability to the fullest. Affability must always be honed as a virtue and not necessarily as a "personality trait."

Guidance for the Marginalized

In recent years, the Church has talked about accompanying the marginalized, but there has been less discussion on guidance for them. In efforts to journey with them, we are encouraged to help guide them in the right direction of their faith and/or other areas of life. This kind of guidance comes through the Holy Spirit which enables Christ's followers to give proper advice in moving forward in their lives. The direction given could be in directing them to seek the counsel of a priest for Confession, or returning to Mass, or

---

[4] United States Conference of Catholic Bishops. *Pope Francis and the Family*. Libreria Editrice Vaticana. 2014, p. 25.

instructing them with catechesis, especially those who have never had any type of religious affiliation. One may also consult with a priest, deacon, religious, or lay person in finding the right type of suggestions needed for one who is away from the faith or who has never been to church or one who is unfamiliar with the Catholic Church.

Efforts to guide the forsaken to the next steps of ongoing healing are encouraged to be kind, affable, and caring. Interactions should be free of prejudice and of anything that separates. Pope Francis writes:

> This open spirit, without prejudice, I would describe as 'social humility,' which is what favors dialogue. Only in this way can understanding grow between cultures and religions, mutual esteem without needless preconceptions in a climate that is respectful of the rights of everyone. Today, either we take the risk of dialogue, we risk the culture of encounter, or we fail.[5]

The Pope's message above is clear that dialogue is the answer we search for. This dialogue is open to the pains and sufferings of others in a spirit of accompaniment and guidance through the Holy Spirit. Although there are risks taken when we open ourselves to hearing the stories of those who have been alienated, through God's guidance, we can discern the best and most effective ways to help them to be healed of past wounds in order to move forward in faith in the present and in the future. We can also educate them on vocation,

---

[5] Ibid., p. 24-25.

service, and in living the baptismal call[6] as followers of Christ. This kind of "guidance" is what gives hope for the future as they discover that no matter what has happened in the past, and despite age, status, or education, God has a great plan for their lives. As faithful Catholics, we can introduce them to a new way of living which is in being an active disciple for Christ and for the Church. One goal is to guide them in the direction to be able to make healthy decisions in the future. We, the faithful, can lead them on the right path so they are not left alone and unable to find their way.

The combination of finding those people who are without support, accompanying them, and offering guidance is an antidote for despair in this world for those who have been cast aside. As we implement the teachings of Pope Francis and of the Catholic Church, we help to continue the mission of compassion and mercy which is needed both now and in the future. This is ongoing work that will continue since we live in a world of sin which will always have its challenges. Even with its pitfalls and times of discouragement, the mission is filled with hope and the love of God which will be a guide. Lead by hope and charity in this process, we can offer direction which is needed in fulfilling God's personal mission for our lives. This is a cause for joy and encouragement.

II. Compassion as Primary in Making Outreach

As the faithful, we demonstrate compassion in going beyond ourselves in unison with those who have gone through times of crisis and adversity. Offering compassion is the initial key to making

---

[6] CCC, 1257.

effective outreach to the marginalized. As outlined in part one of Chapter Ten of this book, to reach those who are rejected and ostracized, we must recognize and accompany them and offer God's guidance. These are ways to accomplish the will of God in preaching the Gospel to the ends of the earth[7] for Christ's sake. Compassion is the nucleus of efforts in helping the marginalized. In understanding this concept more fully, it entails opening wider the doors to those who have left the Catholic Church and those with no religious affiliation at all. This happens when the Church makes a conscious effort to be *active* missionary disciples. There are three suggested ways to practice and develop deeper compassion. These methods are contemplative prayer, a deeper love of God and his will, and in practicing compassion each day.

Contemplative Prayer

Contemplative prayer[8] is the spiritual practice of using our hearts, minds, and thoughts to recognize God's presence and to continue gazing toward him. It is taking the time to listen to God in the stillness of our hearts with hopes of growing closer to him and in doing his will. Contemplative prayer can be exercised in prayerful adoration before the Blessed Sacrament, inside a Church, at home, and in all places where we pray. Location is not so important as the desire to be closer to the heart of God in this prayer. It is the opportunity to "be with God" in the silence of one's hearts in all places. In contemplative prayer, there is a quieting of the heart and mind in

---

[7] Mark 15:15: NOAB.
[8] CCC, 2715.

order to silently listen to the voice of God. It is this spiritual place one can know God's heart in a deeper way and to do as he commands, especially in the important work of evangelization to the marginalized.

In spending time with God, there is a greater awareness of one's surroundings. This helps us, as faithful Catholics, to develop an affable spirit. It occurs in opening our spirits to the ways in which God presents opportunities to serve. The Holy Spirit is a guide in these interactions. Compassion begins to permeate daily existence, and it becomes noticeable to others. In practicing to become a friendlier person, compassion becomes a way of life. Contemplative prayer based on the love of Christ and his teachings, opens hearts and minds to spreading the Gospel in a greater capacity.

Developing a Deeper Love of God Daily

In prayer and awareness, as members of the Church, we begin to love God more. It is the first commandment of the faith that we, as Pope Francis reiterates from the teachings of the faith, can "love God with all of our hearts, mind, and soul, and in loving others as much as we love ourselves"[9]. The awareness of God in our lives experienced through deeper commitment to him and others begins to grow and it fosters growth. Personal relationship with the Lord deepens in love him, and this extends outward to all in the experience of community. A deeper love of God produces joy which is noticeable to others. It is an authentic joy that people are drawn to. This joy is palatable and attractive as it is not dependent on circumstances. The joy of the Lord

---

[9] CCC, 2196.

can be seen and felt even amidst the trials and challenges of life. Pope Frances writes:

> And so, let us ask ourselves: How is it possible to live joy which comes from faith, in the family, today? But I ask you also: It is possible to live this joy, or is it not possible? A saying of Jesus in the Gospel of Matthew speaks to us, 'Come to me, all who labor and are heavy laden, and I will give you rest. (Matthew 11:28).[10]

Pope Francis asks the question if it is possible for this type of joy to come forth from the family today. The answer of course is, yes, it is possible. The way that it becomes "real" is through reflective prayer and in walking with Jesus daily. He offers rest to the weary through his presence. This type of trust in God through prayer enables each person to develop a deeper relationship with Christ. In full trust in the Lord, we, the faithful, are better able to rest with him in all life's outcomes. It is one of the most integral aspects of growth to do the missionary work of the Church which is outreach to those who have been rejected.

Fostering deeper love of God comes through openness in moment-by-moment interactions. Whether a family member, a friend, a neighbor, or a stranger, the faithful can show God's love through affability and relationship with Jesus. Giving witness to the faith, is another way to demonstrate God's unending love. Openness of heart demonstrated through actions is transmitted to those who need to

---

[10] Pope Francis, *Address to the Pilgrimage of Families*. October 26, 2013. www.vatican.va.

know this love. Members of the Church can become instruments of grace, and in deep relationship with Jesus, as an avenue of sharing the good news.

Ways to Make Compassion Real for Others

There are a variety of ways to compassion daily. This comes through prayer and commitment in helping to create a kinder world. Some may ask, what are practical ways to practice compassion? In committing oneself to prayer and closer relationship with the Lord, there are simple ways to accomplish this. Examples are becoming a better listener, doing kind deeds, avoiding selfishness, and exercising affability.

Becoming a Better Listener

This book has discussed the value of becoming a better listener and the ways to develop patterns of "active listening" without passing judgement. It is a gift of grace given to another person in taking the time to sincerely listen and affirm their feelings, especially those who have been marginalized. By offering prayer, care, and attentiveness, we offer *love*. Becoming more active in listening is a skill which must be practiced and perfected over time. The practice of attentive listening is an art which offers the opportunity for healing and charity toward another person. There is excellent value in pausing to let another finish a sentence or a story. Asking pertinent questions where applicable and repeating a story back will demonstrate to the other person that they are heard and respected. This encourages them to continue speaking and gives them a safe place to share feelings and speak of past hurts and injuries which may not be healed. With the help of the Holy Spirit, the faithful can offer prayer or guided advice which may be helpful to them.

Practicing Compassion Daily

The art of living a life of compassion does not always come naturally to everyone. It is to be fostered and practiced. Practicing daily compassion can be done in simple ways such as saying, "thank you," "please," or "I am sorry." In family life, these words are *golden*, and they can help repair hurts which could otherwise explode into arguments or disagreements. Practicing compassion may also include doing a kind deed for a family member or friend. These simple acts of kindness are restorative to relationships and to the Body of Christ, the Church. Forgiveness and reconciliation are the greatest ways to exercise compassion.

Oftentimes when unforgiveness becomes a burden, we lose enthusiasm for the mission of the Church. This may happen in allowing someone or a situation from the present or the past to hold us back from experiencing the full joy of the Gospel. It is not God's will that his people become laden with anxiety over past sins and mistakes. The gift of the Sacrament of Confession enable a fresh start. Once our relationship with the Lord is restored, there is an experience of enthusiasm in the mission of compassion. Pope Francis writes:

> Sometimes we lose our enthusiasm for mission because we forget that the Gospel responds to our deepest needs, since

we were created for what the Gospel offers us; friendship with Jesus and love of our brothers and sisters. If we succeed in expressing adequately and with beauty the essential content of the Gospel, surely this message will speak to the deepest yearnings of people's hearts.[11]

Through the forgiveness of sins, we are released from guilt and shame. Through this forgiveness, we become freer to spread the Gospel in living out our personal mission given by God. The element of forgiveness and ongoing mission fosters joy and fulfillment. It enables us, as members of the Church, to connect on a deeper level with those who have suffered and those who need to experience love God's unconditional love. In exercising ongoing compassion through practicing charity and care, prayerful outreach is offered as a prime way to respond to God's call for our own lives in spreading the Gospel. Through contemplative prayer and fostering a deeper love of the Lord, we, as missionary disciples, come closer to learning how to demonstrate affability which is integral in evangelization. Friendliness is *key* in helping others experience God's mercy through our actions.

---

[11] Pope Francis, *A Year of Mercy with Pope Francis. Daily Reflections.* Our Sunday Visitor. Huntington, Indiana. 2014, p. 130. (This meditation is from *Evangelii Gaudium*.)

III. Friendliness and Charity: God's Call to the Faithful

Friendliness is a valued virtue of the faith, and it falls under justice[12]. As discussed earlier in this book, St. Thomas Aquinas included affability in the context of justice in the *Summa Theologica*. The justice due to others shows respect as a gift from God. Friendly demeanor and charity coincide when the faithful perform kind actions toward those who are away from the Church and those who do not practice the faith. In exercising the virtue of affability, the faithful offer themselves to "be Jesus" to others in all encounters of life. Three ways to offer friendliness in a far-reaching way are: cheerful composure, positive dialogue, and the willingness to befriend those who think differently.

Cheerful Composure

Offering a smile and kindness to others is an effortless way to show God's love. This action is easy and does not even require dialogue. Eye contact and recognizing another's dignity is uplifting, and it demonstrates to another person their value. A cheerful composure which is filled with the love of God shows that they matter not only to the Lord, but to us, as well. Holy Scripture states: "A cheerful heart is good medicine, but a crushed spirit dries up the bones"[13]. This verse from Proverbs offers wisdom for the ages. We, as missionary disciples, can offer a smile to others for no reason other than the joy of the Lord which offers hope. This demeanor is indicative of the

---

[12] CCC, 1807.
[13] Proverbs: 17:22, NOAB.

importance of affability and its relevance in the evangelization efforts of the Church.

Positive Dialogue

Many times, within families and in the political and church arenas, there is a great deal of negativity in daily discussions occurring at home, in the workplace, on social media, and in a variety of other places. Positive dialogue does not mean that one should only speak about "the weather" or neutral topics, it encompasses accepting people where they are on the spiritual journey. Conversing with those who are the opposite side of the spectrum in terms of behavior, tastes, religion, or politics may have a substantial impact on another person if our response to them is charitable. Although there may not be an agreement with one who has a vastly different worldview, we, as members of the Church, can offer respect and kindness. Positive dialogue requires an openness even if both sides are firm on their respective opinions. Doors to demonstrating Christ's love can remain open and available to a person who does not share common values. This also encompasses politeness in response to an opposing view.

Befriending Those Who Think/Act Differently

Sometimes it is easier to make friends with those who are like-minded since normally there is less to be concerned with in terms of differences. In befriending those who may be of a different religion, race, creed, or socio-economic background, we imitate Christ as he made it a point to dialogue with those who were marginalized and on the fringes of society. In communicating with people who do not see or experience life as we do, it is a positive step in terms of evangelization. Oftentimes, people do not open themselves up to those who are on the opposite side of the political arena or those who celebrate another faith to avoid conflict. In making outreach, the faithful are called to minister to the human family, not just to "faithful Catholics" who attend weekly or daily Mass. We follow the pathway of Christ in partaking in evangelizing efforts with this same mentality in our hearts. Pope Francis offers guidance in finding fulfilment:

> The Gospel offers us the chance to live life on a higher plane, but with no less intensity. Life grows by being given away, and it weakens in isolation and comfort. Indeed, those who enjoy life most are those who leave security on the shore and become excited by the mission of life to others. When the Church summons Christians to take up the task of evangelization, she is simply pointing to the source of authentic personal fulfillment. For 'here we discover a profound law of reality, that is attained matures in the measure that is offered up to order to give life the measure that it is offered up to order to others. This is certainly, what mission means.'[14]

In discovering our mission and in living it daily, the faithful become a part of the evangelization efforts of the Catholic Church

---

[14] Pope Francis, *A Year of Mercy with Pope Francis. Daily Reflections.* Our Sunday Visitor. Huntington, Indiana. 2014, p. 80. (This meditation is from *Evangelii Gaudium.*)

(living out our baptismal identity as priest, prophet, and king.). As we make a concerted effort to develop friendships with those who do not look, act, think as we do, we partake fully in this mission. The Church needs its members to help in efforts to minister and care for the poor through sincere charity. Open-ended conversations and dialogue with others which is both friendly and kind displays the light of Christ to those who are separated from the Church. Being open to others makes a world of difference for the domestic and universal Church. This has a tremendous impact on the entire human family including those who are not Catholic.

Cheerful composure in dealing with others, coupled with positive dialogue, and befriending those who are different offers life-giving pathways in which to become compassionate members, sharing in the mission of the Church. The openness of genuine care is what brings about positive change in evangelizing efforts in brining Christ to the unchurched. The virtue of affability is key in doing the will of God both now and in the future. As the Church moves forward, the spiritual concepts of prayer, communication, and virtue will propel efforts of creating a better world for God's sake. In doing so, the Lord will guide, protect, and comfort members of the Church to educate the world on the virtue of affability and its importance in all of the Church's evangelizing efforts.

IV. A Message for the Academic World

Chapter Eight of this book alludes to the fact that religious scholars and those involved in academia have a responsibility to create bodies of work which are not only theologically correct but also understood by average people. Theological findings which are hard for people to grasp and not tangible to their lives are *less applicable*. Church teachings which are not only relevant but easier for those with average intellectual levels to understand help to spread the Gospel in an excellent way. Part of the purpose of this book is to do just that. As mentioned in Chapter Eight, Pope Francis has stated:

> Spirit-filled evangelizers are evangelizers to pray and work. Mystical notions without a solid social missionary outreach are of no help to evangelization, nor are books or social or pastoral practices which lack spirituality which can change hearts.[15]

Book or pastoral practices that "lack spirituality" which can in turn change hearts are an extremely important aspect of evangelization. In an attempt to research properly and create such a piece, monumental efforts were made to refine this project over time in order for this work to be accomplished. These efforts have incorporated within this book: the Church fathers, extended biblical research, added saints, and other needed additions to bring about further enhancements. This was done to center the book in both an academic and pastoral sense. In response to the comment above from Pope Francis, my desire in creating this book on affability and its relevance in modern evangelization is to help to "change hearts" in terms of those who are away from the faith or who feel mediocre about evangelization. In agreement with Pope Francis, my hope is that this piece

---

[15] *Evangelii Gaudium*, p. 126.

Chapter Ten: Faith Interweaved through Action and Charity

will educate an enable all members of the Church to take seriously the role of friendly and open dialogue and to be more aware of how we interact with others in all aspects of daily living. Doing so enables the Church to become more action-oriented to the needs of its people all while staying in line closely with its teachings and doctrines.

In addition to Pope Francis, St. John Paul II has also made statements regarding the importance of the theological world and the responsibility of academia to uphold their responsibility in holding fast to the deposit of faith.

> Theology has always had and continues to have great importance in the Church, the People of God, to be able to share creatively and fruitfully in Christ's mission as prophet. Therefore, when theologians, as servants of divine truth, dedicate their studies and labours to ever deeper understanding of that truth, they can never lose sight of the meaning of their service in the Church, which is enshrined in the concept *intellectus fidei*.[16][17]

The above statement is from John Paul II from his first encyclical *Redemptor Hominis* written in 1979. He is communicating that theologians have a great responsibility and labor of love to be a servant of divine truth. John Paul used the words "creatively and fruitfully" to describe how this service to the Church should be accomplished. Using these words indicates that in developing their creativity, the

---

[16] Pope John Paul II, *Redemptor Hominis. Encyclical Letter.* Kindle Edition. Liberia Editrice Vaticana. March 4, 1979, Location 942-953.

[17] *Intellectus fidei* (Latin) is translated to "the understanding of faith."

fruits of their labor should also accomplish great works for the good of the people of the Church. Although worded differently than Pope Francis, the idea of serving the Church and being high yielding is along the same lines. The theological world has a tremendous responsibility to not only produce truthful and accurate work but also bodies of knowledge that reach the people and make a great difference in their lives of faith. Without this piece, *academia will fail.* In the time period following Vatican II, the so-called "pendulum" may have swung in the direction toward affability without enough proper catechesis to guide members of the Church. The pendulum is now in its proper place, firmly in the middle, backed by years of solid theology in combination with the call to "go and make disciples of all nations"[18] by evangelizing the whole world.

God is Love

To sum up this brief chapter to the academic world, we must never lose sight that *God is love*. In remembering this fact, everything else we do as theologians and people of faith makes more sense. We do not have to search everywhere to understand this concept as it is the most basic theological truth. As Holy Scripture states, "So we know and believe the love God has for us. God is love, and he who abides in love abides in God and God abides in him."[19] Understanding and accepting God as love is *not* incorrect theology with all the complexities of our faith. Holy Scripture states:

---

[18] Matthew 28:19, NOAB.
[19] I John 4:16, NOAB.

Chapter Ten: Faith Interweaved through Action and Charity

> There is no fear in in love, but perfect love casts out fear; for fear has to do with punishment, and whoever fears has not reached perfection in love. We love because he first loved us. Those who say, "I love God," and hate their brothers and sisters are liars; for those who do not love a brother or sister whom they have seen, cannot love God whom they have not seen. The commandment we have from him is this: those who love God must love their brothers and sisters." (I John 4:18-21).[20]

An examination of the above leads to deeper understanding of Christ's teaching on love of God and neighbor. Jesus states there is "no fear in love." As Catholic Christians, the call to love is not something to be afraid of. In addition, it is a command of Christ that *we love everyone*. In doing so we are also loving God since the two Great Commandments are one. Love of God and neighbor are one commandment, and in obeying this command, we are loving him all the more.

In order to accomplish the act of loving both God and others in our lives, we must live always in the Holy Spirit. Hans Urs Von Balthasar states:

> The action of the Holy Spirit in theology sets the final seal on the character of supernatural holiness that befits in virtue its

---

[20] I John 4:18-21, NOAB.

source, its object and its end, which is why the older theologians called theology, in an absolute sense, 'doctrina sacra'.[21]

Lastly, in contemplating the love of God and others, we can also reflect on the teachings discussed throughout this book and the role of affability in modern evangelization. In taking seriously the mission of mercy in the Church in the twenty-first century, we can ponder lessons from Church history, the saints, from Pope Francis and from popes of the modern age. Now is the time to materialize, teach, and spread the word on the momentousness of affability and how to utilize it in all evangelizing efforts. It *can and will* bring the Church to the next level of spreading the Gospel to the ends of the earth.

---

[21] Hans Urs Von Balthasar, *Explorations in Theology. The Word Made Flesh Part I.* (San Fransisco: Ignatius Press, 1989), p. 203.

Conclusion

The topic of this book has focused on the virtue of affability, which is friendliness and openness toward others both in one-to-one interactions and the Church as a whole. The question put forth is, "Does the virtue of affability have significance and overall relevance in the mission of evangelization of the Church?" In other words, is this virtue one to be examined, exercised, and taught to members of the universal Church as one that is not only of prime importance, but also one to be elevated as one of the *primary methods* of reaching further than we ever have before to minister to the marginalized? The term "marginalized" refers not only to the homeless, the poor, and the outcasts of society, it expands to include those within our family units, neighbors, friends, and those who may not appear to be categorized as "rejected" or without support. The book emphasizes the fact that marginalized people are all around us, and the Church needs to do greater outreach in finding those who feel outside the boundaries of our faith communities and have decided to walk away for their own reasons. The primary focus of the book is to gather the facts related to Church teachings and specific areas of human development and psychology to suggest that there is a correlation between affability and healing of the human spirit. This "healing" leads to a relationship with God when those who involved in the evangelizing efforts of the Church understand fully the relevance of friendliness in helping to creating a world of kindness, hope, and most of all love. Primary sources of this book have explored the writings of Pope Francis, including: *Amoris Laetitia*, *Evangelii Gaudium*, *Laudato Si*, and *Fratelli Tutti*. In addition, the Church fathers, modern popes, and the lives of the saints have been studied with a special emphasis on St. Thomas Aquinas. Holy Scripture, human development, psychology, and sociological factors, all of which impact how the Church continues the mission of evangelization, are included in this writing.

In tying all the relevant resources together throughout this book, with primary emphasis on the writings of Pope Francis, it is noted that there is a major gap in the current work of evangelization related to this topic. The idea that there is a of lack sufficient effort within the Church in teaching the relevance of the virtue of affability is discussed in the introduction of this book. This is seemingly evident in the fact that some practicing Catholics do not know enough about the value of this virtue and ways to practice it in daily life. When affability and openness of spirit in dialogue is not taught and included in the catechesis of both new and existing members of the Church, sadly there will be a failure to progress in the missionary efforts to spread the Gospel to the ends of the earth. This book emphasizes that charity must include kind and friendly dialogue with *not just some* but all people we encounter regardless of age, sex, socio-economic background, religion, creed, or any other factors. Openness of heart materializes to something great when the entire Church comes together to give the gift of a smile, to offer care, and genuine compassion. In addition, this book also discusses that the "truths of our faith" should include spiritual formation on the importance of affability as taught by the Church. Even those who are not naturally friendly can be taught to exercise greater care and compassion, which encompasses friendly interactions and a kind demeanor toward everyone. Once this virtue is further understood and

Conclusion

put into practice both inside and outside the Church, evangelization efforts will prosper to the next level in a profound way having a monumental ripple effect on the Church and the entire world.

This book began with the topic of the relevance of positive demeanor and its effects in the work of evangelization. The family is the domestic church, and every individual and family are extremely important to the God, and subsequently, should also be to the Church itself. In this recognition, we understand in a greater capacity that there is an art in accompaniment that must be exercised and prioritized to every member of the Catholic Church. "Accompaniment" is walking alongside a person or family who may be experiencing crises and trauma. In taking time to listen, care, and respond, we are partaking in the evangelizing efforts of the universal Church[1]. Incorporating the virtue of friendliness in conversations and interactions with those who have been cast aside assists in carrying out the commands of Christ as given in the Beatitudes and in chapter twenty-five in Matthew's Gospel where Christ separates the sheep from the goats[2] symbolizing those who cared and ministered to the poor and those who did not. The "poor" consists of not only those who are materially poor but also the poor in spirit and those who have lost faith or never had it to begin with. The art of accompaniment reflects an understanding of the Gospel considering Christ's commands to love and care for the rejected. This is a key component of our universal call to holiness and in loving our neighbor as much as we love ourselves.

---

[1] CCC, 811.
[2] Matthew 25:32, NOAB.

This book also explored the Church's teaching on love of God and neighbor. Both in Holy Scripture and in the Catechism of the Catholic Church, there is much emphasis on love of God and of our brothers and sisters.

In response to the question about the first of the commandments, Jesus says, 'The first is, Hear, O, Israel: The Lord our God, the Lord is one, and you shall love the Lord your God with all your heart, and with all your soul, and with all your mind, and with all your strength.' The second is this, 'You shall love your neighbor as yourself.' There is no other commandment greater than these." The apostle St. Paul reminds us this: 'He who loves his neighbor has fulfilled the law. The commandments, 'You shall not commit adultery, You shall not kill, You shall not steal, You shall not covet,' and any other commandments, are summed up in this sentence, 'You shall love your neighbor as yourself.' Love does no wrong to a neighbor, therefore love is the fulfillment of the law.[3]

Love being the fulfillment of the law is an inclusion of the way we not only how we make outreach to others but also how we exercise affability in our lives as a valuable virtue. In doing so we carry out Christ's mission on earth as we focus on the importance of accompaniment with true charity and friendship with those who need it most. We do not act out of obligation only, but rather because it is an honor to serve God and others. With this intention deep in our hearts, the good that we do to befriend the lost and forgotten comes

---

[3] CCC, 2196.

across with authenticity. When good deeds are done only for the sake of pursuing a checklist mentality, the recipients of charitable efforts are keenly aware of the falsehood of heart when it is not displayed as openness and friendliness to them.

In addition to the prominence of Church teachings and mission, this book integrates how affability has affected ecclesiology and soteriology. Ecclesiology is the study of the Church itself, and its leadership. The book points to the Holy Eucharist[4] as the source and summit of our faith and how we gain strength as a people to carry out the mission of the Church. The Eucharist is discussed in Chapter Two of this book with theology from Pope Benedict XVI.

Soteriology has to do with the doctrine of salvation of our Catholic faith. In terms of ecclesiology, since affability is a Christian virtue all interactions with the Church and its people have a lasting impact on what is known as ecclesiastical works and studies. Soteriology asks the question, "What does the Church teach about salvation and the virtue of affability?" The answer is given in this book as we commit ourselves to live as sacramental people who love God above all, and our neighbor as ourselves. This book highlights the life of our Blessed Mother Mary as the Mother of God who gave her fiat and changed history through her "yes" in doing God's will. Mary is a model for every person as the greatest saint of the Catholic Church, and the instrument God chose to institute our salvation. Ecclesiology and soteriology come together to recognize these truths of the faith. We are Eucharistic people, and we learn from our Mother Mary how to love God above all. Mary exercised an openness of heart and spirit in her relationship with God which directed her to say yes to

---

[4] Ibid., 1384.

becoming the Mother of our Savior. This openness is another way of expressing an affable spirit, which of course, is the main thesis of this book. The areas of study of ecclesiology and soteriology suggest that within the realm of the virtue of justice is the affability, an openness of demeanor, thought, and action enables God to work in our hearts. Ecclesiology and soteriology have benefited from the valuable teachings on affability which are found in the doctrines of the faith and in all its salvific efforts.

The desire to love is expressed both on an individual level, in relationship with God, and in a communal way. In every human heart there is a thirst to know God and to be with him. This desire of heart to express love comes to fulfillment first within the domestic church and extending out into community and to the entire world. This book sheds light on the fact that the desire to love would benefit by practicing the virtue of friendliness in daily life. In doing so, the fulfillment of communion with God becomes a reality. Perfecting the virtue of affability takes time as each person has a different personality and unique way of expressing themselves to the world. The key to knowing oneself and becoming more virtuous is through prayer, living a sacramental life, and in adherence to the will of God. In doing so, the faithful open up to the movement of the Holy Spirit and the desire to live in peace. Holy Scripture and the life of Christ points to this fulfillment, as well.

The biblical references discussed in this book point to varied areas of scripture where affability has been prevalent in the lives of the Lord's followers. From Genesis through Revelation, the virtue of affability has played an integral part in salvation history since the beginning. In this book there are examples of how biblical characters of both the Old and New Testaments demonstrated affability through prayer and obedience to God. Affability is also evident in the relationships with others[5] as there are valuable lessons on human relationships in scripture which lend itself well to understanding how and why affability was and continues to be influential in our openness with God and others. The life of Christ Jesus clearly offers the most prevalent example in the New Testament of affability in action especially in his relationship with the marginalized. Repeatedly, Jesus points to caring for the least among us in offering our very selves to them as a gift. This task cannot be accomplished without getting to know the poor and in making outreach to them. The example of Christ through the Paschal Mystery[6] of our faith points to the invitation Jesus gives to each one of his followers. This mystery ties into the call to be missionary disciples. We are all called to mission, and this work includes being open of heart to the needy and to those who do not have the love and the support they deserve. As we say "yes" to Christ in becoming involved in this ministry, we are also responding to the call to be more affable and open to new people encountered each day and to those for whom we are already acquainted. Friendliness of spirit and of heart is necessary in the evangelizing work of the Church, which is evident in Holy Scripture, and through the life of Christ. It is a call to conversion of heart for the sake of the marginalized of the world.

---

[5] "Relationships with others" refers to *all* human relationships encountered in daily living. It includes family, community members and those we do not know personally.

[6] CCC, 571.

In Chapter Four, Part One of this book, we explore human development and psychology through the lens of faith. The Church cannot ignore the importance of understanding the human person on a deeper and more holistic level considering the varied facets of personalities, experiences, cultures, and all areas which encompass who we are as human beings. In infanthood, one of the first positive signs given to parents and caretakers is when a baby smiles, laughs, and interacts. Although seemingly small, this aspect of displayed happiness points to affability as a valued piece of the larger picture of human development. As life progresses, happiness has continual value. The human smile shines God's love and life into its people. This book speaks of the neuroscience of emotion[7] since studies point to the essentiality of happiness especially to those who have undergone trauma. Understanding, exercising, and bringing happiness to others aids in giving hope and healing to those who suffer. Active listening and accompanying those who lack support are ways that the faithful can practice this type of charity in recognizing their pain and in being there during times of trauma and adversity. A great saintly example of imitation of Christ is St. Teresa of Calcutta who lived a life of poverty in giving of herself to the poorest of the poor. This is discussed in Chapter Four, Part Three of this book. Her life of prayer and of openness to the destitute and those without hope is a beautiful example of faith in action and affability, which is openness of spirit toward others. Additional saints of our faith are included in this book on topics related to this valuable virtue.

---

[7] Diana Fosha, Daniel J. Siegel, Marion F. Solomon, *The Healing Power of Emotion. Affective Neuroscience, Development and Clinical Practice* (New York: W.W. Norton and Company, 2009).

Conclusion

Living a virtuous life is the goal as we strive to know, love, and serve Jesus each day and in finding those people whom God calls us to serve and care for. This mission is not only important, but also integral in *driving forward* the Church's evangelizing efforts. In doing so, the Church imitates Christ in day-to-day missional efforts. The virtuous life includes adherence to God's will, love of the sacramental life, and in becoming active disciples. Since we live in a world of sin, there will be continual challenges in executing this mission. The virtues of the faith as taught in the Catechism of the Catholic Church help to guide us along the proper path. The Catechism states:

> Human virtues are firm attitudes, stable dispositions, habitual perfections of intellect and will that govern our actions, order our passions, and guide our conduct according to reason and faith. They make possible ease, self-mastery, and joy in leading a morally good life. The virtuous man is he who freely practices the good. The moral virtues are acquired by human effort. They are the fruit and seed of morally good acts, they dispose all the powers of the human being for communion with divine love.[8]

These firm dispositions help followers to attain true happiness which is found only in God. The teaching above solidifies the importance of affability which can be taught and perfected over time. Although some people may tend to be either extraverted, introverted or in between, the faithful can learn to practice the virtue of affability

---

[8] CCC, 1803.

through genuine friendliness and openness. It may seem impossible to change one's personality, but through prayer and practice even the most inward or self-aware person can learn skills to become affable and open to the needs of the marginalized. Sincerity is a key factor. If this idea is understood, perfected, and spread, doors will begin to open to those who have left the Church and evangelization will flourish. It will take time, but efforts put forth can make a difference in reaching beyond all barriers.

Bullying is also a topic in this book as it is a dominant area of concern sociologically in the twenty-first century. Discussed in Chapter Five, Part Two of this book, bullying[9] is repeated and aggressive behavior toward a person or a group with the intention of intimidating someone. The acts done may be either verbal or physical, and may include emotional, psychological, or spiritual as discussed in this book. When someone has been bullied, effects may include depression, anxiety, and even suicidal thoughts or actions. Bullying occurs everywhere in society: home, within extended families, schools, workplaces, neighborhoods, and within the confines of the Church. Another effect of bullying is alienation which happens because of negative and/or abusive behavior toward a person or group. Victims become left out of the larger group or community leaving them alone without the support of friends or someone to confide in, resulting in grief which may require professional help from a therapist or doctor. Those affected by bullying may feel victimized and may choose to isolate themselves from others. Additionally, those affected may feel forced to confine themselves from the

---

[9] American Psychological Association. "Bullying." Adapted from APA Dictionary of Psychology, 2023.

presence of their perpetrators. Families who are away from the Church may not consider reaching out a local parish or priest for counsel which can possibly lead a spiritual void. These traumatic experiences cause other life adversities such as relationship issues, substance abuse, and further alienation from society. As a Church, we can make concerted outreach to those who have been marginalized through prayer, care, and in exercising friendliness and compassion to those who are wounded by the hurts of life. Healing takes time, but the effort put forth to pray and accompany another is worth the effort. The magnitude of effects that occur in exercising friendliness and openness is massive in making a difference for others.

The way that we help individuals and families through tragedies such as bullying and traumatic experiences is by striving for holiness ourselves. As we seek to become better people through the gifts of the Holy Spirit and God's grace, we can exercise virtue and joyfulness. This book speaks about the teachings of Pope Francis on holiness of life; which is something to be put into practice every day. Pope Francis reminds us that there is joy in spreading the Gospel to others. Evangelizing does not have to be a "chore;" it is missional work. This work takes patience. It happens when we make it a point to put others first in our daily lives. Pope Francis states:

> Being patient does not mean letter ourselves be constantly mistreated, tolerating physical aggression or allowing other people to use us. We encounter problems whenever we think that relationships or people ought to be perfect, or when we put ourselves at the center and expect things to turn out our way. Then everything makes us impatient, everything makes

us react aggressively. Unless we cultivate patience, we will always find excuses for responding angrily. We will end up incapable of living together, antisocial, unable to control our impulses, and our families will become battlegrounds.[10]

The above writing by Pope Francis in *Amoris Laetitia* draws a picture which explains why patience is one of the most precious virtues. Patience helps us to wait and let the Lord work both within our own hearts and in the hearts of those around us. This virtue helps us to see the anger within ourselves and to take a step back to allow the Holy Spirit to work. In the same way, we must let the Lord work in order to learn to become more affable, especially toward those who have suffered. In doing so, the Holy Spirit will teach the faithful to be more compassionate in a variety of ways. In addition, there must be better understanding of the deep hurts that people have endured.

In Chapter Six, Parts One, Two, and Three of this book, we explored *Summa Theologica*[11] written by St. Thomas Aquinas which explains that the virtue of affability as a justice given to others. Justice, of course, is through due respect and equity. This relates to openness of the heart toward others. St. Thomas refers to affability as a virtue which we can strive for in relation to others in fair treatment of them. St. Thomas Aquinas utilized a method of presenting questions and answers as a way of teaching and catechizing. He included affability in his most well-known writing, the *Summa Theologica*.

---

[10] *Amoris Laetitia*, p. 75.

[11] St. Thomas Aquinas. *Summa Theologica*. Volume II. Christian Classics. Westminster, MD, 1948.

Chapter Seven of this book discusses Pope Francis' teachings on how we can exercise mercy and sensitivity toward others in ministry. Pope Francis' catechesis in *Amoris Laetitia* encompasses teachable topics related to practicing mercy. He says that without patience and charity, we will find it hard to continue the mission of peace within family life. It takes work each day, and this book details the practical methods of missional mercy which can be accomplished and placed into action in Chapter Seven.[12] *Amoris Laetitia* focuses primarily on the domestic church, the family, and ways to minister and support family life, especially to those who have undergone various trials. Pope Francis speaks extensively about the love between husband and wife, and how this love extends to their children, to all family members and friends, and ultimately to the world. He speaks about the virtues in depth, and he reminds his audience that we must take care within families to pray for one another. Pain and challenges will be present, but serving together as a family brings joy.

Chapter Seven, Part Four is devoted to discussing the "Practicality of Mercy"[13]. This is an area of relevance related to affability and how the Church can reach beyond its limits. In learning about the mercy of God, we can begin to exercise greater charity beginning within the family. Pope Francis speaks about the sensitivity we must strive to understand and live out since vast numbers of people are affected by relationship problems, divorce and separation, and traumas. He says the first step in helping them is to take a step back and to open our hearts to their pain to offer direction and help. This cannot be done without instituting mercy and to "be Christ" to others.

---

[12] Ibid.
[13] *Amoris Laetitia*, p. 239.

On-going conversion is a major part of the full dynamic and mission of the work at hand. This type of conversion entails self-inventory. Are we open to helping other people, or are we too occupied to be of any assistance to those who lack support? These are good questions in learning how to navigate to help the marginalized. The baptismal call to holiness impels the love of God fully and other people as gifts. As we do this, we can then help the suffering of the world. We are all part of the body of Christ, and each member has eternal value to God. *Lumen Gentium* speaks of this unity we have as believers:

> As all the members of the human body, though there are many, form one body, so also are the faithful in Christ. Also, in the building up of Christ's Body various members and functions have their part to play. There is only one Spirit who, according to his own richness and the needs of the ministries gives His different gifts for the welfare of the Church. What has a special place among these gifts is the grace of the apostles to whose authority the Spirit Himself subjected even those who were endowed with charisms. Giving the body unity through Himself and through His power and inner joining of the members, this same Spirit produces and urges love among believers, from all this follows that if one member endures anything, all the members co-endure it, and if one member is honored, all the members together rejoice.[14]

---

[14] *LG*, p. 2.

All members of the human family are invited to partake in the mission of mercy. Together, we cry with those who grieve and have gone through trials, and we rejoice with those who have experienced happiness. Affability is the reaction and openness shown to others, and it matters to those who feel neglected. It is also respectful to help other people to endure hardships that occur in life. This respect is a way to foster love and care during a time of sadness and of pain.

Chapter Eight, Section Three of this book is dedicated to young and newly initiated Catholics on conversion of life. Those individuals who become Catholics as young adults or later in adulthood learn that conversion is a calling to be taken seriously. It is one accomplished through prayer and commitment to following the teachings of Christ. In ministering to the young[15], we learn what is meaningful to them and how to speak their language. As evangelizers, the guidance of the Holy Spirit assists the faithful to find creative ways to engage younger people. Although younger people may be tempted by promiscuity and worldly lifestyles, we can "meet them where they are" by recognizing their gifts and talents even amidst the confusion put forth by the culture. Members of the Church can communicate to them their value and gifts and invite them to partake in the mission of the Church. This makes a tremendous difference in their lives of faith. Older people can mentor younger adults on the importance of loving the faith and in living it. The faith is passed on by those who care deeply about its mission. Older Catholic adults are frequently interested in handing on the truths of the faith to the younger generation, and this gives everyone a particular mission. When affability

---

[15] "Young" refers to the age groups of teenage years through young adulthood (late teens through 30's).

is included in the dialogue between the young and the old, the results will be a positive outcome. Healing and reconciliation come about over time to individuals of all ages with the help of God's grace and mercy.

All dialogue is suggested to exhibit an attitude of care, gentleness, and mercy. Gentleness is key since those who feel they have been marginalized may feel a sense of alienation from the Church and its members. Gentleness encompasses the understanding that some people have gone through horrific trials which can cause great challenges in their lives. These adversities can often lead to poor decisions and sinful choices. In understanding these concepts more fully, the faithful can exhibit compassion in hearing their stories of pain. In listening and guiding them, members of the Church may lead them in finding professional help such as counseling or therapy. These steps help to build a support system for those who do not have the proper care from their family, community, or from the Church.

Chapter Nine, Part One of this book is on loving and serving as Catholics. One person's actions have a monumental effect toward others in the evangelizing work of the Church. Partaking in this mission creates a gentler world of mercy. This encompasses discovering our God-given gifts. There may be a tendency to view "gifts and talents" as musical talent, or in being able to create something. It is true that talents may consist of those extra-curricular activities of life. "Talents" are often virtues that we have learned to exercise in caring for those in need, helping the poor, and being a mentor to another person. Virtues are also gifts which can be exercised and perfected. This book offers examples of the lives of several saints in Chapter Nine, Part Two, who have lived lives of heroic virtue. The saints offer us a reason to hope as they made a conscious decision to love the Lord at all costs. In addition, the saints exercised deep love and commitment to the neglected, and this includes the poor in spirit. The love of the saints is an openness of spirit toward people which made a tremendous difference to those without hope. The saints oftentimes gave their lives in martyrdom, as well. Sacrificial love encompasses affability *to an extreme* which suggests the deep importance of this valuable virtue.

The concluding chapter of this book, Chapter Ten, speaks of faith interwoven through daily actions and sincere charity. It also discusses outreach to the marginalized, compassion as a key component, and friendliness and charity as a call to the faithful. All these aspects draw a picture of the virtue of friendliness as integral in the mission of the Church. This understanding begins with an introspective comprehension of Church teachings and of our own personal missions. It entails using our gifts and talents. These aspects help all members of the Church to move forward in this mission of love and care for those who suffer to become more affable.

As this book concludes, the final question is "How do we, as Church, go forward in bringing all of these aspects in unison and putting them to practice?" The answer begins with prayer. In prayer, we communicate with the Lord. Whether prayer is done in communion with others, in adoration before the Blessed Sacrament, or in the depths of one's heart, prayer will guide us in the proper direction in doing God's will. This relationship is *ongoing* and requires attention to be in his presence and in doing his will. God will guide us through every prayer, sacrifice, and all moments of life, especially through frustrations. Prayer life is where the faithful hear his voice and understand his love in living out our vocations and in evangelizing efforts.

One major piece of prayer is in living out the sacramental life of the Church. In committing oneself to going to Confession regularly, and in receiving Jesus in the Eucharist at Mass we encounter the most basic tools of the faith to move forward in love. Reliance on Him who loves us and who created us is the beginning of a closer relationship with the Lord in the sacramental journey. As we develop a closer love of Jesus, we can pray to his Mother Mary as the greatest saint of our faith and of the Church. In praying the "Hail Mary," it enables us to understand the love of our Holy Mother who guides us and points to her son Jesus to find all the answers to life's questions. In our prayer life, we, the faithful, may also find a patron saint to intercede to, along with Mary, to help to live our best for God's sake. The prayers of a particular saint, of our own choosing, may assist us to walk this road ahead. This is the path of the cross in our own lives.

In addition to prayer, this "call to action" in living out our personal missions with God includes going outside of the boundaries of our hearts. We, as Christ's followers, are called to meet others where they are. As we do this, we will encounter people who have been rejected, hurt, and cast aside. These people may be homeless or poor, or they may also be the "poor in spirit." Oftentimes those who lack faith are those we know and interact with daily. Whether the marginalized person is a family member, friend, co-worker, or someone else, the faithful can learn to become more caring and compassionate toward everyone. This is the work of the Church which is in taking responsibility for care of the ostracized of our world. Doing so helps to make a monumental difference in being true missionary disciples.

The ultimate step in making affability real and palatable is in teaching others about this virtue. Unless members of the Church take this calling seriously, it will be challenging for us to make an impact. By praying, in going outside of confines, by teaching others, this mission can be accomplished. We must be witnesses of the mercy of God to others. Pope Francis states:

> In God's great plan, every detail is important, even yours, even my humble little witness, even the hidden witness of those who live their faith with simplicity in everyday family relationships, work relationships, friendships.[16]

The words above from Pope Francis encourage us to see and understand that every detail has meaning, and that small and mundane aspects of daily life have immense importance. Relationships are meaningful to God since human interactions are where the Lord dwells. As we, the faithful, recognize this in both small and greater ways, we can partake to a fuller extent in the mission of the Catholic Church.

Finally, in this mission of love, Pope Francis reminds us that it is a work in progress. As we pray, we keep ourselves open to the needs of others, and in helping to spread love and charity, we actively make the world a better place to live. We may wish to consider, also, the fact that it is not always an easy task, and family life is not perfect. Pope Francis states:

---

[16] United States Conference of Catholic Bishops. *Pope Francis and the Family*. Libreria Editrice Vaticana. 2014, p. 31.

> This never-ending vocation born of the full communion of the Trinity, the profound unity between Christ and his Church, the loving community which is the Holy Family of Nazareth, and the pure fraternity existing among the saints of heaven. Our contemplation of the fulfillment which we have yet to attain also allows us to see in proper perspective the historical journey of our interpersonal relationships a perfection, a purity of intentions and a consistency which we will only encounter in the Kingdom to come.[17]

These words of Pope Francis remind us to pray to the Holy Family and to be in communion with the mission of the family in interpersonal relationships. The Holy Trinity, Father, Son, and Holy Spirit are with us throughout the journey of life, and Pope Francis' mention of the loving community of the Holy Family is that of wisdom. As families commune together, pray, and take on a missional attitude of living, this is where the Holy Spirt dwells in helping to make these ideas come to fruition for the Church and the world.

Everything begins with a personal "yes" to Jesus in the daily walk with him. When we wake in the morning, we give our day to him and begin with a prayer asking for his grace to do his will. We open ourselves to his love, and we dedicate each moment to helping to bring more love and peace into family life and the world. This "yes" mimics the affirmative response that the Mary, the Mother of God gave to the angel Gabriel[18] when she was asked to be the Mother of the Lord. In giving our "yes" to the Lord in all these things, we

---

[17] *Amoris Laetitia*, p. 255.
[18] Luke 1:26-38, NOAB.

Conclusion

include the virtue of affability which is our openness to others. Affability is the friendliness shown to strangers, the kindness displayed to those in need, and the patience exhibited to family members who may frustrate us at times. Affability is a valuable virtue needed by the Church today in excelling forward throughout the twenty-first century and beyond. It will enable the faithful to break the barriers of division and to make greater outreach to the marginalized in ways never done before. In accepting this mission of love and care, let us continue to do the will of God in being kind and affable to everyone we encounter for God's sake. In doing so, in the spirit of Pope Francis, we can move ahead with joy knowing that we have done *all that we could* to propel the mission of the Church to the next level of love and care for the marginalized.

Bibliography

Primary Resources

Aquinas, Thomas. St. Thomas Aquinas *Summa Theologica*. Volume Two. Christian Classics. Westminster, Maryland. 1948.

Boer, Paul A. (Editor). St. Augustine of Hippo. *City of God*. June 24, 2012.

Catechism of the Catholic Church. Second Edition. Liberia Editrice Vaticana. 1994.

Communio International Catholic Review. Vol. XLVII. No. 2. Summer 2020.

Ewing, Addison, A. "Thomas Aquinas Doctor and Saint." The Sewee Review. Vol. 23, No. 4. The John Hopkins University Press. October 1915, pp. 305-408.

Kempis, Thomas. *Imitation of Christ*. Tan Book and Publishers. May 3, 1895.

Nathan, Peter E. Gorman, Jack M. Salkind, Neil J. *Treating Mental Disorders. A Guide to What Works*. Oxford University Press. 1999.

Newman, Barbara M. Newman, Phillip R. *Development Through Life. Psychosocial Approach*. Brooks/Cole Publishing. 1995.

Oesterle, John A. *St. Thomas Aquinas Treatise on the Virtues*. University of Notre Dame Press. Notre Dame. 1966.

Pope Benedict XVI. *Caritas in Vertitate. Charity in Truth*. Liberia Editrice Vaticana. June 29, 2009.

Pope Benedict XVI. *Deus Caritas Est. God is Love*. Liberia Editrice Vaticana. Kindle Version. December 25, 2005.

Pope Benedict XVI. *Spe Salvi. Saved in Hope.* Liberia Editrice Vaticana. November 30, 2009.

Pope Francis. *Amoris Laetitia. The Joy of Love.* Liberia Editrice Vaticana. October 1, 2015.

Pope Francis. *Evangelii Gaudium. The Joy of The Gospel Apostolic Exhortation on Love in the Family.* March 19, 2013.

Pope Francis. *Fratelli Tutti. On Fraternity and Social Friendship.* Libreria Editrice Vaticana. October 3, 2020.

Pope John Paul II. *Familiaris Consortio. Apostolic Exhortation.* Kindle Edition. Libreria Editrice Vaticana. November 22, 1981.

Pope John Paul II. *Redemptor Hominis. Encyclical Letter.* Kindle Edition. Liberia Editrice Vaticana. March 4, 1979.

Pope Paul VI. *Lumen Gentium. The Dogmatic Constitution of the Church.* 1964.

Ratzinger, Joseph. Pilgrim Fellowship of Faith. Ignatius Press. 2005.

Saint Maria Faustina Kowalska. *Divine Mercy in My Soul. Diary.* Marian Press. Stockbridge, MA. 2004.

St. Francis of Sales. *Introduction to the Devout Life.* Cosimo Publications. 2007.

St. Therese of Lisieux. *The Story of a Soul.* Saint Benedict Press. Tan Books. Copyright 2010.

St. Thomas Aquinas. *Summa Theologica.* Volume II. Christian Classics. Westminster, MD, 1948.

The Counseling Sourcebook. A Practical Reference of Contemporary Issues. Crossroad/New York. 1997.

The New American Annotated Bible. College Edition. An Ecumenical Study Bible. Oxford University Press. 2010.

United States Conference of Catholic Bishops. *Connecting Young Adults to Catholic Parishes. Best Practices for Catholic Young Adult Ministry.* USCCB Publishing. Washinton, D.C. 2010.

United States Conference of Catholic Bishops. *Pope Francis and the Family.* Libreria Editrice Vaticana. 2014.

Secondary Sources

Alva, Reginald. "The Catholic Church's Mission with the Marginalized. An Analysis in the Light of Pope Francis' Teaching on Evangelii Gaudium." *International Review and Mission.* Vol. 109. Issue 1. May 2020. https://doi.org/111/irom.12313

American Psychological Association. "Bullying." Adapted from APA Dictionary of Psychology. 2023.

Aquinas, Thomas. St. Thomas Aquinas *Summa Theologica.* Volume Two. Christian Classics. Westminster, Maryland. 1948.

Azarius, Brother. "Aristotle and the Christian Church. An Essay." The Brothers of Christian Schools. Published by William H. Sadlier. New York, NY. 1888. https://www3.nd.edu/~maritain/jmc/etext/aatcc.htm

Boer, Paul A, Sr. *A Catholic Interlinear New Testament. Volume I. The Four Gospels and the Acts of the Apostles in Latin, English, and Greek.* Kindle Edition. Veritatis Splendor Publications. 2012.

Boer, Paul A, Sr. *A Catholic Interlinear New Testament. Volume II. The Epistles of St. Paul the Apostle in Latin, English, and Greek.* Kindle Edition. Veritatis Splendor Publications. 2012.

Boer, Paul A, Sr. *A Catholic Interlinear Bible. Old Testament Polyglot.*

Vol. I. Genesis, Exodus, and Leviticus in English, Latin, and Transliterated Greek and Hebrew. Kindle Edition. Veritatis Splendor Publications. 2013.

Boer, Paul A, Sr. *A Catholic Interlinear Bible. Old Testament Polyglot. Vol. X. Isaiah, Jeremiah, Lamentations and Baruch in Latin, English, Greek, and Hebrew.* Kindle Edition. Veritatis Splendor Publications. 2013.

Boer, Paul A, Sr. *A Catholic Interlinear Bible. Old Testament Polyglot. Vol. VII. Job & Psalms in Latin, English, Greek, and Hebrew.* Kindle Edition. Veritatis Splendor Publications. 2013.

Boer, Paul Sr. A. *Catholic Interlinear Bible. Old Testament Polyglot. Vol. VIII. Proverbs, Ecclesiastes, and Song of Solomon in Latin, English, Greek, and Hebrew.* Kindle Edition. Veritatis Splendor Publications. 2013.

Catechism of the Catholic Church. Second Edition. Liberia Editrice Vaticana. 1994.

Cherian, Antony Augustine, O.P. "The Friendliness Called Affability." The Dominican Friars. February 3, 2023.

Chu Ilo, Stan. "Poverty and the Economic Justice of Pope Francis." Bulletin of Mission Research. DePaul University. Vol. 43. Issue 1. 2019. https://doi.org/10.1177/239699318810698

Ciancio, Susan. "The Reality of Bullying: A Pro-life Perspective." The Catholic World Report. August 11, 2023.

Cicero, Marcus Tullius. *Treatises on Friendship and Old Age.* Good Press. 2022.

Clark, Meghan, J. "Pope Francis and the Christological Dimensions of Solidarity Social Teaching." St. John's University. Vol. 80(1), 102-122. 2018.

Coleman, Rev. Gerald, DPSS. "Pope Francis and the Meaning of Marriage." *The National Catholic Bioethics Quarterly*. October 16, 2016. https://doi.org/10.5840/ncbq20161614

Danaher, Edward M. "A Comparison of the Theories of Aristotle and St. Thomas Aquinas Regard to the Existence of God." Marquette e-publications. Marquette University. 1938. https://epublications.marquette.edu/bachelor_essays/124/

Degges-White, Suzanne, Ph.D. "Friendology: The Science of Friendship." *Psychology Today*. May 29, 2018.

DiLorenzo, Maria. *Blessed Pier Giorgio Frassati. An Ordinary Christian*. Pauline Books and Media. 1973.

Drexel, Mother Mary Katharine. *Reflections on the Life in the Vine found in the Writings of Mother M. Katharine Drexel*. Drexel Guild. 1982.

Dutton, Marsha L. Aelred of Rievaulx Spiritual Friendship. Cistercian Publications. 2010.

Ewing, Addison, A. "Thomas Aquinas Doctor and Saint." The Sewee Review. Vol. 23, No. 4. The John Hopkins University Press. October 1915, pp. 305-408.

Fenton, Francesca Pollio. "10 things you should know about Blessed Carlo Acutis." *National Catholic Register*. October 12, 2023.

Fosha, Diana. Siegel, Daniel J. Solomon, Marion F. *The Healing Power of Emotion: Affective Neuroscience, Development and Clinical Practice*. New York: W.W. Norton and Company, 2009.

Frances, Sr. Anne, At LE, OP. "Ludus Sequen's Saint Thomas Aquinas on Evangelical Poverty and Christian Perfection." Center for Thomistic Studies. March 25, 2014.

Frassati, Luciana. *A Man of the Beatitudes. Pier Giorgio Frassati.* Ignatius Press. 2001.

Gafford, Joe Aaron. "The Life and Conversion of Augustine of Hippo." Harding University. *Tenor of Our Times.* Vol. 4. Article 4. Spring 2015, pp. 12-23.

Hajduk, Ryszard. "Pope Francis, Renewal of Pastoral Care in the Logic of Mercy." University of Warmia and Mazury in Olyzlyn. 2021. https://doi.org/10.31648/sw.6378

Hanson, Rick, Ph.D. *"Be Friendly. Friendliness is a down-to-earth approach that is welcoming and positive."* Psychology Today. November 7, 2012.

Hasseldine, Julian. "Friends, Friendship, and Networks in the Letter of St. Bernard Of Clairvaux." University of Hull. Department of History. Academia.edu. 2006.

Jourdain, Charles. "The Philosophy of Saint Thomas Aquinas." The Crayon. Vol. 5. No. 11. pp. 306-308. November 1858. https://doi.org/10.2307/25527818

Jones, Jeffrey. "Church Attendance Has Declined in Most U.S. Religious Groups." Gallup. March 24, 2024. https://news.gallup.com/poll/642548/church-attendance-declined-religious-groups.aspx

Jones, Jeffrey. "U.S. Church Membership Falls Below Majority for First Time." Gallup. March 29, 2021. https://news.gallup.com/poll/341963/church-membership-falls-below-majority-first-time.aspx

Juliet, Sr. Jennifer. *The Prayers, Quotes and Sayings of Saint Teresa of Calcutta (Mother Teresa).* Kindle Edition. September 13, 2016.

Kempis, Thomas. *Imitation of Christ*. Tan Book and Publishers. May 3, 1895.

Kennedy, D.J. Summa Theologica Parts I and II. Pars Prima Secudae. Kindle Edition. Jazzybee Verlag. July 21, 2012.

Lambery, Kim. "The Art of Accompaniment." An International Review. Vol. 43. Issue 3. 2015. https://doi.org/10.1177/0091829614563062

LaMorte, Michael. *From the Voyages of St. Francis Cabrini*. Catholic Treehouse. January 31, 2024.

McInerny, Ralph. "A First Glance of St. Thomas Aquinas." Chapter Two: St. Thomas and Aristotle. Jacques Maritain Center. University of Notre Dame Press. 1990. https://www3.nd.edu/~maritain/jmc/etext/peeping.htm

Mett, Sarah. "The Church's Mission: Evangelizing like Mother Teresa in the Year of Mercy." Catholic Exchange. January 21, 2016.

Merutiu, Monica D. "Pope Francis and the Caring Society." *Journal of Interdisciplinary Studies*. Catholic Exchange. Vol. 30. Issues 1-22. Summer-Autumn 2018. https://doi.org/10/5840/jis2018301-22.

Messingue, Jean. McNamee, Sheila. "Positive Family Pastoral Care and Counseling. A Reading of Pope Francis Apostolic Exhortation Amoris Laetitia." American Theological Library. University of Belgium, University of New Hampshire. 2016. https://doi.org/10.2143/CS.26.1.3285227

Mother Agnes of Jesus. *The Story of a Soul. The Autobiography of St. Therese of Lisieux*. Tan Books. 2010.

Nathan, Peter E. Gorman, Jack M. Salkind, Neil J. *Treating Mental Disorders. A Guide to What Works.* Oxford University Press. 1999.

Neumann, Vincent. *Blessed Pier Giorgio Frassati. Chronicle of a Man of Beatitude.* Kindle Edition. Sacred Lives Collections. February 6, 2024.

Newman, Barbara M. Newman, Phillip R. *Development Through Life. Psychosocial Approach.* Brooks/Cole Publishing. 1995.

Nouwen, Henri J.M. *You are the Beloved. Daily Meditations for Spiritual Living.* Convergent Books. 2017.

O 'Collins, Gerard, S.J. "The Joy of Love (Amoris Laetitia): The Papal Exhortation in its Context. Sage Theological Studies. Vol. 77(4). 905-921. 2016. DOI: 10.1177/0040563916666823.

Oesterle, John A. *St. Thomas Aquinas Treatise on the Virtues.* University of Notre Dame Press. Notre Dame. 1966.

Pieper, Josef. *The Four Cardinal Virtues.* Harcourt, Brace, & World, Inc. 1965.

Pew Research Center. "Leaving Catholicism." February 2011. https://www.pewresearch.org/religion/2009/04/27/faith-in-flux3/

Pope Francis. *A Year of Mercy with Pope Francis. Daily Reflections.* Our Sunday Visitor. Huntington, Indiana. 2014.

— Address to Pilgrimage of Families. www.vatican.va. October 26, 2013.

— General Audience. www.vatican.va. October 2, 2013

— General Audience. www.vatican.va. October 4, 2013.

— General Audience. www.vatican.va. March 16, 2014.

— General Audience. www.vatican.va. June 14, 2014.

— General Audience. www.vatican.va. June 16, 2014.

— General Audience. www.vatican.va. June 19, 2014.

— General Audience. www.vatican.va. August 29, 2019.

— *I Ask You, Be Shepherds. Reflections on Pastoral Ministry.* Crossroads Publishing. 2015.

— Regina Caelia Audience, www.vatican.va. May 4, 2014.

— "The Threat of Gossip." Morning Meditation in the Chapel of Domus Sanctae Marthae. www.vatican.va. September 2, 2013.

Pope John Paul, II. *Theology of the Body in Simple Language.* Kindle Edition. Philokalia Books. April 30, 2014.

Pope, Stephen J. "Integral Human Development from Paternalism to Accompaniment." *Theological Studies.* Vol. 80(1). 123-147. 2019. https://doi.org/10.177/0040563918819798

Richardson, Cyril. St. Ignatius of Antioch. Letter to Smyrnaeans. An interpretation. 110 AD. https://www.orderofstignatius.org/files/Letters/Ignatius_to_Smyrnaeans.pdf

Saint Theresa of Lisieux. *The Story of a Soul.* Tan Classics. 2010.

Scannone, Juan Carlos. "Pope Francis and the Theology of the People." Sage Publications. Vol. 77. Issue 1. March 2016. https://doi.org/10.1177/00450563015621141

Shields, Oliver. *Biography of Aristotle by Ptolemy.* December 14, 2021.

Smith, Innocent, O.P. "Liturgical Prayer and the Theology of Mercy in Thomas Aquinas and Pope Francis." Sage Journals. University of Regensburg, Germany. Vol. 79 (4). 782-800. 2018. https://doi.org/10177/0040563918801329

Socks, Pete. *Mother Teresa. Carrier of God's Mercy.* Operando. October 19, 2016.

Saint Thomas Aquinas Collection (22 Books). Aeterna Press. September 16, 2016.

St. Aelred of Rievaulx. Spiritual Friendship. Cistercian Fathers Series Book 5. Translated by Lawrence C. Braceland, S.J. Cistercian Publications. Liturgical Press. Collegeville, MN. 2010.

St. Bernard of Clairvaux. *On Loving God*. Fordham University. June 11, 2009.

St. Bernard of Clairvaux Collection of 8 Books. Aeterna Press. September 22, 2016.

St. Teresa of Calcutta. *Be My Light*. St. Anthony Messenger Press. 2007.

Tadie, Joseph Lawrence. "Between Humilities: A Retrieval of Saint Thomas Aquinas on the Virtue of Humility. A Book." Boston College. February 2006.

The Writings of St. Francis of Assisi. Kindle Edition. E-Bookarama. February 12, 2023.

Trendowski, Edward. "The Six Tasks of Catechesis in the Catechumenate – Inspired Stages of Catholic Marriage Preparation. A Book. Catholic University of America. 2021. https://hdl.handle.net/1961/cuislandora.2322302

Veneration, Fr. Vincent X. *St. Francis Cabrini Novena, Detailed Biography, Novena And Devotion to St. Francis Xavier Cabrini*. Amazon Kindle Book. November 3, 2023.

Whitworth, Patrick. *Three Wish Men from the East, the Cappadocian Fathers and the Struggle for Orthodoxy*. Sacristy Press. 2005.

United Stated Conference of Catholic Bishops website. "The New Evangelization." March 2024.

https://www.usccb.org/beliefs-and-teachings/how-we-teach/new-evangelization

Von Balthasar, Hans Urs. *Explorations in Theology. The Word Made Flesh Part I*. Ignatius Press. San Fransisco. 1989.

www.ingramcontent.com/pod-product-compliance
Lightning Source LLC
Chambersburg PA
CBHW050851160426
43194CB00011B/2114